THE

BELIEVER'S

DAILY REMEMBRANCER.

BY

THE REV. JAMES SMITH.

From the Thirty-eighth London Edition.

NEW YORK·

ROBERT CARTER & BROTHERS,

No. 530 BROADWAY.

1872

PREFACE.

THE present humble work is a pastoral effort, flowing from love to the Lord's people, and a desire to honor His great name. It is an acknowledged fact, that many of the Lord's people are living far below their privileges; and are walking as men, not aiming singly at the Lord's glory. This is to be regretted; and while none but the Lord the Holy Spirit can produce the change we desire to witness, yet the means are to be used, and we must stir up their pure minds by way of remembrance. In this little work, I aim to speak in the closet, in the cottage, in the kitchen, and even in the field, to the different classes of the Lord's family; endeavoring to draw them nearer to their God and gracious Father. My desire is to promote the POWER OF GODLINESS; and these little pieces are written to convince, comfort, and correct; to fan the flame of devotion, and to produce holiness of heart and life. To this end some degree of sameness in the pieces, and a repetition of some important truths, appeared absolutely necessary. Habitual dependence upon God for all we need, acknowledging the hand of God in all we receive, and walking with God, notwithstanding all that may happen to us below, enter into the very vitals of genuine Christianity; and it is only while we are thus acting that we enjoy peace with God, and walk in the comforts of the Holy Ghost. That the Lord, who often uses weak things to confound the mighty, may bless this little work to thy good and His glory,

Is the prayer of,
Dear Reader,
Yours in the Lord Jesus
JAMES SMITH.

DAILY REMEMBRANCER.

JANUARY 1.

Look unto me. Isaiah xlv. 22.

A NEW year's morning opens upon us, and we are still exposed to sorrow, Satan, and disappointment; sin lives in us; and a thousand things are ready to distress us; but our God says, "LOOK UNTO ME." Look unto me TO-DAY. I have blessings to bestow. I am waiting to be gracious. I am your Father in Jesus. Believe that I am deeply interested in your present and eternal welfare: that all I have promised, I will perform: that I am with you, purposely to bless you. I cannot be unconcerned about anything that affects you; and I pledge myself to make all things work together for your good. You have looked to self, to others, in time past; but you have only met with trouble and disappointment: now look unto me ALONE, to me FOR ALL.

> Our helper, God! we bless thy name,
> Whose love forever is the same;
> The tokens of thy gracious care
> Open, and crown, and close the year.

4. 24. 22

5

Be ye thankful. Col. iii 15.

WHAT cause to be thankful, what reason to be grateful have we! Surrounded by mercies, both temporal and spiritual. If we look back, we ought to rejoice that God. hath chosen us in Christ Jesus, before the foundation of the world; that He sent His only begotten Son into the world, to be a propitiation for our sins; that He sent His Holy Spirit into our hearts, to convince us of sin, lead us to Jesus, and make us meet for heaven. We have His word in our hands, His grace in our hearts, His mercies in our houses, and His heaven before our eyes. O for a thankful heart! But let us take our poor, hard, ungrateful hearts to Jesus; He can soften them and fill them with gratitude. Let us confess our ingratitude before Him, and mourn over our unthankfulness at His feet He is ready to forgive. He can sanctify us wholly He will hear our cry, and pity our complaints. O Jesus, grant us a deep sense of our utter unworthiness, and of Thine unmerited goodness, that our souls may daily praise Thee with joyful lips. May we live as thoughtful dependants; as grateful, loving children, before our Father and our God; and daily be thankful.

Through all eternity, to Thee
A joyful song I'll raise;
But, oh! eternity's too short
To utter all Thy praise.

JANUARY 3.

A Mediator. Gal. iii. 20.

GOD is and must be the eternal enemy of sin He cannot be reconciled to it : it is the abominable thing which He hates. He cannot look upon it but with abhorrence. How then can God receive, bless, or commune with us? Only through a Mediator; Jesus fills this office; He stands between God and us; He honors all the Father's perfections; and renders us and our services acceptable through His glorious righteousness and precious blood. God can only love us, receive us, commune with us, or bless us, in Jesus. He represents us to God, and we are accepted in the BELOVED; He represents God to us, and we prove Him to be gracious. When going to the throne of grace, never forget that Jesus is the Mediator; the middle man; present your persons, your petitions, and your praises to God through Him. You have nothing to fear, for Jesus wears your nature; He has a heart that beats in unison with yours; He calls you BROTHER; He uses all His influence with the Father on your behalf; all He did and suffered is employed for you; and at this moment He pleads your cause

> Oft as guilt, my soul, torments thee,
> Turn thine eyes to Jesus' blood ;
> This will comfort, cheer, and cleanse thee,
> Seal thy peace, and do thee good :
> Peace and pardon,
> Flow to thee through Jesus' blood.

Blessed are ye poor. Luke vi 20

THE Lord's people are all poor; they see and feel that sin has stripped them of every excellence; and has left them wretched, and miserable, and poor, and blind, and naked. They can do nothing of themselves, they can procure nothing; but free grace has made ample provision for them, and the gospel informs them that Jesus has everything they want, and all He has is for them. When they look at, or into themselves, they are discouraged; but when they look to Jesus they rejoice. He has riches of grace, and riches of glory; and He says, " Every one that asketh, receiveth." He giveth liberally and upbraideth not. Here then is the present blessedness of the Lord's poor; Jesus has all they need; He is their Friend; and they that seek Him shall not want any good thing. Am I poor? If so, Jesus bids me come to Him, and buy gold, clothing, wine and milk; all that is necessary to comfort and support in time, and render me happy throughout eternity. Poor in self, rich in Jesus. Poor at present, rich by-and-bye; for theirs is the kingdom of heaven. " All things are yours, ye are Christ's, and Christ is God's." " All things are for your sakes.·"

What want shall not our God supply,
From His redundant stores ?
What streams of mercy from on high,
An arm almighty pours !

4.27.22

JANUARY 5.

The fear of death. Heb ii 15.

ALL must die, but all do not die alike; some are cut off suddenly, others by a lingering illness; some die only safe, others happy. Some fear death all their lives, others do not. But death must be viewed through Jesus, or fear it we shall, if we think seriously. Death is a separation from the body; the second death is a separation from God. The former we *must* pass through, not so the latter. What shall separate us from the love of God? DEATH? No, we are more than conquerors through Him that hath loved us. Death only opens the prison-door, and sets the captive free. It is an answer to our many prayers for deliverance, for freedom from sin, for perfect happiness. If we are united to Jesus by a living faith, death cannot disunite us; but will only introduce us into His presence, that we may forever enjoy His love. If we walk with God; if we believe the Saviour's word; if we look beyond the valley; we shall not fear death. Jesus will not leave us then. He will be present according to His word, and we shall prove His faithfulness, veracity, and love. "Thanks be unto God who giveth us the victory, through our Lord Jesus Christ."

Why should I shrink at pain and woe,
  Or feel at death dismay?
I've Canaan's goodly land in view,
  And realms of endless day.

JANUARY 6

Be careful for nothing. Phil iv 6.

THE Lord careth for us. He knows our wants, and has promised to supply them; our foes, and will deliver us from them; our fears, and will make us ashamed of them. All creatures and things are in His hand, and at His disposal; all circumstances are absolutely under His control; He directs the angel, feeds the sparrow, curbs the devil, and manages the tempest. He is thy FATHER. His love to thee is infinite. Thou art His DELIGHT, His dear son, His pleasant child. Will He neglect thee? Impossible. Cast then thy cares upon Him Tell out all thy desires, fears, and troubles to Him; let Him know everything FROM THEE, keep nothing back: and then in the confidence of faith expect Him to fulfil His word, and act a parent's part. Bless Him for all He has given, for all He has promised; plead with Him for all you may need; but never for one moment, or under any circumstances, distrust Him. He cannot love thee more. He is a present help. He will make all His goodness pass before thee. He will rejoice over thee to do thee good, with His whole heart, and with His whole soul.

Then let me banish anxious care,
Confiding in my Father's love;
To Him make known my wants in prayer,
Prepared His answer to approve

10

JANUARY 7.

Let him deny himself Matt xvi 24

IT is required by Jesus that every disciple should practise self-denial; we must deny and crucify the workings of self-righteousness, and venture alone upon His work and worth for salvation; and we must mortify the pride of reason and intellect, and believe as His word reveals, and walk as His word directs. Our nearest relatives, dearest friends, and choicest comforts, must be resigned, if they are opposed to His glory and the furtherance of His cause. A Christian must lay everything at the feet of Jesus, and say, " Lord, do with it as thou wilt." We are not our own, nor is anything we have our own; it is the Lord's. Our appetites, pleasures, and pursuits, must all be brought into subjection to the obedience of Christ. His glory is to be sought at all times, in all things, under all circumstances, and when this is done, we are safe and happy. The servant must obey his Master, and the child submit in all things to the wise, judicious, and loving Father. But for whom am I called to deny myself? For Jesus, who lived and died to save me, and is now in heaven interceding for me; and who is the great pattern of self-denial, having humbled Himself even unto death.

Beloved self must be denied,
The mind and will renew'd ,
Passion suppress'd, and patience tried,
And vain desires subdued.

11

JANUARY 8.

I will help thee.   Isaiah xli. 13.

WHEREVER the Lord leads us, He will support us; nor shall the difficulties of the way, or the weakness we feel, be too much for us. His hand is stretched out to us, and it is for faith to lay hold and proceed, confident of assistance. The arm of His power is the protection of His people in danger, and the strength of His people in weakness. He is a very present help in trouble. A God at hand. Are you weak, or in difficulty? Plead His word; it is plain, positive, and sure; He cannot lie; He will not deceive. His strength is made perfect and is glorified in your weakness. Fear not, underneath are everlasting arms. He will strengthen you with strength in your soul. He can help, for He is omnipotent; He will help, for He has given you His word. Trust in the Lord at all times; yea, trust in the Lord forever, for in the Lord Jehovah is everlasting strength. That strength is promised to you, and will be employed for you in answer to prayer. Why then are ye so fearful? Why cast down? He says, "I WILL HELP THEE." "He hath said, and shall He not do it? He hath spoken, and shall He not make it good?".

Fear not, I am with thee; oh, be not dismay'd !
I, I am thy God, and will still give thee aid ;
I'll strengthen thee, help thee, and cause thee to stand,
Upheld by my righteous, omnipotent hand.
 12

JANUARY 9.

Gethsemane. Matt. xxvi. 36.

THIS was a garden at the foot of Mount Olivet; here Jesus, as the SUBSTITUTE of His people, received the cup of wrath from the hand of His offended Father. It was the wrath of God, all we had deserved, the punishment we must have endured; the Son of God in our nature, in our stead, for our salvation, was punished by divine justice. No human hand touched Him, no human voice spake to Him, when He sweat great drops of blood falling down to the ground. It was the baptism He expected, and oh, how great was His love! The baptism He longed to undergo. See the wonderful sufferer, hear His dreadful groans, listen to His heart-breaking sighs; heaven and hell are astonished, only man remains unaffected Beloved, it is our SURETY; He is paying our debt, redeeming our souls, purchasing our happiness, and making our peace. He went to GETHSEMANE that we might not go to hell; He was punished that we might be glorified. Often, very often, visit this sacred spot; here have fellowship with Christ in His sufferings by faith O my soul, I charge thee to visit Gethsemane, and visit it very often, for fellowship with Jesus! •

> The Father heard,—and angels there
> Sustained the Son of God in prayer,
>   In sad Gethsemane;
> He drank the dreadful cup of pain,
> Then rose to joy and life again.

5.8.22

13

JANUARY 10.

I am a worm Psalm xxii. 6.

MAN is naturally poor and proud, but grace
strips him and humbles him in the dust. Here
the highly favored David, the man after God's
own heart, cries out, "I am a worm." How
little, how despicable he appeared in his own
eyes. Every one that humbleth himself shall
be exalted. You have looked at Bible saints,
and have sighed out, "Ah! they were not like
me!" My brother, are you not a poor, weak,
worthless worm? Do you not feel so? Well,
so did David. The less you are in your own
eyes, the more fit you are for the Lord Jesus,
and the more welcome will you be at the
throne of grace. But this was the language
also of David's Lord; this was the view the
Jews had of Him, and they treated Him ac-
cordingly. The brightness of glory is compared to a vile reptile; the express image of
the Father's person is treated with the greatest contempt. But it was for us men, and for
our salvation. O mystery of mercy! Jesus is
reduced to a level with the worm, that he may
be raised higher than the angels.

> From Bethlehem's inn to Calvary's cross—
> Affliction mark'd His road;
> And many a weary step He took,
> To bring us back to God,
>
> By men despised, rejected, scorn'd,
> No beauty they can see,
> With grace and glory all adorn'd,
> The loveliest form to me.

14

5.9.02

JANUARY 11.

He invites me in ♡

JESUS calls thee to His throne ; He is there waiting to hear, relieve, and bless you.♡ You are to go to Him just as you are, and receive from Him all you need. He will give you wisdom, to direct your steps ; peace, to keep your hearts ; strength, to do His will ; righteousness, to justify your souls ; and rest, unspeakably sweet. He is glorified in bestowing these blessings upon you. He calls you this MORNING, this MOMENT, to receive without money and without price. What a precious Saviour is Jesus ! What a kind and tender Friend ! Let us go boldly to the throne of grace, that we may obtain mercy, and find grace to help in time of need. "Come," He says, "come to me ; go not to self, to the world, to the empty cisterns which creatures idolize ; but come unto me, and I will do for you exceeding abundantly above all you can ask or think. Your sins I will pardon ; your graces I will revive ; your comforts I will restore ; your holiness I will increase ; your efforts to glorify me I will crown with success ; I will bless you, and you shall be a blessing." "Oh, how great is thy goodness which thou hast laid up for them that seek thee ; which thou hast wrought for them that trust in thee, before the sons of men !"–

> Jesus, with thy word complying,
>   Firm our faith and hope shall be ;
> On thy faithfulness relying,
>   We will cast our souls on Thee

5, 11, 22

JANUARY 12.

I go mourning Psalm xxxviii. 6.

Bur what is the cause of your mourning? There is nothing apart from Jesus worth mourning for, or beside sin worth mourning over. Is it because of the unevenness of thy walk with God? On account of the deep depravity of thy nature? Because men keep not God's law? Or because Jesus hides His face, and your evidences fade and wither! You may well mourn after Jesus, but you must not despond; for He will turn again, He will have compassion upon you. The depravity of the heart is enough to make an angel weep; but forget not the precious blood that cleanseth, or the promised grace that sanctifies. Look not too much at the defects which appear in your walk, nor at the corruption which works in your heart; but deal with the blood and grace of Jesus, as the means of thy cure. Read and believe His promises; confess and plead at His throne; wait and watch in His ways; be careful lest by inordinate mourning you grieve His Spirit. He cannot be unkind, He never will forsake you. He was anointed "to comfort all that mourn."

Why should the children of a king
  Go mourning all their days?—
Great Comforter! descend, and bring
  Some tokens of thy grace.
Dost thou not dwell in all the saints,
  And seal the heirs of heaven?

16

JANUARY 13.

Let him ask in faith.   James i. 6.

THE believer's prayers should be regulated by God's promises ; he often fancies he wants what would only do him harm; and, therefore, if he ask he is denied, not in anger but in love. God has promised all good, and only good, to His beloved people. Ask for what God has promised to bestow, and ask believing that God will honor and fulfil His own precious word. He cannot deny Himself; all He hath promised He will perform. You can therefore have no reason to doubt whether the Lord will give you, if you really need it, and he has plainly promised it; therefore ask desiring, and expecting, and then look to receive. What are thy wants this morning? Where hath God promised such things in His holy word? Search out the promise, take it to His throne, plead in the name of Jesus for its fulfilment, and never doubt for one moment but that the Lord will make it good. Stay yourself therefore on the word of the Lord; but if you will not believe, surely you shall not be established. Faith honors God by trusting Him ; and God always honors faith by answering it. "Come boldly to the throne of grace, that you may obtain mercy, and find grace to help in time of need."

Beyond thy utmost wants,
His love and power can bless
To praying souls He always grants
More than they can express.

B

JANUARY 14.

be careful & consider all circumstances & possible consequences.

Walk circumspectly. Ephes. v 15.

You are in an enemy's land; surrounded by temptations, and have a heart that is deceitful above all things, and desperately wicked. *To honor Jesus in your spirit, communications, and every action, should be your constant aim. You are to live UNTO the Lord, FOR Him who died for you and rose again. To this end, provision was laid up in the everlasting covenant, for this purpose the precious promises were made, and with this design the Holy Spirit is given; that you may serve Him in righteousness and holiness all the days of your life. This world is not your home; Satan's family are not to be your associates; riches, honor, or pleasure, are not to be your objects; you are to walk as in the midst of snares; watchful, prayerful, depending upon Jesus, and cultivating fellowship with Him. Oh, keep your eye on Jesus as your example; walk by His word as your rule; be not venturesome or presumptuous, but avoid the very appearance of evil. Never leave the Lord's ways or ordinances, to join the world's parties or please a carnal fancy. Keep close to Jesus, and follow on to know the Lord. Act as a loving child going home to his father'-house.

So let our lips and lives express
The holy gospel we profess,
So let our works and virtues shine,
To prove the doctrine all divine.

"18

JANUARY 15.

But thou art the same Ps cii 27. ♡

EVERYTHING, below is liable to change; health may give place to sickness, pleasure to pain, plenty to poverty, love to enmity, honor to disgrace, strength to weakness, and life to death. Remember the days of darkness, for they shall be many. But though all our circumstances and friends should change, there is one who never changes; He is in one mind, and none can turn Him. With Him is no variableness. He is the same yesterday, to-day, and forever; and He is our best friend, our nearest relation, our gracious Saviour. Yesterday, His name was Jesus; His nature was love; His purpose was to do us good with his whole heart and soul: to-day, He is the same; we cannot expect too much from Him, or be too confident in Him, if we are walking humbly with Him; He will be our God and we shall be His people. Let us cultivate intimacy with Him, dependence upon Him, concern to please Him, fear to offend Him, zeal to glorify Him; and it must be well with us in health and sickness, plenty and poverty, life and death; for He is the same, and will never turn away from doing us good, but remain the fountain of love and holiness forever. Praise ye the Lord. *yes - Praise ye Lord!*

This God is the God we adore,
Our faithful—unchangeable friend,
Whose love is as large as His power,
And neither knows measure nor end.

what a glorious God you are!

5/9/22

JANUARY 16.

Is it well with thee? 2 Kings iv **26.**

Is Jesus precious to thy soul? Are you mourning over sin, or after the presence of your beloved Saviour? Are you strong in faith, giving
glory to God? Are you panting for communion
with your heavenly Father? Is the world beneath your feet? Are you glowing with love
to all saints? Are you seeking first the kingdom of God and His righteousness? Are you
lying at the feet of Jesus in trouble, crying,
Lord, help me? If so, it is well with thee:
there is spiritual life in thy soul, and the blessed
Spirit is thy teacher. But if the world is pre-
ferred to Jesus, the pleasures of time to fellowship with God, if self-examination is neglected,
and the Bible is become dry and unsavory, it is
not well. Health of soul is manifested by HABIT-
UAL prayer, zeal in the Lord's cause, an appetite
for the bread of life, and activity in the Lord's
ways. Is thy soul sick? If so, apply at once
to Jesus, as the great physician; and plead
with Him to restore unto thee the joys of His
salvation, and to uphold thee with His free
Spirit. He will heal thy backslidings, and love
thee freely.

'Tis well, my soul is fill'd with joy,
Though in myself a feeble worm;
For Jesus will His power employ,
And save my soul in every storm:
He will His gracious word fulfil,
And guard my soul from every ill.

S. 24 22

JANUARY 17.

I would do good. Rom. vii. 21.

EVERY believer has experienced the renewing of the Holy Ghost; sin has not dominion over him. He perceives the beauty of holiness, and loathes himself on account of sin. He would be internally holy, and externally conformed to the precepts of the Bible. He would pray with fervor; praise with gratitude; believe with confidence; war against sin, Satan, and the flesh, with courage; and glorify God by every feeling, thought, word, and action. Thus he feels, and for this he prays in his best moments; but he finds that he needs the frequent renewing of the Holy Spirit, for he is prone to sink into coldness, deadness, darkness, and stupidity, and he is obliged to cry out, " My soul cleaveth unto the dust; quicken thou me according unto thy word." The Lord must work in us to WILL as well as to DO; for by nature we are unwilling, and the desire after holiness, proved by effort to obtain it, is from God. Beloved, you must be coming to Jesus daily for fresh supplies of the Spirit, or you will find yourself not only weak but careless; not only will the power of godliness decline, but you will become indifferent. Watch against temptation. Watch unto prayer .

O Lord, assist me through the fight,
  My drooping spirit raise;
Make me triumphant in thy might,
  And thine shall be the praise.

5.22.22

21

JANUARY 18.

Evil is present with me. Rom. vii 21.

But what a mercy that it does not reign in you and over you; it did once, and would now but for free and sovereign grace. If sin makes you groan, leads you to the throne to plead with God, and to the fountain of the Saviour's blood to be cleansed from it, it does not, it cannot reign. It may disturb your peace, distress your mind, hinder you in duty, mix with all your duties and efforts to do good; and even make you cry out, "O wretched man that I am, who shall deliver me?" But even then you should not doubt; Jesus still loves you, grace will reign in your experience, and you shall be more than a conqueror. Paul had known the Lord many years, he had been in the third heaven, and daily triumphed in Christ; yet he felt just as you feel; when he would do good evil was present with him, and he could not do the things that he would. If sin annoys you, is your burden, and causes you grief; holiness lives in you, and the present painful conflict will end in everlasting peace. You may even now sing, "Thanks be unto God, who giveth us the victory, through our Lord Jesus Christ.' Live upon Christ, and you will live down all evil.

Oh! the rich depths of love divine,
Of bliss a boundless store!
Dear Saviour! let me call thee mine;
I cannot wish for more.

JANUARY 19.

AND who is the brother of Jesus? Every one who does the will of His Father. Every believer who proves the truth of his faith by the goodness of his works; who shows the excellence of his nature, by the piety, benevolence, and charity of his life. Believer, Jesus calls thee BROTHER. He has for thee a brother's love. Oh, how tender! Oh, how tried! Stronger than death; passing knowledge. He bears with thy infirmities, reproves thy follies, encourages thy faith, forbids thy fears, and will certainly provide for thy wants. Joseph in Egypt supplied his brethren during the famine, and shall not Jesus supply His. If He seem to speak roughly, He will act kindly, and perform a brother's part. He has all power in heaven and in earth, He doeth according to his will, and He is not ashamed to call us brethren. He will correspond with us, and bids us daily, yea hourly, correspond with Him. Oh, remember, when you go to the throne of grace, that your BROTHER fills it. He calls you to it, and will withhold no good thing from you. Precious Lord Jesus, manifest to me a brother's love; and help me to rely on thy fraternal kindness.

Our nearest friend, our Brother now,
Is He to whom the angels bow;
They join with us to praise His name,
But we the nearest interest claim.

23

The wisdom of the just. Luke i. 17.

THE Lord's people are justified freely, by **His** grace, through the redemption that is in Christ Jesus. The work of Jesus is their justification before God: in this they trust: this they plead: and in this they rejoice. Taught by the Holy Spirit, they manifest wisdom in readily believing God's faithful word, and trusting Him to make good the same to them. They resign themselves and all they value into His hands for preservation, and to be entirely at His disposal, persuaded that His wisdom and love will do better for them, than they possibly could for themselves. They refer all things to God for His decision, and cheerfully abide by His sentence. They live in simple, child-like dependence upon His providence and grace, for body and soul, for time and eternity, seeking to make His will theirs. They walk in charity with their fellow-christians, who differ in some things from them, and would do good to all, especially to them that are of the household of faith. Beloved, do you manifest this wisdom? Do you walk by this rule? Do you mind the same things? Have you the wisdom that is from above, which is pure, gentle, easy to be entreated, full of mercy and good fruits?

> Boundless wisdom, power divine,
> Love unspeakable, are thine;
> Wisdom, Lord, to me be giv'n,
> Wisdom pure, which comes from heav'n.

JANUARY 21.

Ye cannot serve God and mammon. Matt vi 24.

OUR God is a jealous God. He requires the devotion of the heart, the consecration of all the powers, and we cannot enjoy religion without these. Persons who try to unite God and the world, the service of sin and the service of God, cannot be happy. We must be decided Well, who is to be God TO-DAY? Who is to have the heart, the talents, the affections TO-DAY? Is gain, carnal pleasure, or worldly company to be the idol to-day? Or, is Jesus to have the thoughts, the desires, and the talents? Shall we seek His glory, and aim at His honor? Or, shall we say to some worthless bramble, Come thou and reign over us? Choose you, whom will you serve? Attempt not to reconcile opposing claims, but let God or mammon have the whole. Surely you are ready to cry out,— "Thine am I, Jesus, and thee only will I serve!" But you can only serve Him acceptably, as you serve Him with the grace He imparts; He has provided, promised, and invites you to receive. Let us therefore have grace whereby we may serve God acceptably with reverence and godly fear. Serving God in the spirit of adoption is true happiness.

Oh, let Thy love my soul inflame,
And to Thy service sweetly bind;
Transfuse it through my inmost frame,
And mould me wholly to Thy mind.

I am thy shield. Gen xv. 1.

THEY that believe are blessed with believing Abraham · the promises God made to him, He will fulfil to us. We are surrounded by foes; fiery darts fly in every direction; but Jehovah, in Jesus, interposeth Himself as our shield. Our safety and protection is from our relation to Him; we should soon be overcome if He did not preserve and defend. How safe and how happy we feel, when we realize that our God is our defence, and the most high God our protector! If foes alarm, or dangers affright, yet remember, " The name of the Lord is a strong TOWER," you may run into that and be safe. Faith is the arm; Jehovah is the shield; with Satan, sin, and the world we are in conflict; but we are preserved as in a garrison by the power of God, through believing, unto salvation. My brother, look to Jesus through this day as thy shield, and expect safety and protection alone from Him; He is present to protect thee, and answer thy prayers He will thus preserve thy going out and coming in, from this time forth, and even for evermore. He will give thee the shield of His salvation, and His gentleness will make thee great.

His righteousness to faith reveal'd,
Wrought out for guilty worms,
Affords a hiding-place and shield,
From enemies and storms.

Why are ye so fearful? Mark iv. 40

THE disciples appeared to be in danger, and fear filled their hearts ; they did not realize that they were the care and charge of Jesus, or else knowing Him their fears could have had no place. Beloved, you are in the hands of your loving Saviour ; He has charge of you and all your concerns ; He has numbered the very hairs of your head, and watches over you every moment, by night as well as by day. He is ever present, His eye cannot be diverted from you, His omnipotence is engaged to defend you, His fulness to supply you, His wisdom to guide you, and His perfections will be glorified in your everlasting holiness and happiness. He says, "I am glorified in them." Why are ye so fearful? Jesus is a very present help, He is a friend that loveth at all times. He is your SHIELD, and will be your exceeding great reward. But perhaps you have wandered from Him; your conscience accuses, and Satan tempts you to despond ; go, go and return unto Him, delay not a moment, cast yourself guilty as you are at His feet, confess all, and give yourself to Him afresh. He will receive you graciously, love you freely, and restore the joys of His salvation.

The saints should never be dismay'd,
 Nor sink in hopeless fear ;
For when they least expect His aid,
 The Saviour will appear.

Ye are not your own. 1 Cor. vi. 19.

No—Jesus has purchased you with His own blood, quickened you by His Spirit, espoused you to Himself, and intends to glorify you with Himself forever. He claims you, and says, "I have called thee by thy name; thou art mine." He will provide for you as His own, and spare you, as a man spareth his own son that serveth him. You are His beloved bride. His portion. A member of His· body, of His flesh, and of His bones. In loving you, He loveth Himself. He requires you to live under the daily conviction that you are His; that all you have is His. You have nothing of your own; all you have He freely gave, and all you have you profess to have surrendered to Him. Think more of Jesus than of His gifts, cleave to Him, and not to what you may be called to surrender. He will never take anything from you, but He will give you something better. If He strip you, it is to teach you; to lead you to live upon Himself; and to find your heaven in His company, grace, and offices. Do you live, walk, and act, so as to leave the impression upon the minds of observers that you are the Lord's? Do you expect Him to preserve, guide, and supply you?

Lord I am I thine, entirely thine?
Purchased and saved by blood divine!
With full consent thine I would be,
And own thy sovereign right in me.

JANUARY 25.

Ye are my friends John xv. 14

> [> attitude of patronizing superiority]

WHAT infinite condescension in Jesus, to call
us worms, His friends! But He not only calls
us so, but treats us as such, and expects us as
friends to do whatsoever He commands us.
Is Jesus thy friend? Then visit Him often, let
him hear thy voice in prayer and praise; then
trust Him confidently, let him see a proof of
thy faith in thy dependence; then walk with
Him in love, let Him enjoy much of thy company; then expect Him to be thy friend in
sickness and health; in poverty and plenty; in
life and in death. If Jesus is our friend, we
can never be destitute; if father and mother
forsake, He will take us up and take us in; we
can never be miserable, He will receive us and
be a Father unto us; we can never be neglected, for He will never fail us nor forsake us,
but will do for us all He has promised in His
word. He will defend us from foes, visit us in
sickness, and cheer and support us in death.
Precious Lord Jesus, be thou my friend, call
me thy friend, and treat me as such, in life, in
death, at the judgment, and before thy Father's
face forever.

> Oh let us make His name our trust,
> He is a Saviour wise and just;
> On His Almighty arm depend,
> He is a tried and faithful friend;
> And all His friends shall shortly prove
> The power and glory of His love.

29

JANUARY 26.

I will instruct thee Psalm xxxii 8.

Aт best we know but little, and we are slow to learn : but as the Lord has promised to instruct us, we may yet expect to be made wise unto salvation. The Lord's teaching always produces humility, self-loathing, confidence in God, zeal for His glory, and devotes the heart to His praise. It brings us to the feet of Jesus, and delivers us from the present evil world. Under divine instruction we learn the true nature of sin, the vanity of the world, the emptiness of creatures, and the fulness and preciousness of Christ. Is God willing to instruct us? Then let us be early and often at His throne, praying as the Psalmist did, "Lead me in thy truth, and teach me : for thou art the God of my salvation ; on thee do I wait all the day." Then shall we exclaim as Elihu did, "Behold, God exalteth by His power : who teacheth like Him?" The Lord will teach us to profit, and sanctify us through the truth He imparts. Christ is our great lesson, and to know Him rightly is life, peace, and joy. Is Jesus thy teacher? Then sit at His feet, treasure up His words, and show forth His praise. He says, "Learn of me." Learn to know Him, love Him, and obey Him.

Eternal life thy words impart,
On these my fainting spirit lives :
Here sweeter comforts cheer my heart,
Than the whole world around me gives.

JANUARY 27.

Lacked ye anything? Luke xxii. 35.

THE Lord will always provide for His own people, who keep His company, do His will, and aim at His glory. If He sends us, though He chooses to carry the purse, our bread shall be given, and our water shall be sure. The disciples went out unfurnished, but then Jesus commanded them; they return and confess that they lacked nothing, the God of providence supplied them. If we are in the Lord's way, we may rest assured that we shall meet the Lord's messengers bringing our supply. They that seek the Lord shall not want any good thing. He notices our wants, remembers His promises, times His mercies, and proves Himself a faithful God. Have you lacked anything? for body? for soul? He who has supplied the past will provide for the future. Jesus is full of grace; go and receive, that your joy may be full. Jesus is the God of providence; look to Him, trust in Him, plead with Him, and you shall never be destitute. Believe His word, "He cannot deny himself; trust in His faithfulness, and He will put honor upon thy faith, fulfilling His own word. " Thy bread shall be given thee, and thy water shall be sure."

E'en down to old age, all my people shall prove
My sovereign, eternal, unchangeable love,
And when hoary hairs shall their temples adorn,
Like lambs they shall still, in my bosom, be borne.

31

JANUARY 28.

We have an Advocate. 1 John ii. 1.

YES—-Jesus pleads for us in heaven; by His own blood He entered once into the holiest, there to appear in the presence of God FOR US. He pleads for us against Satan, answering all his accusations; and for us with the Father, that we may be kept, supplied and glorified. O what a comfort when the heart is straitened in prayer, when the mouth is closed by guilt, when the spirit is harassed by temptation, to know that Jesus as our Advocate appears and pleads for us above! Beloved, Jesus is before God for you this morning, and every morning; and the benefit of His intercession you daily enjoy. When doubting and fearful, put your cause afresh into His hands, and leave Him to carry it; He can plead well; His arguments are powerful, and His manner is divine. Keep Jesus before thee this day as thy Advocate; rejoice in His office and name, and remember He is saying, "Father, I will that those whom thou hast given me, be with me where I am, to behold my glory." Him the Father heareth always; and all for whom He pleads are safe, and shall be happy.

Look up, my soul, with cheerful eyes,
See, where the great Redeemer stands
The glorious Advocate on high,
With precious incense in His hands;
And on His pleading still depend,
Who is your Advocate and Friend.

JANUARY 29.

Search the Scriptures.   John 7. 39.

THE Bible is God's book, a favor bestowed on man; intended to lead him to a knowledge of the nature, perfections, purposes, will, providence, and salvation of God. It contains all that is really necessary to be known. It should be read carefully, prayerfully, frequently, and in course; every part of the Bible should be read, meditated upon, and prayed over It makes us wise unto salvation, through faith which is in Christ Jesus. We cannot understand the Scriptures, or gather spiritual profit therefrom but by the Holy Ghost; nor should we expect to be taught the mind of God but by the Scriptures. Praying, reading, and thinking, should go together; and no one but he who has proved it, can possibly tell the profit which may be thus gained. Let the Bible be the every-day book. In it God speaks to your soul; by it He will sanctify your nature, direct your steps, and give you joy and peace Let not the works of man occupy the place of the book of God; but search the Scriptures daily, and exercise faith therein. "Open thou mine eyes, that I may see wondrous things out of thy law." Unfold to me the riches of thy grace.

O may thy counsels, mighty God,
  My roving feet command;
Nor I forsake the happy road,
  That leads to thy right hand.

JANUARY 30.

And shalt thou be delivered? Isa. xxxvii. 11.

This is plainly the language of an insulting foe; he had triumphed, and now he boasted, but his power was bounded, and his pride procured his fall. Often when in trouble, when distressed, when tried by a sense of sin and unworthiness, unbelief and Satan join, and pointing to others who have fallen, and to our acknowledged unworthiness, insultingly ask the question, "And shalt thou be delivered?" Yes, Satan, we shall be delivered; the God of Hezekiah is our God, and He hath said, "I will deliver thee in six troubles, and in seven I will not forsake thee." We believe His word, we rely on His faithfulness, we plead at His throne: and so sure as He CAN deliver He WILL. He hath often done so in times past, He doth deliver all His praying people now, and in Him we trust that He will deliver us. Not on account of anything in us, or of anything done by us, but because He hath said, "I will be with him in trouble, I will deliver him and honor him; I will set him on high, because he hath known my name." He is faithful, His word cannot fail, nor should our faith be shaken. Deliverance is certain, for God hath spoken, and God is true.

> The same His power, His love the same,
> Unmoved the promise shines;
> Eternal truth surrounds His name,
> And guards the precious lines.

34

JANUARY 31.

We joy in God. Rom v. 11.

THIS is every believer's privilege; G*d is reconcil*d to him in the person and through the work of Jesus: all charges against him are blotted out; all his sins are freely and fully forgiven; he is justified from all things; and stands before God in Christ, accepted, beloved, and blessed. To him God is love; with him God is at peace; and he is now a son *daughter* of God. If this is believed on the testimony of God, and realized in the soul as the effect of faith; then God becomes our exceeding joy, and we rejoice with joy unspeakable and full of glory. If we joy in frames, they change; if we joy in friends, they die; if we joy in possessions, they are vanity; but if we joy in God, though the exercise of joy may be interrupted, yet the object remains eternally the same, and we shall joy for evermore. Beloved, look at Jehovah in Jesus; there you see Him as the Father of mercies and God of all comfort; joy and rejoice in him as your God, your portion, your everlasting all. Throughout this day, joy in God as your Father, your Friend, and your Saviour.

> Joy to find, in every station,
> Something still to do or bear:
> Think, what spirit dwells within thee;
> Think, what Father's smiles are thine;
> Think, what Jesus did to win thee ,—
> Child of heaven! canst thou repine!

6.15.22

FEBRUARY 1.

Immanuel. Matt. i. 23.

CONSIDER Jesus through this day as God with thee; God in thy nature; God become man for thy salvation and consolation. None but God was able to save; thy Jesus is God: it was necessary that the Saviour should be man, and Jesus is man. He has the nature of His Father, here is His ability; He has thy nature also, here is His suitability. Jesus is God with thee, to hear thy prayers, check thy fears, redress thy grievances, sympathize with thee in thy sorrows, and be thy every-day friend. God is with us, observing our conduct, directing our ways, reproving our follies, providing our supplies, and making all things work together for our good. Always remember, Jesus is with me; every sin is committed under His eye, against His love, and goes to His heart; think, when tempted to sin, that you hear Immanuel, the suffering, bleeding, dying, reigning Saviour, say, "Oh, do not that abominable thing which I hate." Walk before Him in love, peace, holiness, and zeal, for his glory and praise. He is God for thee, as well as with thee. Look to His wisdom, power, and love, for safety and supply; and with filial confidence trust his word. *assuming the relation of a child*

Sweeter sounds than music knows
Charm me in Immanuel's name;
All her hopes my spirit owes
To His birth, His cross, His shame.

36

6.17.22

FEBRUARY 2.

The spirit of supplication. Zech. xi. 10

ALL spiritual prayer is produced by the Holy Spirit; He convinces us of need, discovers to us the fulness of Jesus, leads us to the throne of grace, and helps our infirmities there. The very desire to pray is from Him, and the liberty we enjoy in prayer is His gift. But how dreadful a thing is sin, and how condescending is the Holy Spirit! He sympathizes with us, and maketh intercession for us, with unutterable expressions of distress; with groanings which cannot be uttered. Sin has rendered us so vile, that no sacrifice but that of the Son of God Himself, could atone for us; and so weak, that none but the Holy Spirit can enable us to pray with fervor, faith, and success. See, beloved, how deep are your obligations, and how great your dependence upon this blessed Spirit of grace and supplication. Be careful lest you grieve Him by your lightness, worldliness, or lukewarmness; but sow unto the Spirit and ye shall reap life everlasting. He will testify to you of Jesus, and bless you with liberty and peace.

I want a heart to pray,
To pray and never cease;
Never to murmur at thy stay,
Or wish my sufferings less.
I want a godly fear,
A quick discerning eye,
That looks to thee when sin is near,
And sees the tempter fly.

Cleave unto the Lord. Acts xi 23.

EVERY believer is united to Christ, and is one with Him. Jesus is the vine, he is a branch; Jesus is the husband, he is the bride. Satan's design is to lead him from the Lord; he knows well he can do little or nothing, while the Christian cleaves to Jesus. Oh, then, cleave to Him by faith, in love, with perseverance! Cleave to His truth, to His people, to His ordinances, to His word, and to His throne. Think of Jesus as the affectionate child thinks of his beloved father, as the tender bride thinks of her devoted bridegroom, as the way-worn traveller thinks of his cheerful home. Let Jesus be uppermost in thy thoughts, let His love rule thy heart, and let nothing steal away thy affection from Him. Live upon His fulness, live according to His word, live in the element of His love; no living safely, no living happily, but as you cleave unto the Lord. Never let Satan find thee at a distance from Jesus, or he will assuredly be too much for thee. He is ever on the watch to find thee wandering, that he may worry, deceive, and distress thee. Therefore cleave unto the Lord, with full purpose of heart. Cleave to Him as the ivy to the oak, or the child to the mother's breast.

Saviour, let me cleave to thee;
Love the bond of union be;
And, lest I should e'er depart,
Keep thy dwelling in my heart.

38

6.19.22

FEBRUARY 4.

Precious faith. 2 Peter i. 1.

FAITH is the gift of God. It is the fruit of everlasting love, the effect of grace; we believe through grace The faith which is the evidence of salvation, includes giving credit to the gospel report, of a free and full salvation for poor unworthy sinners; an application to Jesus on the throne of grace, founded on that report; and a trusting on the word, work, and death of Jesus, for life and salvation. This always produces love to Jesus, and leads the soul to obey Him out of gratitude. It is precious; being scarce, few thus believe; being valuable, without it we cannot please God, cannot be justified, cannot rejoice in hope, or enjoy gospel blessings; but he that believeth is entitled to every precious promise, to all the fulness of Christ, to enjoy God in every new covenant relation, and shall never see death. He is passed from death to life, and shall never come into condemnation. Gracious God! give unto thy people, and unto me especially, much precious faith, that believing in Jesus, I may rejoice with joy unspeakable and full of glory. Oh, to believe this day without wavering! Oh, to be strong in faith, giving glory to God!.

Oh, for a strong, a lasting faith,
To credit what th' Almighty saith!
To embrace the message of His Son,
And call the joys of heav'n our own.

6.2022

FEBRUARY 5.

Precious blood. 1 Pet. i. 10.

THE blood of Jesus is the price of our redemption, the object of our faith, the ground of our peace, the subject of our meditation, and our constant plea at the throne of grace. It satisfied divine justice, and speaks peace to the humbled sinner's heart. It overcomes Satan, and cleanseth from all sin. It purges the conscience from dead works, and leads us to joy in God. We build on it as our foundation, flee to it as our refuge, look to it as the cure for sin, and sing of it as the joy of our heart. It has made a perfect, a satisfactory, an infinite atonement; and no sinner can perish who relies upon it, washes in it, and pleads it before God. It is indeed precious blood! It is invaluable! Whenever you feel guilt on your conscience, fears rising in your mind, or a gloom come over your spirit; look to, meditate upon, make use of the precious blood of Jesus. It made peace, it gives peace, and it secures peace. It cleanses, heals, and sanctifies; and we could not live happy one day without it. The blood of Jesus Christ cleanseth us from all sin. To this alone we must look as the foundation of our hope, and the ground of our peace.

> Dear dying Lamb, thy precious blood
> Shall never lose its power;
> Till all the ransom'd church of God
> Be saved to sin no more.

40

FEBRUARY 6.

He is precious. 1 Pet ii. 7.

YES—Jesus is precious to every believer: however Christians may differ upon some points, they all agree in this, JESUS IS PRECIOUS. They cannot always feel towards Him as they wish, but they have always one and the same opinion of Him. He is precious in His person, word, work, blood, righteousness, and intercession : as prophet, priest, and king ; in every name He wears, every character He bears, every relation He fills, and every office He sustains; so precious that none can be compared with Him. His people love Him, but none of them think they love Him enough; they adore Him, but mourn over their want of fervor when addressing Him; they prefer Him above all things, and consider Him altogether lovely. Do you find Christ precious this morning? If He was to be sold, what would you give for him? If you could be gratified, how would you feel towards him? He is precious to poor sensible sinners ; to strong believers; to holy angels; and to God our heavenly Father. Is He so to you? Live near to Him, be intimate with Him, and you will feel Him precious. The more you know of Him, the more you will prize him.

Hail, thou ever blessed Jesus,
  Only thee I wish to sing ,
To my soul thy name is precious,
  Thou my Prophet, Priest, and King

6. 22. 22

41

FEBRUARY 7.

My times are in thy hand. **Ps. xxxi. 15.**

Every event is under divine control; nothing is left to chance. The hand of God is in all that occurs; directing, overruling, or sanctifying to our good. He appointed all that concerns us, and appointed all in infinite wisdom and love; therefore we should not judge rashly, or conclude hastily. We know not what may occur to-day, but we know that the purpose of God cannot be frustrated, nor can His promise fail. He worketh all things after the counsel of His own will. He says, "My purpose shall stand, and I will do all my pleasure." But this is our comfort, that He taketh pleasure in His people, and in the prosperity of His servants. Let us consider, then, everything passes under our Father's eye; is overruled by our Saviour's power; is directed by the Holy Spirit to do us good. It shall not be as our enemies wish, or as our hearts fear; but as our God and Father pleases and has ordained. Be not therefore anxious, troubled, or cast down; the Lord God omnipotent reigneth, and He is God. He shall preserve thee from evil, He shall preserve thy soul.

I know not what may soon betide,
But Jesus knows, and He'll provide·
My life is by His counsel plann'd,
And all my times are in His hand:
I'll therefore trust, nor yield to fear,
But cast on Jesus all my care.

42

FEBRUARY 8.

That I may win Christ. Phil iii 8

THE aim of men in general is to make a fortune, enjoy the world, and live respectably: the aim of the believer is to win Christ. Jesus possesses all He desires, and to possess Christ would satisfy every wish. We have now a title to Him, we receive much from Him, and we often enjoy His love; but we want to be present with Him, and to have full possession of Him as our everlasting all. He is set before us as our mark, He is held out as the prize, and is promised as the everlasting portion of every overcomer. Where is the heart this morning? Which way do the desires tend? . What is to be the object of pursuit to-day? If Jesus is the principal object, failing in our pursuit after other things, losses, or crosses, will not much affect us; but our conduct will say, "I aim to win Christ; if He is mine, all is well, other things are but trifles compared with Him." Keeping Jesus in view thus, will prevent murmuring, cure our impatience, and keep our hearts in comparative peace. O may our every action cry in the ears of every observer, "THAT I MAY WIN CHRIST." He who has Christ, has an infinite portion; unsearchable wealth.

Not softest strains can charm mine ears,
Like His beloved name ,
Nor aught beneath the skies inspire
My heart with equal flame.

Be watchful. Rev. iii. 2

SATAN is watching to ensnare us, the world is watching to exult over us, and God is watching to protect us. Jesus our best friend says to us. "BE WATCHFUL." Watch against the spirit of the world, against thy easily besetting sins, against seasons of temptation, and against Satan the sworn enemy of thy soul. Watch for opportunities to do good, for answers to prayer, for the appearance of God as a God of providence. Unite prayer to God, dependence on His holy word, and watchfulness together; pray to be kept *from* sin, *in* temptation, unspotted from the world; trust in God to answer, but do not leave the throne; and then watch as though all depended upon thy diligence and efforts. Blessed is He that watcheth and keepeth his garments. "Watch ye therefore and pray always." But trust not thy watchfulness, but while watching trust in God. He that keepeth thee will not slumber: He is with thee when on guard, as well as when thou art feasting on His word and rejoicing at His table. He withdraweth not his eyes from the righteous. "The eyes of the Lord are upon the righteous, and His ears are open to their cry." Watch ye, therefore, and pray always.

> Oh! watch, and fight, and pray;—
> The battle ne'er give o'er;
> Renew it boldly every day,
> And help divine implore.

God is for me. Psalm lvi 9.

BELOVED, the greatest mercy a sinner can enjoy is to have God on his side, engaged in his quarrel, and employed in his most important concerns; this mercy is yours. God is for you: He chose you in Christ before the world began: He formed you to show forth His praise: He preserved you in Christ until He called you by grace: He quickened you by His Spirit, and led you to Jesus: He has given you His Son, and promised every additional good. He has said to you, " Thou art mine." You have said, "I am thine." He is now your refuge and strength; He is tenderly concerned for your welfare, devotedly attached to your cause, and observes every step you take. He may try your faith, but will certainly supply your wants. He may exercise your patience, but will never turn a deaf ear to your cries, except you indulge iniquity in your heart. No parent ever felt so deeply interested in the welfare of a beloved child, as thy God does in thine. He says, "Fear thou not; for I am with thee; be not dismayed, for I am thy God: I will strengthen thee; yea, I will help thee; yea, I will uphold thee with the right hand of my righteousness." *Amen, TY Lord!*

God is our refuge and defence,
In trouble our unfailing aid;
Secure in his omnipotence,
What foe can make our souls afraid!

FEBRUARY 11.

I will spare them. Mal iii 17.

PRECIOUS assurance·! But whom will the Lord spare? All His children,—especially those who speak of His goodness, witness to His faithfulness, think upon His name, and honor Him before an evil generation: He says, "They shall be mine, in that day when I make up my jewels, and I will spare them as a father spareth his obedient son." If we are aiming at the Lord's glory, and walking by the Lord's word, we have nothing to fear from any of His dispensations. He will shield us from danger, sanctify our troubles, and secure our best interests. If we are living to His praise, we may safely leave our wants and our comforts in His hands; He will supply the one and preserve the other. He says, "Fear thou not, for I am with thee." "Bring every trouble to my throne, every want to my fulness: I am EL-SHADDAI, God all-sufficient: enough in the absence of every one and everything. I am your God; I may punish the nations, but I will spare you. Believe this and be happy. Rejoice in this and you glorify me. You are no more a servant, but a son; and if son, then an HEIR of God through Christ. Though I punish the world, I will spare you."

Jesus, my Saviour and my Lord!
  'Tis good to trust thy name:
Thy power, thy faithfulness, and love,
  Will ever be the same.

46

FEBRUARY 12

Hope thou in God Psalm xlii 11.

HOWEVER gloomy the day, however strange the trials, however distressing the visitation, hope thou in God. He is with you, He is your God, He has promised to befriend you, He is the faithful God. He will turn darkness into light, make crooked things straight, and make all grace abound towards you, so that you, having all sufficiency, may abound to every good work. The changes that affect you, cannot affect him. You cannot rely too simply upon Him, or expect too much from Him. If all within and without seem to conspire to distress you, still say, "I will hope in God." Expect Him to be to you all a gracious and powerful God can be; expect Him to do all a loving Father and infinite God can do. Hope for light in darkness, for relief in distress, for strength in weakness, for joy in sorrow, for deliverance when sinking beneath the wave, and for life in death. Hope for all you need, and for all God has promised. Hope thou in God, and in God alone. Hope because God has spoken, because he is true and faithful, and you cannot hope in vain. The foundation of your hope is laid in the blood of Jesus, and the oath of God.

Ye fearful saints ! fresh courage take ;
The clouds ye so much dread
Are big with mercy, and shall break
In blessings on your head.

FEBRUARY 13

Search me, O God. Ps. cxxxix. 23.

NONE can search the heart but God; none are desirous or willing for the heart to be searched but real Christians. A believer desires to know the worst. He dreads deception. Grace has made him honest, and he prays, "Lord, search me." If a man was to search, he would expose, irritate, and injure us; but if God search, He will humble, strengthen, and heal us. The man who sees himself in the light of truth, and knows himself as the effect of divine searching, cannot trust himself for one moment; he flies from self to Jesus; from law to grace; he loathes himself; and while he confidently trusts in Jesus, and rejoices in hope, he walks humbly with his God. He cannot boast, he dares not presume; but walks in holiness, and ascribes all to free grace. Beloved, take the heart to Jesus to be searched. He says, "I am He that searcheth the hearts and trieth the reins." If He search you, He will save you from deception, self-righteousness, and every false way. Be this your daily prayer, "Search me, O God, and lead me in the way everlasting. Examine me, O Lord, and prove me: try my reins and my heart." Let a man examine himself. You need searching.

> Lord, search my heart, and try my ways,
>   And make my soul sincere;
> Then shall I stand before thy face,
>   And find acceptance there.

FEBRUARY 14.

The Lord delighteth in thee. Isa. lxii. 4.

AND is it possible, that such poor, depraved, unworthy creatures, can be the objects of Jehovah's delight? Yes—the infinite love of God has been fixed upon us from eternity: because He loved us, He sent His only begotten Son to die for us; He sent His Holy Spirit into our hearts; and gave us a good hope through grace. Hear the Apostle: "But God, who is rich in mercy, for His GREAT LOVE wherewith He loved us, even when we were DEAD IN SINS. hath quickened us together with Christ: by whose grace ye are saved." Jehovah views us in Jesus, and loves us with an infinite love. Yea, He has loved us as He has loved Him. Every believer, though his faith may be weak, his fears many, his corruptions strong, his troubles great, and his temptations sore, is the object of Jehovah's delight. Let us therefore endeavor to pass through this day, yea, and every day, believing and realizing, "I am Jehovah's delight; the object of His highest love; the subject of His sweetest thoughts; and His portion for evermore." O incomparable privilege! Source of comfort, holiness, and love! Thou hast more cause for gratitude than an angel

God, the eternal mighty God,
To dearer names descends;
Calls you his treasure and his joy,
His children and his friends.

D

FEBRUARY 15.

Grieve not the Holy Spirit. E[hes. iv. 30.

WE are absolutely dependent upon the Holy Spirit for life, light, teaching, and sanctification. Without His presence, power, and operations, we are dead, dark, ignorant and carnal. We should therefore be very careful not to grieve, or dishonor Him. We do so when we neglect, slight, or make any improper use of God's holy word; when we indulge in hard thoughts of God, or low thoughts of the Lord Jesus; when we mind the things of the flesh in preference to spiritual things; when we trifle with, or indulge in any sin of omission or commission; when we slight His intimations, abuse His gifts, and listen to Satan, the world, or the flesh, in preference to Him. When He is grieved He suspends His influence, and we find no assistance in duty; we get cold, carnal, and indifferent; we taste no sweetness in spiritual things, and the ministry of the word becomes dry and lifeless; the Bible is a sealed book; there is no power in prayer; no gratitude for mercies received; and religion becomes a task. Oh grieve not the Holy Spirit of God, by whom ye are sealed unto the day of redemption; but sow unto the Spirit, and ye shall reap life everlasting.

Return, O holy Dove! return,
Sweet messenger of rest!
I hate the sins that made thee mourn,
And drove thee from my breast.

7.31

FEBRUARY 16.

I will be to them a God. Heb. viii. 10.

THAT is, to all His people. The object of their adoration and trust, the subject of their meditation, and the source of all their happiness. To be our God, is more than being our friend, helper, or benefactor; (creatures may be so;) He engages to do us good according to His all-sufficiency, to bestow upon us blessings which none else can. He will pardon us, and pardon like a God—He will sanctify us, and sanctify us like a God—He will comfort us, and comfort us like a God—He will glorify us, and glorify us like a God. If He is our God, He is our all, and all He has is ours. He is our inheritance, and a glorious inheritance He is. Consider, when in danger, in darkness, in distress, in temptation, in duty, or in pain; God will be to you a God, delivering, enlightening, comforting, strengthening, and sanctifying you. Make a God of Him, look to Him for all He has promised, which is all you want; adore his divine perfections, and rejoice that they are all engaged to make you blessed. Live to His glory, walk by His word, and He will glorify Himself in your present and everlasting welfare. He rejoiceth to do good unto His people, He delights to bless them. .

> Here would I dwell, and ne'er remove,
> Here I am safe from all alarms;
> My rest is " everlasting love,"
> My refuge, " everlasting arms."

51

FEBRUARY 17.

Now is the day of salvation. 2 Cor **vi. 2.**

WHAT an unspeakable mercy to live at such a period. We are poor, lost, ruined sinners; but this is the day when salvation is freely bestowed, without money and without price. The Lord saves from the love, power, and consequences of sin; gives His Holy Spirit, writes His law in the heart, and directs our feet into the way of peace. He gives us Jesus, who is the Saviour; gives us grace, which conquers sin; and gives us heaven, to enjoy when the journey of life is ended. This is the day in which He works deliverance for His people; He employs His power, His wisdom, His word, His providence, and His angels, for our deliverance. What then shall we fear? Of whom shall we be afraid? Let us go to His throne, remembering that it is the day of salvation; let us plead for deliverance from all that mars our peace, prevents our enjoyment, or hinders us in our christian course. Let there be no despondency, for this is a day of good tidings; it is, believe, and be saved; pray, and be delivered; wait on the Lord, and He will strengthen your heart. "By grace are ye saved, through faith; and that not of your selves, it is the gift of God.".

Salvation! O the joyful sourd,
'Tis pleasure to our ears;
A sovereign balm for every wound,
A cordial for our fears.

FEBRUARY 18.

Be ye also patient. James v. 8.

OUR God is a God of patience. The Lord Jesus is the great example of patience. The Holy Spirit is the agent producing patience. Trials, troubles, and disappointments, are the means which exercise and strengthen it. The patience required, is a disposition to bear all that God has appointed for us, without complaining; yea, with resignation and hope: to wait God's time for the mercies we need, or for answers to the prayers we put up. Patience is the daughter of faith; and it is only as we believe that God has appointed, overrules, or commands, for our good and His glory, that we can be patient. Patience produces self-possession, shuts the mouth from complaining, keeps back the heart from seeking revenge, and is a principal point in self-government. Are you impatient? Then confess it, and mourn over it before God; it will make you miserable, and lead you to dishonor God. Watch against it; the coming of the Lord draweth nigh. Look at the prophets, apostles, martyrs, at Jesus; and be ye also patient: "In your patience possess ye your souls."

> Thus trusting in thy love, I tread
>   The path of duty on :
> What though some cherished joys are fled,
>   Some flattering dreams are gone ?
> Yet purer, brighter joys remain ;
> Why should my spirit then complain ?

FEBRUARY 19.

He careth for you. 1 Peter v. 7.

THE Lord knows all his people, their persons, wants, and trials; He thinketh upon them to benefit, deliver, and supply them. He keeps His eye upon them in all places, at all times, and under all circumstances. He has them in His hand, and will not loose His hold. He looks upon them always as His own; the objects of His love, the purchase of His Son's blood, the temples of the Holy Spirit. They are precious in His sight. He knows they are weak, fearful, and have many enemies. He teaches them to cast themselves and all their cares into His hands: and He has given them His word, that he will care for them. It is a Father's care which He exercises. It is wise, holy, tender, and constant; therefore all will be well, only trust. Believe that He cares for you this day; carry all your concerns to Him in the faith of this; leave all with Him, persuaded that He will manage all by His infinite wisdom, and bring all to a good issue by His omnipotent power. Cast all your cares upon Him as fast as they come in; be anxious for nothing. "Cast thy burden upon the Lord, and He shall sustain thee; He will never suffer the righteous to be moved."

Cast, my child, on me thy care,
'Tis enough that I am nigh;
I will all thy burdens bear,
I will all thy wants supply.

54

FEBRUARY 20.

Is the Lord's hand waxed short? Num xi 23

No—what He hath done, He can do; and all He hath promised, or His people need, He will do. He has all power. He knows no difficulty. Why then are we cast down? Because we do not believe His word, depend simply on His veracity, and expect all we need from His hand. He was displeased with Moses when he questioned His power, and He is displeased with us when we doubt His love, distrust His providence, or ask, "How can this thing be?" Whatever may be your difficulty, trial, or want, plead with the Lord and confidently expect deliverance; and if any temptation is presented to weaken your faith, rouse your fears, or disturb your tranquillity, meet it with this question, "Is the Lord's hand waxed short?" Beloved, look not to the hand of man, but look simply to the hand of God; man may disappoint you, God will not. He is faithful that promised. He is a God at hand. He will be near you throughout this day; His hand is able and ready to help you; therefore trust and be not afraid.

In heaven, and earth, and air, and seas,
He executes His firm decrees;
And by His saints it stands confess'd
That what He does is ever best:
Then on His powerful arm rely,
And He will bring salvation nigh.

The Lord trieth the righteous. Ps. xi 5.

WHERE the Lord gives grace, He always tries
it; therefore His own people must expect to
pass through the fire. He will try our faith,
of what sort it is; our love, of what strength it
is. He will also try our patience and our constancy. Let us not therefore be surprised at
trials, nor let us be discouraged by them; for
He tries out of pure love, with the best design,
according to a wise rule, and at the fittest
season. He considers our frame, our circumstances, and our foes; He does nothing rashly or
unkindly. He would not put us to pain if we
did not need it; trials are preservatives or re-
storatives; they keep us back from evil, or are
intended to bring us out of evil into which we
have fallen. Thy trials then are from the Lord;
His wisdom selected, His love appointed, and
His providence brings them about. If you ask,
" Why, Lord, am I tried thus?" the answer is,
" To humble thee, and to prove thee, and to do
thee good at thy latter end." Receive every
trial as from God, and go to Him for strength
to bear it, grace to sanctify it, and deliverance
from it; and so all will be well. It is not for
His pleasure, but for your profit, that you are so
tried.

> The clouds of deepest woe,
>   A sweet love-message bear;
> Dark though they seem, we cannot find
>   A frown of anger there.

FEBRUARY 22.

He delighteth in mercy. Mich. vii. 18.

THE proper object of mercy is misery ; sin has rendered us miserable, and God has revealed Himself as merciful. He delighteth in mercy ; it is a pleasure to Him to have mercy upon us ; He delights to pardon our sins, relieve our necessities, and save our souls. His own glory being secured, He delights to bless His people. He is styled THE FATHER OF MERCIES ; and as a father takes pleasure in his children, so does our God in showing mercy. He always delights in mercy, therefore He does so this morning ; go then and mourn over thy sins which have grieved Him, and rendered you miserable ; go and plead for mercy at His throne, nor doubt for one moment His pity, His kindness, or His grace. Have you obtained mercy ? Be zealous, to glorify God in the day of visitation ; be honest, and ascribe all to mercy which is her due ; and be active to spread the good news abroad, assuring poor miserable sinners, that GOD DELIGHTETH IN MERCY. With this check thy fears, repel thy temptations, and comfort thy heart. Believe it as an undoubted truth, plead it as a powerful argument with God, and daily rejoice in it. It is sweet to be an infinite debtor to mercy.

'Tis mercy in Jesus exempts me from hell ;
Its glories I'll sing, and its wonders I'll tell ;
'Twas Jesus, my friend, when He hung on the tree,
Who open'd the channel of mercy for me.

Who loved me. Gal. ii 20.

AND what was Paul? A blasphemer, a perse-
cutor, one who injured the church of God
And did Jesus love Paul? Yes—He loved me.
Then the love of Jesus is free, and not on account of anything man is. The cause of love
is in God, not in the objects loved You may
have looked for some reason to conclude that
God has loved you, but you have been disappointed; the Lord says, "I will love them freely." When we were dead in sins, He quickened us because He loved us; He revealed Jesus
to us because He loved us; He has given us His
Holy Spirit because He loved us. Whom once
He loves He never leaves Jesus loves us this
morning with a free, infinite, and eternal love.
He loves our persons apart from our graces and
acts; these are the effects of His love, and not
strictly the objects of His love. O Holy Spirit!
whisper to our hearts this morning, "Jesus
loved THEE, even thee." Oh, to love Him in return! to love Him above health, wealth, comfort,
yea, life itself! Oh, to show forth the praises
of His love by humility, faith, constancy, and
zeal!

> Great God, to thy almighty love
> What honors shall I raise?
> Not all the raptured songs above,
> Can render equal praise.
> Thy love to me surpasses thought,—
> Oh could I praise thee as I ought!

8.13

FEBRUARY 24.

Who gave Himself for me. Gal. ii 20.

JESUS was our substitute. He lived, suffered, and died in our stead. Our sins were imputed to Him, punished in Him, and removed by Him. God had cursed us, but Jesus gave Himself to bear the curse in our stead; every threatening of the law was executed on Him; every one of the claims of justice was answered by Him; and now God is just and yet the justifier of every one that believeth in Jesus. The debt-book is crossed, the handwriting that was against us is destroyed, and every foe is overcome. Do we think of the law we have broken, of the justice we have provoked, of the hell we have deserved? Let us also think, Jesus gave Himself for me. He satisfied justice, fulfilled the law, and brought glory to God, in my nature, name, and stead; and God is infinitely more honored by the life and death of my substitute, than He could have been either by my obedience had I never sinned, or by punishing me for sin. This is our rejoicing, that God can be just in justifying us who believe in Jesus. Thanks be unto God for His unspeakable gift.

Oh! let my trembling soul be still,
While darkness veils the sky,
And wait thy wise, thy holy will,
Wrapt yet in mystery.
I cannot, Lord! thy purpose see,
But all is well since ruled by thee.

FEBRUARY 25.

Christ is all Col iii 11.

Yes—this is God's purpose, which cannot be frustrated, that Christ shall be all. He is all in our justification and sanctification, for we are justified and sanctified IN HIS NAME He is all in our preservation and glorification, for we are kept by His power, and enter heaven through His merits He should be all in our pursuits, pleasures, hopes, motives and aims. Many put their comforts in the place of Christ, and then God puts comfort out of their reach : others put their graces in the place of Christ, and then faith, hope, and love are concealed by a cloud. There must be nothing between God and us, but Jesus; we must look away from sin, from graces, and from works, and expect to be accepted, blessed, and honored, only in the name and for the honor of Jesus. Christ is our conquering weapon, by which we overcome our foes; our plea, by which we prevail with God; our righteousness by which we are justified, and our peace, which supports and comforts us in life and in death. Christ is all we want, or God can give. He is our sun and shield ; our present joy, and endless portion.

Saviour ! the knowledge of thy love
Into my soul convey
Thyself bestow ! for Thee alone,
My all in all I pray
I would be only, always thine,
And prove the power of love divine.

Ye do dishonor me. John viii. 49.

THIS is a complaint brought against us by our Lord Jesus Christ. Let us listen to it. He has assured us of His love, that He seeks our good, that He will not be wroth with us; we dishonor Him, therefore, by our fretfulness under trials and troubles; by our murmuring when all is not as we wish; by our impatience to be delivered from pain; by our unbelief in reference to His promises and providence; by our unthankfulness for the many mercies we receive; by employing His favors in Satan's service; by limiting His power or His goodness; by omitting duties from want of love, or zeal; by relying on our services instead of free grace; and by looking to others, instead of looking only and always to Him for all. Dishonoring Jesus must be a great sin; it produces deadness, darkness, and misery; let us realize its criminality, lament it before God, seek repentance for it, and forgiveness of it. Oh, let us aim to honor Jesus by gratitude, patience, faith, love, forbearance, penitence, zeal, and constantly aiming at His glory! To honor Him in life, death, and forever!

> Lord, draw my heart from earth away,
>   And make it only know Thy call;
> Speak to my inmost soul, and say,
>   "I am thy Saviour, God, thine all!"
> Nor let me more dishonor Thee,
> But thy devoted servant be.

FEBRUARY 27.

All things come of Thee   1 Chron. xxix 14

Every good gift and every perfect gift is from above; creatures apart from God are empty cisterns, dry wells, deceitful brooks All good dwells in thy God, and flows from Him to thee. Every crumb is from Christ. What He gives freely, cost Him groans, sweat, and blood to procure for thee. View Him as the source of all good, and His atonement as the medium through which all flows to thee. He gives thee thy temporal mercies, and thy spiritual blessings; He gives thee also the ability to enjoy them, and employ them for His glory. He directs all events, whether pleasing or painful. "Be not angry with yourselves," said Joseph to his brethren, "it was not you but God." To Him, therefore, your mind should be directed, in prayer, dependence, and praise. Look above creatures and see the Lord's hand, as did Job, Eli, David, and Paul. Rest with unshaken confidence and filial resignation on His word, power, providence, and love ; ever remembering that all things come of Him. The Lord will give us that which is good, and a blessing with it, if we are looking to, and walking with Him. Every good gift and every perfect gift is from above,—from Jesus.

He sank beneath our heavy woes,
  To raise us to His throne;
There's ne'er a gift His hand bestows,
  But cost His heart a groan.

62

FEBRUARY 28.

I am He that liveth. Rev. i. 18.

JESUS once died in our stead; He now liveth **at** the right hand of God. He is the fountain of life. Because He lives, His people shall live also He lives in heaven to see of the travail of His soul, in the regeneration, sanctification, preservation, and glorification of His beloved family. He lives to intercede for them, to sympathize with them, and to pour down blessings upon them. He lives to watch over them, to counsel and direct them, and to save them for evermore. He lives to execute the purposes of the Father, to manage all the concerns of His church, and to glorify us with Himself for evermore. Gracious Saviour! earthly friends may die, but Thou livest; temporal comforts may be lost, but we have still a place in Thy heart; Thou art our Friend before Thy Father's throne. May we ever remember, Jesus liveth who was dead; and He is alive for evermore, and has the keys of hell and of death. Oh to live for Him on earth, who lives for us in heaven! Oh, to live like Him, that as He is, so we may be in this world—representatives of God and holiness! Oh, to live by faith on Him, in sweet and holy fellowship with Him.

He lives—the great Redeemer lives !
What joy the blest assurance gives!
And now, before his Father-God,
Pleads the full merits of his blood.

63

FEBRUARY 29.

Love not the world.   1 John ii. 15

WHAT is the world? A shadow. A deception. The enemy of God What can it do for us? It may enchant, but it will deceive. It may please for a time, but it will sting in the end. It is an enemy's country; we must pass through it, but we should not be too intimate with the inhabitants of it. It crucified our Saviour; it is in open rebellion against our God; it has allured, deceived, and injured many of our brethren; it is reserved unto fire at the judgment of the great day. We *shall* soon be called to leave it, we *may* be called to-day; "For what is our life? It is even as a vapor, which appeareth for a little while, and then vanisheth away." Let us fix and spend our love upon a worthier object; let us turn our thoughts to heaven, to Jesus; and let us seek grace that we may daily and heartily say, "Whom have I in heaven but Thee, and there is none upon earth I desire beside Thee." Precious Saviour! engross our attention, fix our affections, and be always our ALL IN ALL! None but Jesus, none but Jesus, should be our motto every day. He alone is worthy of our love; and He is worthy of it, for He died and lives to win it.

Lord, from this world call off my love,
Set my affections right,
Bid me aspire to joys above,
And walk no more by sight.

64

MARCH 1.

Thy Maker is thine husband Isaiah liv 5.

SWEET assurance! Surprising condescension. Does Jesus, by whom all things were made, fill this sweet relation? Is He my nearest and dearest relative? Yes—He loves thee more than any other: He is more closely united to thee, and more deeply interested in thee. He is the bridegroom, thou art the bride; He has espoused thee to Himself, has made full provision for all thy present wants, and is gone to prepare thy everlasting habitation, where thou art to dwell with Him and enjoy His love. The relation really subsists: He regards thee as His beloved bride, and He would have thee live daily in the recollection that He is thy Lord. O, love Him above all. Call upon Him with confidence. Look for Him with ardent longing. He will come to be glorified in His saints, and admired in all them that believe. Think not that He will ever forget the person, neglect the concerns, or turn a deaf ear to the requests of His beloved, blood-bought bride. His love is infinite, and the whole is set on thee; and will remain fixed on thee forever. He is in one mind, and none can turn Him. Having loved thee, He will love thee unto the end.

Jesus, my Shepherd, Husband, Friend
My Prophet, Priest, and King,
My Lord, my Life, my Way, my End,
Accept the praise I bring.

E   65

MARCH 2.

Resist the Devil. James iv. 7.

E\ERY believer must expect to be visited by Satan ; he is our adversary ; he is always watching for an opportunity to injure us. He first tempts us to sin, and then accuses us of sinning. He misrepresents every subject. He endeavors to make the world appear lovely, sin trifling, death terrible ; he generates hard thoughts of God, perverts His Holy Word, and leads believers into bondage. His fiery darts are very terrible. Thoughts the most blasphemous, horrible, and unnatural, are often thrown into the mind by him ; and then he lays them to our charge, and distresses our souls on account of them. But we are called upon to resist him steadfast in the faith, believing what God is to us ; what Christ has done for us ; what He has promised to give us ; and that God will bruise him under our feet shortly. The triumphing of this WICKED ONE is but short ; for we shall overcome him by the blood of the Lamb, and the word of His testimony. Look to Jesus, call upon thy God, and oppose the blood and righteousness of Jesus to all his charges. He is mighty, but thy Jesus is ALMIGHTY. Take this shield of faith, and thou shalt quench all the fiery darts of the wicked one.

Temptations everywhere annoy ;
And sins and snares my peace destroy :
Lord, let thy presence be my stay,
And guard me in this dangerous way.

66

MARCH 3.

Let us have grace. Heb. xii. 28.

WE daily need grace to sustain us in troubles; to subdue our corruptions; to sanctify our tempers; to preserve us in temptation; to quicken our languid affections; to enlarge our experience; to render us useful to others; to enable us to endure to the end; and to meet death with confidence and joy. Our God is the God of all grace. Jesus is full of grace, and He giveth more grace. He has promised it, "He will give grace;" He has invited us to come and receive it, "Come boldly to the throne of grace, that ye may obtain mercy, and find grace to help in time of need." His grace is sufficient for us; but without grace we are dull, lifeless, and sure to fall. Oh let us look to Jesus for grace to strengthen us, sanctify us, and make us useful. Let us never attempt anything in our own strength; but let us receive from the Lord, that we may live to the Lord; and ascribe all that we do that is good, to the grace of God which is with us. Grace is always free. It is free for us, for us this morning, and our God bids us come and receive. Come then boldly to the throne of grace, and you SHALL obtain mercy, and find grace to help you this day.

On me, my King, exert thy power,
  Make old things pass away;
Transform and draw my soul to Thee,
  Still nearer every day.

MARCH 4.

Only believe. Mark v 35.

THAT is, take God at His word Give Him credit for meaning what He says, for being faithful to his own word; and then what will become of your fears? God speaks to you in language which you can understand; He promises all you can possibly need, He bids you put Him in remembrance, and plead with Him; and He pledges His character for the comfort of your heart. If you believe not, you make God a liar; you bring darkness on your own soul; you give Satan an occasion against you; and a thousand doubts, fears, and suspicions distress you. Is it any wonder? Can you offer a greater insult to God than deliberately to disbelieve His word? But you ask, Are the promises made to me? Yes, to every one that believeth, and to you if you believe. And the Spirit is promised to work faith in your heart; complain not then of the difficulty of believing, or of the power of unbelief; but go to thy God and plead with Him, crying, "Lord, increase my faith:" and go to His word, as to the word of a gracious Father, and endeavor to believe it.

Why, my soul! art thou perplexed!
Why with faithless trouble vexed!
Hope in God, whose saving name
Thou shalt joyfully proclaim,
When his countenance shall shine
Through the clouds that darken thine.

MARCH 5.

Fear thou not. Isaiah xli. 10.

THE Lord's people are all prone to fear because they do not realize their relation to God, their interest in the promises of God, and that they are always in the presence of God. How graciously our God forbids our slavish fears, and encourages confidence in Himself! Our slavish fears dishonor Him, our filial confidence glorifies Him. He loves to be trusted! He is grieved by our doubts and fears. We should fear nothing but sin; and if we fear sin follow holiness, and preserve a conscience void of offence toward God and man; if we live upon His word, daily use the open fountain and cultivate communion with our God, we will have no cause to fear. Beloved, leave all your distrust, and slavish fear, to the poor, godless werldling; but trust thou in the living God always, and everywhere. Hope in God; wait upon God; expect from God; follow hard after God: and all you want will be given, and all that would injure you will be frustrated. Be not afraid, only believe: Jesus is with thee, and will preserve, bless, and keep thee; therefore, " FEAR THOU NOT."

And art Thou with me, gracious Lord,
To dissipate my fear?
Dost thou proclaim Thyself my God,
My God forever near?
Then farewell, anxious, gloomy care,
Since God forbids my soul to fear.

Walk worthy of God. 1 Thess. ii. 12.

God hath called us with an holy calling, to enjoy a holy Saviour, believe a holy gospel, possess a holy nature, and walk in a holy way. All the provisions of free grace, all the promises of infinite love, and all the precepts of reigning holiness, unite to require us to be a holy people unto the Lord our God. We are to imitate the conduct of our God; He feeds His foes, loves His people, and always acts becoming His glorious character. Enemies will lie in wait to deceive you, errors will be broached to mislead you; but beware, lest being led away by the error of the wicked, ye fall from your own steadfastness. Consider your character,—children of God; your high privileges,—united to Jesus, temples of the Holy Ghost, companions of saints and angels, the friends of God; your destination,—to fill a throne of glory, wear a blood-bought crown, and reflect the praises of Jehovah forever. Walk worthy of God, suitable to your character, profession, and destination. Walk with God; walk as Jesus walked; walk circumspectly; walk in love; walk honestly as in the day; so will you adorn your profession, and secure to yourself comfort and peace. .

Oh ! for a closer walk with God,
A calm and heavenly frame,—
A light to shine upon the road
That leads me to the Lamb !

MARCH 7.

Ephraim my dear son. Jer xxxi 20.

Poor fickle, backsliding Ephraim, is thus called by our infinitely gracious God. Adopted by grace into the heavenly family, taught by the Spirit and united to Jesus, God views us through Him ; and having predestinated us to be conformed to the image of His Son, He views things which are but purposed as accomplished, and we are comely through the comeliness He has put upon us. His love to us is wonderful; He says, " He that toucheth you, toucheth the apple of His eye." He rejoices to do us good, and gives His angels charge over us. He will not suffer any one really to hurt us; but, lest this should be the case, He will keep us night and day. Let us then abide in Jesus; let us cultivate communion with this gracious God; let us follow on to know the Lord; trust in Him at all times; wait upon Him continually; and rejoice in this delightful fact, that God calls us "HIS DEAR SONS, HIS PLEASANT CHILDREN." He not only calls us so, but treats us as such; and addresses us as such in His holy word. Let us call Him our Father, and look to Him for all we need; so shall we honor Him, conquer Satan, and enjoy peace. Our Father is God : our God is our Father.

If I've the honor, Lord, to be
One of thy numerous family,
On me the gracious gift bestow,
To call Thee ABBA, FATHER ! &c

They need not depart. Matt. xiv. 16.

How many things concur to lead or drive us
away from Jesus! But we need not depart
from Him; He has everything we can possibly
want, for body or soul, for time or eternity.
He gives grace and glory, and no good thing
will He withhold from them that walk uprightly.
Having called us, and drawn us to Him, He
wishes us to abide with Him; and if tempted
to leave Him, to whom can we go? He will
supply every want, sanctify every trial, enable
us to overcome every difficulty, and make us
happy in His own love. The world will allure
you, Satan will try to drive you, and inward depravity will prompt you to wander; but keep
near to Jesus this day; think of Him, look to
Him, call upon Him, converse with Him; make
Him your Companion, Friend, and God. There
is no real happiness, or solid peace, but in the
presence and blessing of Jesus; and when He
giveth quietness none can make trouble. If you
wander, if you look to others, if you set your
affections on anything below, you cannot justify
your conduct, for you need not depart. He is
all. He has all. He will give all. You have
only to believe His word, and your wants shall
be all supplied. ·

Oh, let us ever walk in Him,
And nothing know beside;
Nothing desire, nor aught esteem,
But Jesus crucified.

MARCH 9.

Hear ye Him. Matt. xvii 5

Jesus speaks to us in His word; He tells us all His mind; and the Father commands us to hear Him. He speaks to us in a variety of subjects, He instructs, exhorts, warns, directs, and comforts. He always speaks in love. Every word is intended to do us good. Let us then take up His word and say, " I will hear what God the Lord will speak " How much better this than to listen to Satan, unbelief, carnal reason, or men. Let us believe what He says, for He speaks truth; expect what He promises, for He intends to bestow; practise what He commands, for His ways are peace; and abstain from what He prohibits, for it is sure to be injurious. Hear Him, and plead His word in prayer. Hear Him, and oppose what He says, to fear, Satan, and appearances. Hear Him, and compare all doctrines with His word Hear Jesus every day, give Him your attention at least for a few minutes; you can hear nothing better than what He speaks; no one that has a greater claim upon your attention. Hearing Jesus with attention, prayer, and faith, will prevent a great number of real evils.

Jesus, my Prophet, heavenly Guide !
Thy sweet instructions I will hear;
The words that from Thy lips proceed,
Oh how divinely sweet they are !
Thee, my great Prophet, I would love,
And imitate the blest above.

MARCH 10.

TROUBLE and the Christian are seldom far apart, or long apart; this may sound discouraging; but Jesus and the Christian are never apart. He will never leave us, and trouble is intended to prevent our leaving Him, or to bring us back if we have already wandered. The loving heart guides the hand which smites; and nothing is done by Him, or permitted, but that it may be overruled for our good. Trouble may be near, but the throne of grace also is near; His word of promise is near; and He is near who justifieth us. In trouble God can glorify His grace, deepen His work in your heart, brighten your evidences, and fill you with joy and peace in believing; plead with Him to do so, let not trouble fill you with confusion, weaken your faith or drive you from Him; but listen to, and act upon His word. He says, "Call upon me in the day of trouble, I will deliver thee, and thou shalt glorify Me." "I will be with him in trouble, I will deliver him and honor him." "Hath He said, and shall He not do it? He hath spoken, and shall He not make it good?" Every trouble is intended to endear Jesus to your heart.

This land thro' which His pilgrims go,
  Is desolate and dry:
But streams of grace from Him o'erflow,
  Their thirst to satisfy:
Jesus has all His saints can want,
And when they need He'll freely grant.

MARCH 11.

Beloved, now are we the sons of God.
1 John iii. 2.

WHAT surprising grace is this. For what are we? Poor, vile, depraved, unworthy sinners So base by nature that we had not one redeeming quality, and even now, apart from the work of the Spirit, there is in us no good thing But we were predestinated to the adoption of children; we were born again of the Spirit; and grace has put us among the children, for its own glorification. Beloved, now, while we feel so much corruption, while despised by the world, harassed by Satan, tormented with fears, now are we the sons of God. And will God neglect or disregard his beloved sons? No—let us then cherish the thought, believe the fact, and rejoice in the relationship. Let us walk and act as the sons of God, coming out from among the formal, the self-righteous, and the profane; and devoting ourselves entirely to the Lord's service and glory. Let us remember in trouble, in sickness, and in death itself, God is our Father, Jesus is our brother, and heaven is our home Let us approach God as children, and plead with Him as sons. He says to us, "Come near unto me, my son, that I may bless thee."

The God who reigns above, we call
 Our Father and our Friend;
And, blessed thought! His children all
 Shall see Him in the end.

MARCH 12.

We shall be like Him. 1 John iii. 2.

LIKE whom? Like Jesus in His glorified humanity. As free from sin, as perfect in holiness as completely happy. His likeness will appear in every believer. What a contrast with the present! Now we appear to ourselves, at times, as like Satan as possible. Oh, the depth of depravity we discover, the powerful corruptions we feel, the fearful opposition to God we sometimes experience! But we shall be like Him. God has purposed it, the gospel plainly reveals it, and the Holy Spirit is engaged to effect it. Every evil shall be purged out, every virtue shall be produced and perfected, and we shall be pure as He is pure. Let us then look forward to, and anticipate that glorious period: let us consider the end of our election, redemption, and calling; and let us pray, pant, and strive to be holy. If holiness is our element, heaven will be our home, and unspeakable happiness our eternal portion. But we know not what we shall be, only that we shall be like Him, for we shall see Him as He is. If we suffer, we shall also reign with Him.

Oh! glorious hour!—Oh! blest abode!
I shall be near, and like my God,
And flesh and sin no more control
The sacred pleasures of the soul.

My flesh shall slumber in the ground,
Till the last trumpet's joyful sound:
Then burst the chains, with sweet surprise,
And in my Saviour's image rise.

MARCH 13.

Seek those things which are above. Col. iii. 1.

AND what are the things which are above? Holiness—or conformity to Jesus, and entire devotedness to His service. Happiness—flowing from the manifestation of Jehovah's glory, the presence of Jesus, and the soul's delight in His will. Unity—saints above realize close, intimate, and indestructible union to Father, Son, and Spirit; they enjoy sweet and constant union with each other, and the holy angels; they have unity of design, work, and enjoyment. Seek those things which descend from above; as faith—which believes, trusts, and prefers God's word: love—which has God for its author, Christ for its principal object, and spiritual things for its chosen subjects; fellowship—with Father, Son, and Spirit, and all spiritual persons and subjects. In a word, all spiritual gifts, graces, and operations. Seek them earnestly, principally, and constantly. Think much and often upon them. Highly value and esteem them. Constantly prefer them to earthly things. Labor to possess and enjoy them. God giveth liberally, and upbraideth not. You have not, because you ask not. Ask and receive. Receive and be happy. Your God bids you " REJOICE."

> Rise, my soul, and stretch thy wings,
> Thy better portion trace;
> Rise from transitory things,
> Towards heaven, thy native place.

10,9

MARCH 14.

By nature he is an enemy to God, in open rebellion against Him, and justly condemned by Him. He is in love with sin, a slave to lust, a servant of Satan. He is blind to his best interests, deaf to the calls of God, and dead in trespasses and sin. He is an open sepulchre, a mass of wretchedness and disease, abominable and filthy beyond description. And can such a creature be the object of Jehovah's love, the purchase of a Saviour's blood, and the habitation of the Holy Spirit? Yes—as such, they were chosen to salvation—as such, Jesus was sent into the world to redeem them—as such, the Holy Spirit came to quicken, cleanse, justify, and save them! O amazing grace! Astonishing mercy! And will God in very deed dwell with such creatures upon earth? Yes—"To this man will I look, and with him will I dwell, that is poor, and of a contrite spirit, and that trembleth at my word." Well may the patriarch exclaim, "What is man that Thou shouldest magnify him? and that Thou shouldest set thine heart upon him?"

> Oh, what is feeble, dying man,
>   Or any of his race,
> That God should make it his concern
>   To visit him with grace !
> That God, who darts His lightnings down,
>   Who shakes the worlds above,
> And mountains tremble at His frown,
>   How wondrous is His love !

A Christian. 1 Peter iv. 16

A CHRISTIAN wears the name, possesses the nature, breathes the spirit, lives the life, and devotes himself entirely to the glory of Jesus. All Christ has is his, all Christ has done was for him, and all Christ has promised he may expect. Are you a Christian? Is the matter doubtful? Does Jesus live in you? Are you living by faith upon Him? Is He your daily bread? Do you find that you could as well live without food, as without Jesus? This is a sure evidence. This is the certain effect of the Spirit's work. If you are a Christian, you pant, pray, and strive to be Christ-like; to bear about in your body the dying of the Lord Jesus, that the life also of Jesus may be made manifest in your mortal body. You put off the old man which is corrupt, and put on the new man which is created in righteousness and true holiness. You may live in newness of life, as one raised from the dead; exhibiting the effects of His death in deadness to the world, love to immortal souls, bearing testimony to the truth, and looking for, and hasting to, the coming of the day of God.

> Father, in me reveal thy Son;
> And in my inmost soul make known
>   How merciful Thou art:
> The secret of Thy love reveal,
> And by Thine hallowing Spirit dwell
>   Forever in my heart.

MARCH 16.

Thy God reigneth. Isaiah lii. 7.

JESUS has power over all flesh. He is upon the throne of the universe. He superintends all things. His will cannot be frustrated. His designs must be accomplished. Nothing is left to chance. His hand is in every event. He rules over the world by His power. He rules in the church by His word. He rules in the heart by His Spirit. He reigns to crush or convert thy foes; to secure thy well-being and His glory. Let this truth calm and compose thy mind at all times: "My God reigneth." He sitteth above the water-floods, He remaineth a king forever. He is entitled to all honor. He is the proper object of thy fear, faith, and love. See Him on His throne and rejoice; for it involves thy safety, happiness, and honor. Do men oppress? does Satan annoy? are things going cross? This is thy comfort, God reigneth: He directs and controls every being and every event. Gracious God! may I ever live believing that the reins of government are in Thy hands; and that Thy counsel shall stand, and that Thou wilt do all Thy pleasure. My God, reign in me!

His kingdom cannot fail;
He rules o'er earth and heaven;
The keys of death and hell
Are to our Jesus given
Lift up the heart, lift up the voice,
Rejoice aloud, ye saints, rejoice

80

MARCH 17.

God was manifest in the flesh 1 Tim. iii 16.

THE manifestation of God is in the person and work of Christ, and we are herefrom to learn what our God is, and what we may expect Him to do for us. What Jesus was to those about Him, such Jehovah is; what Jesus did and was willing to do, that our God is willing to do for us. In Jesus we see tender love, melting compassion, and gracious forbearance; mercy and power, rectitude and pity, holiness and long-suffering, justice and harmlessness, united. Such is our God. Fury is not in Him. Love is His name and His nature. And can you slavishly fear such a God? Can you wilfully sin against and grieve such a being? Cannot you believe his word, depend upon His veracity, rejoice in His name, and expect from Him every promised good? For this purpose His word was written, His name is published, and Jesus died. Always look at God in Christ; attempt not to learn God from nature. "No man hath seen God at any time; the only begotten Son, which is in the bosom of the Father, He hath declared Him." "I HAVE MANIFESTED THY NAME."

> Till God in human flesh I see,
>   My thoughts no comfort find;
> The holy, just, and sacred THREE,
>   Are terrors to my mind:
> But if IMMANUEL'S face appear,
> My soul surmounts each slavish fear.

MARCH 18.

But He answered her not a word. Matt. xv. 23.

DELAYS are not denials. Jesus delayed to answer, but He did not deny her request. He hath said, "Ask, and it shall be given you. Whatsoever ye shall ask the Father in my name, He will give it you." Heaven and earth may pass away, but His word must stand forever. He delays the answer to try our faith, patience, and perseverance; but when He sends the blessing He proves His faithfulness, pity, and love Be not discouraged though your prayers remain unanswered for a time; it will not be always so. This poor woman had to wait, though her case was very trying, and her request very urgent; but at last Jesus commended her faith publicly, and dismissed her with, "Be it unto thee even as thou wilt." Prayer will prevail, if it is the prayer of faith. Pray on, then, and do not faint. Say as Jacob on the plains of Peniel, "I will not let thee go except thou bless me." Plead with Him; be importunate; wait His time; be willing to receive in His own way; be concerned that He should be glorified in giving to you, or doing for you; and you cannot fail. His mercy is from everlasting to everlasting, upon them that fear Him.

> Then let us earnest cry,
>   And never faint in prayer
> He sees, he hears, and, from on high,
>   Will make our cause his care.

MARCH 19.

In His favor is life. Psalm xxx. 5.

THAT is, in the favor of God in Christ. If He have a favor towards us, all will be well; but He has, and as a proof of His favor He gave Jesus for us, and to us; He sent the Holy Spirit to quicken, teach, and sanctify us. By believing we enter into the enjoyment of His favor: and enjoying His favor we learn to despise all that is opposed to it. Our spiritual life flowed from His favor; our happiness stands in the enjoyment of His favor; and heaven will be the full display and realization of His favor. To His favor we ascribe all our present comfort and future hopes. By the favor of God we are what we are. By His favor we are saved. This is the source of every good, the joy of every true believer's heart. Let us endeavor to ascertain beyond a doubt, that we are the favorites of God; let us prize His favor above thousands of gold and silver; and let our daily prayer be, "Remember me, O Lord, with the favor that thou bearest unto Thy people: O, visit me with Thy salvation, that I may see the good of Thy chosen, that I may rejoice in the gladness of Thy nation, and glory with Thine inheritance. Amen, even so, Lord Jesus."

> Early, my God! without delay,
> I haste to seek thy face;
> My thirsty spirit faints away,
> Without thy cheering grace.

MARCH 20.

The Lord is risen Luke xx.v. 3 4.

JESUS once died for our sins, and He rose for our justification. He lay in the grave as our substitute, He rose as our representative. He died that we may live. He lives, and we shall live through Him, and with Him forever. He is risen, having conquered death, reconciled us to God, perfumed the grave, and finished the work which the Father gave Him to do. As He arose, so shall we. As He is gone into heaven, thither should our thoughts, our hopes, and our affections ascend. Jesus has risen, to plead our cause; manage our affairs; fulfil His precious promises; and to prepare for us mansions in our Father's house. Sin was atoned for by His death, heaven is secured by his life. He is our risen, ascended, and reigning BROTHER. He is our conquering and crowned CAPTAIN. Oh, let us think of, speak for, and devote ourselves to JESUS. He is above the world; let us live above its vanities, amusements, and trammels; let us look beyond death to that glorious resurrection, when we shall be raised from the dead, and possess bodies which shall be incorruptible, glorious, powerful, and spiritual.

Jesus triumphs! sing His praises;
  'Twas by death He overcame.
Thus the Lord His glory raises;
  Thus He fills His foes with shame.
    Sing His praises!
  Praises to the Victor's name.

MARCH 21.

I will give you rest   Matt. xi 28

THERE is no rest for the Christian in the world There will be always something to disturb, perplex, or distress him : it is an enemy's land. But Jesus says, "I will give you rest." He does so by enabling us to rely on His word, recognize His hand, submit to His will, and trust in His perfect work. He assures us that our sins are forgiven us ; that our persons are safe in His keeping ; that His presence shall always be with us ; and that all things shall work together for the best. We can rest on His faithfulness ; He has been tried, and found faithful We can rest on His love, for it knows not the shadow of a turn We can rest on His power ; it is ever engaged on our behalf. We can rest on His covenant. it is ordered in all things and sure. We can rest on His blood ; it speaketh peace, pardon, and acceptance with God. We can rest at His feet ; there we are safe, and can never be injured. We cannot rest on our graces, on our comforts, on our friends, or on our possessions ; but we may rest on Jesus— we should rest on Him with unshaken confidence, and ardent love ; for His promises are plain, His power is infinite, and His love passeth knowledge.

> God is thy rest,—with heart inclined
> To keep His word, that word believe,
> Christ is thy rest,—with lowly mind,
> His light and easy yoke receive

Precious promises. 2 Pet i. 4.

The promises of scripture are the promises of the great God; they are all of free grace; they are confirmed by the blood of Jesus; and are exceeding great and very precious. They are so plain that a child can understand them; and so great that no angel could fulfil them. There is such a variety that they meet every case; and such a fulness that they include every want. They are breasts of consolation for the poor, tried, and distressed believer; and are the strength and support of every child of God. They are our plea at the throne of grace, our confidence in the hour of trial, and our rejoicing in prospect of death. Beloved, God's promises are to be your daily comfort; it is for you to search them out, store them up, believe them, trust in them, plead them, and be assured of their fulfilment, because, "He is faithful who promised." The promises are more precious than gold or silver; sweeter than honey or the honey-comb; more lasting than the earth; and more stable than the pillars of heaven. Let us think of them, plead them, and expect their fulfilment to-day; our God is a faithful God, keeping covenant and mercy unto a thousand generations.

Praise to the goodness of the Lord,
Who rules His people by His word;
And there, as strong as His decrees,
He sets His kindest promises.

MARCH 23.

Where is your faith? Luke viii. 25

THE disciples were in a storm, surrounded by danger, and filled with fear; they apply to Jesus—this was right; they doubt His care, question His love, and cry, "We perish."—This was wrong. Jesus demands, "WHERE IS YOUR FAITH?" May He not put the same question to us? We have His word, but do we heartily believe it? We speak of His love, but do we confidently trust it? We read of His care, but do we see our safety in it? We often seem to believe any one sooner than Jesus; to trust any word more than His word; and therefore we are cast down, fearful and distressed. Let us this day endeavor to fix our faith steadily upon His precious word; let us believe in His particular providence; let us commune with Him as our firm and faithful friend. He says, "Let not your hearts be troubled, ye believe in God, believe also in Me." He is worthy of credit, He cannot deceive; He deserves our confidence, He will not neglect; He encourages our hope, and promises, "If ye ask anything of the Father in My name, I will do it." Do you believe this? Do you believe it when you pray?

Oh, how wavering is my mind,
Toss'd about with every wind,
Oh, how quickly doth my heart
From the living God depart:
O my God, thy grace impart,
To fix and bind my wandering heart.

87

MARCH 24.

Thy sins are forgiven. Luke vii 48.

Whose sins ? Thine, if thou believest in Jesus.
For to Him give all the prophets witness, that
through His name whosoever believeth in Him
shall receive remission of sins   If we confess
our sins, God is faithful and just to forgive
us our sins, and to cleanse us from all unrighteousness   God pardons, for Christ's sake
every one who believeth, confesseth, and for
saketh sin.   He thus proves Himself ready to
forgive, plenteous in mercy, and full of compassion to all who call upon Him   He never
refuses to pardon, nor manifests the least re-
luctance.   Nor ought we to doubt for one moment upon the subject, seeing His word is so
plain, His grace is so great, His mercy is so
free ; and His faithfulness so clearly proved.
What then do we want?   Only faith to believe
God's word, that we, being believers in Jesus,
having confessed sin at His throne, and prayed
for pardon in Christ's name, are forgiven all our
trespasses.   And this is needful, for we can
never mortify sin, live above the world, rejoice
in God, and honor the gospel, but as we believe
these sweet words of Jesus, "Thy sins are forgiven thee."

How high a privilege 'tis to know
  Our sins are all forgiven !
To bear about this pledge below,
  This special grant of heaven !
O Lord, this privilege bestow,
  Teach me while I dwell below.

88

MARCH 25.

OUR compassionate Lord was surrounded by a starving, fainting multitude; His disciples had only five small coarse loaves, and two little fishes, and yet He had bidden them to feed the company. The commands of Jesus are often intended to try our faith, and bring us as children to His feet. He says, " Bring them to Me." Things are not what they appear, but what Jesus makes them. His blessing produces a wonderful change. He bids you bring everything to Him. Have you a family? He says, " Suffer the little children to come unto Me, and forbid them not." Have you trials? Take them to Him; His blessing sweetens and lessens trials. Are you in poverty? Carry your poverty to Him; He can increase your little, and bless it with a peculiar flavor. Whatever troubles you this day, or any day, think that you hear Jesus saying, " Bring it hither to Me." Carry all things to Him, small things as well as great ones; it is only by so doing, that you can surmount trials; conquer foes; glory in tr'bulation; and joy in God.

The privilege I greatly prize,
Of casting all my care on Him,
The mighty God, the only wise,
Who reigns in heaven and earth supreme,
How sweet to be allowed to call
The God whom heaven adores my Friend;
To tell my thoughts, to tell Him all ,
And then to know my prayers ascend.

He giveth power to the faint Isa xl 29.

THE Lord's people often feel faint, being burdened with a body of sin and death, pursued and
assaulted by Satan, tried and hindered by the
world ; but though faint they continue to pursue. Waiting on the Lord they renew their
strength. The Lord has said, "I will strengthen
thee." Brother, remember the promise and
faithfulness of thy God ; yield not to fear, or
you will surely faint. Believe because God is
true. David says, "I had fainted unless I had
believed to see the goodness of the Lord in the
land of the living." Power is given in answer
to prayer. Strength is proportioned to the day.
The back is fitted for the burden. Our God
will not lay upon us more than He will enable
us to bear. He strengthens by His word, by
His Spirit, and by His presence ; expect Him
to be and do according to His word ; this will
honor Him, and He will strengthen you with
might by His Spirit in the inner man. Go
forth, however weak you may feel, assured that
God will give you strength and courage ; strength
to do and suffer His will, and courage to face,
fight and overcome every foe.

Whence do our mournful thoughts arise ?
  And where's our courage fled ?
Have restless sin, and raging hell,
  Struck all our comforts dead ?
Chase, chase thy gloomy fears away,
Strength shall be equal to the day.

Ask, and ye shall receive. John xvi. 24.

THESE are the words of Jesus. He addresses them to us this morning. They suppose want, and inability to supply ourselves. They intimate that provision is made and may be obtained. They invite us to ask with confidence, assuring us we shall receive. Jesus has a boundless fulness of blessings, and a loving tender heart to bestow them. He will supply all our needs. Let not want, then, lead you to despond, but look to Jesus; He has, He gives, He tells you to ask and receive. Can any terms be more easy, more suitable, more encouraging than these? But ask in faith, believing because Jesus has promised; ask with earnestness, as though you valued the blessings; ask with importunity; go again and again, until you obtain them. Go to Jesus for all you want; make everything a matter of prayer; in everything, by prayer and supplications, with thanksgiving, let your requests be made known to God. Doubt not, for His word is plain; He is full of compassion; He waits to be gracious; and He has thousands of witnesses to attest His faithfulness, veracity, and love. Look to the generations of old. Did any ever seek the Lord in vain? No: every one that asketh receiveth.

> My soul, ask what thou wilt,
>   Thou canst not be too bold,
> Since His own blood for thee He spilt
>   What else can He withhold?

MARCH 28.

I am the Lord's. Isa. xliv. 5.

Not only because He has chosen me from others, in Jesus His beloved Son; nor merely because I am redeemed from among men, by the precious blood of Immanuel; but also be cause I have surrendered myself up into the Lord's hands, with all I have and am, to b taught by His Spirit, ruled by His word, sup plied by His providence, and devoted to Hi praise. The Lord claimed me, and I wa enabled to acknowledge the claim; He has right to me, and that right should never be for gotten by me. Am I tempted to sin? to murmur? to despond? Let this be m preservative, "I AM THE LORD'S." How base ungrateful, and wicked for ME to yield to sin for me to complain of any of His dispensations or for me to doubt His goodness or His grace I am the Lord's, for life; I shall be the Lord' in death; and then (O delightful thought!) shall be the Lord's for evermore. He will guid me by His counsel, and afterwards receive m to glory. I have only to aim at His glory, wal by His word, and live at His throne, until H takes me to Himself. My only business o earth is to please God, and my heaven will b to enjoy Him forever.

Jesus, thy boundless love to me,
 No thought can reach, no tongue declare,
Oh, knit my thankful heart to Thee,
 And reign without a rival there!

MARCH 29.

Cease ye from man. Isaiah ii. 22.

NEVER trust him, for his heart is deceitful; never expect from him, for he is an empty cistern; never follow him, for he is a false guide. Cursed be the man who trusteth in man, and maketh flesh his arm, and whose heart departeth from the Lord. Trust ye not in a friend. One object of trust is enough: He has all you want, and has offered to give whenever you ask. He never did deceive, He never can. It is impossible for God to lie. Looking to man, dishonors His fulness; trusting in man, is pouring contempt on His word; expecting from man, is overlooking His agency. If you neglect this loving direction, expect to suffer; if you walk by it, your peace will be like a river, and your soul like a well-watered garden. He knows what is in man, you do not. He cautions you, because he loves you. He would save you from disappointment, sorrow, and woe. Come then to the conclusion of the prophet, "Therefore will I look unto the Lord; I will wait for the God of my salvation: my God will hear me."

Happy they who trust in Jesus!
　Sweet their portion is, and sure:
When destruction others seizes,
　God will keep His own secure;
　　Happy people!
Happy though despised and poor.

93

Yea, He loved the people. Deut xxxiii 3.

AND what were the people whom He loved? Poor, oppressed, rebellious, stiff-necked, hard-hearted, unworthy creatures Just such are His people by nature now. Such are we. Yet He loves us ; pities us ; and distinguishes us from others around us. He spared not his own Son, but delivered Him up for us all ; and with Him He will freely give us all things. Though He has not yet all His people with Him, yet He has Jesus sitting at His right hand, who is their representative ; the express image and exact likeness of His elect. All the rays of His love centre in Him, who is the head of His body the Church. All the streams of delight empty themselves into Him, and through Him flow down to every believer on earth. As He loveth Christ, so He loveth us; while He loveth Jesus, He will love us ; for Christ and we are one. What is done to us, is done to Him, and what is done to, or bestow-ed upon Him, as man and Mediator, is done to and bestowed upon us. Oh, glorious mystery of infinite and eternal love ! Oh, direct my heart into this love of God ! .

O love of unexampled kind !
That leaves all thought so far behind;
Where length, and breadth, and depth, and height,
Are lost to my astonished sight :
Lord, shed abroad that love of Thine
In this poor sinful heart of mine

94

MARCH 31.

I will be with him in trouble. Ps. xci. 15.

Sin is the parent of trouble; all sorrow origi-
nated in departing from God. It is generally
occasioned by transgression, or sent as a preventative to a greater evil; it may be occasioned by good, for saints are sometimes persecuted for righteousness' sake. It is intended
to correct, improve, and to bring us near to
God. Whatever may be our trouble, if we are
the Lord's, He is with us; and with us for the
most gracious purposes. He fixes the period of
our troubles, nor can they continue longer than
He sees needful. He regulates the heat of the
furnace, nor will He suffer us to be tried more
than we are able to bear. He sanctifies our
troubles, and causes them to work our good.
He delivers out of trouble, when the purposes
of His love are accomplished. In every trouble,
remember, God is now especially present; He
is with you to hear your prayer, increase your
strength, direct your way, and make you a conqueror. His grace is sufficient; His presence
is sure; your deliverance in His time and way
is certain. Therefore, "wait on the Lord, be
of good courage; He will strengthen your heart;
wait, I say, on the Lord."

He that hath made his refuge God,
Shall find a most secure abode,
Shall walk all day beneath His shade,
And there at night shall rest his head.

95

APRIL 1.

The Lord is my shepherd. Ps. xxiii. 1.

THEN David was one of the Lord's sheep. All His sheep know him, love Him, and follow Him. They possess His disposition; He was meek and lowly in heart. Are you a sheep of Christ? Are you looking to, following of, and rejoicing in your Shepherd? If so, it is his province to lead you, feed you, protect you, and heal you. Your person, life, health, comforts, and safety, are committed to His care. He is the good shepherd, He laid down his life for His sheep; He searches and seeks out His sheep wherever they have been scattered; He feeds His flock; He gathereth the lambs with his arms, and carrieth them in His bosom. He loved His sheep more than his own life; He cares for His sheep more than for all the world beside. He feeds them in the most suitable pasture, and leads them in the paths of righteousness for His name's sake. Oh, view Jesus as your Shepherd, expect Him to lead you, feed you, fold you, and present you to His Father with exceeding joy. Cleave to Him; let nothing tempt you to leave His feet, His flock, or His fold. He will never leave you, nor forsake you.

Jehovah is my Shepherd's name,
Then what have I, tho' weak, to fear?
My sin and folly I proclaim,
If I despond while He is near:
In every danger He is nigh,
And will my every want supply.

96

APRIL 2.

I shall not want   Psalm xxiii. 1.

THIS was David's conclusion, from the belief that the Lord was his shepherd. If we are the sheep of Christ, He will supply us. He has all things in His possession, the silver and the gold are His, and the cattle upon a thousand hills. His private mark is upon all. All spiritual blessings are in His possession also; and He has a kind, tender, and liberal heart. He will give. He has engaged to supply, conduct, protect, and present His flock upon mount Zion. He has promised to be to us, do for us, and bestow upon us, all that our circumstances require. His conduct towards His flock in old times is a sufficient guarantee; when ever were the righteous forsaken; or His sheep left neglected and unheeded? Did David ever want? Few passed through greater changes, or severer trials; yet upon his dying bed he tells us, he had all his desire. If you belong to Christ, you may safely conclude, "I SHALL NOT WANT." Your fears are follies; your anxieties are groundless; your forebodings are sinful; you have a God to provide for you, and you ought to rejoice. "My God," says the Apostle, "shall supply all your needs, according to His glorious riches." *yes & amen!*

> What want shall not our God supply,
> From His redundant stores?
> What streams of mercy from on high
> An arm almighty pours!

I flee unto thee to hide me   Ps cxlii 9

THIS implies DANGER—the Christian may be in danger, from sin, self, foes. FEAR—his fears may be groundless, but they are often very painful. INABILITY — to defend himself, or overcome his opposers. FORESIGHT—he sees the storm in the distance, and looks out for the covert. PRUDENCE—he hides before the storm, ere the enemy comes upon him. A laudable CONCERN for safety and comfort. The believer, if wise, will at all times flee to Jehovah. Jacob flies to Laban; the manslayer to the refuge; the bird to his mountain; and the Christian to his God. Asa may seek to physicians; Ephraim to King Jareb; and Saul to the witch; but the believer looks to his God. The Lord receives, befriends, and secures. Let us flee to Him by prayer, in faith, with hope, for salvation: and He will receive us, shelter us, and be our refuge and strength. Flee from sin, from self, from the world; but flee to Jesus. His heart is ever toward us, His ear is open to us, and His hand is ready to help, protect, and deliver us. His throne is our asylum, His promise our comfort, and His omnipotence our guard.

Happy soul, that free from harms,
Rests within his shepherd's arms!
Who his quiet shall molest?
Who shall violate his rest?
He who found the wandering sheep,
Loves, and still delights to keep.

APRIL 4.

It is I, be not afraid. John vi. 20

=a command

THE fears of the Christian are a dishonor to his Lord, a denial of his creed, and a fruitful source of distress to his own soul. All things are of God, He worketh all things after the counsel of His own will, and in every event He says to us, "IT IS I, BE NOT AFRAID." If friends turn to foes and distress us, if death enters our dwellings and bereaves us, if sickness lays us aside and fills us with pain, He says, "It is I, be not afraid." If losses, crosses, and sore trials come upon us, and discourage, distress, and perplex us, He says, "It is I, be not afraid." If death approaches and calls upon us to leave the body, and close our eyes upon our beloved relations, friends, and connections, He says, "It is I, be not afraid." Should we hear the pillars of heaven crack, and feel the strong foundations of the earth give way; should the heavens be rolled up like a scroll, and the great white throne appear; still, amidst the wreck of matter and the crush of worlds, He cries, "Be not afraid, it is I." Happy Christian! thy fears are groundless, and thy brightest hopes well founded.

Oh, that I might so believe,
Steadfastly to Jesus cleave;
Only on his love rely,
Smile at the destroyer nigh;
Free from care and servile fear,
Feel the Saviour always near.

APRIL 5.

Without Me ye can do nothing. John xv. 5. *That's right!*

NEVER forget that the Lord is our righteousness and strength. We are not sufficient to think rightly of ourselves, but through Him we can do all things. Never attempt anything without looking to Jesus for power. Let a knowledge and constant sense of weakness keep you near to Him; sensibly depending on Him; and ascribing all good unto Him. You cannot, He can. You have destroyed yourself, in Him is your help found. It is only by union to Him, and receiving from Him, that you can glorify God, adorn your profession, enjoy your privileges, and obey the holy precepts of the gospel. Never presume, but come up out of the wilderness, leaning on Him, your beloved. Live as one deeply sensible of your dependence upon, and obligation to, the Lord Jesus. He is the strength of the poor, the strength of the needy in his distress; and your strength too. Beloved, Jesus is your life-giving Head, the Fountain from which you are to draw all your supplies, and the Friend to whom you are to carry all your cares. He will work in you to will and to do of His own good pleasure.

Jesus, immutably the same!
  Thou true and living vine!
Around thy all-supporting stem
  My feeble arms I twine:
Thou art my strength, my life, my hope,
Nor can I sink with such a prop.

2/9/23

Worthy is the Lamb that was slain. Rev. v. 12.

THIS is an ascription of praise to Jesus, thy Jesus, as the sacrifice for sin, the atonement of the church, the Saviour of His body. Jesus who died for thy sins is worthy to receive power, and riches, and wisdom, and strength, and honor, and glory, and blessing. We never can ascribe too much to Jesus. But He is worthy also to be BELIEVED, in preference to Satan, unbelief, the world, or appearances; to be TRUSTED with all, for all, before all; to be LOVED, more than any other, in opposition to any other that would rival Him: to be OBEYED, though he commands us to cut off a right hand, or pluck out a right eye; to be FOLLOWED, wherever He may lead us, through evil report and good report; to be PRE-FERRED, to ease, pleasure, wealth, health, to anything and everything. Jesus is worthy to be our example, our confidant, our king, and our all. He is worthy of all He requires, all we can give, all His people have done for Him, or suffered in His cause. Believe His word, trust His grace, love His name, obey His com-mands, and prefer Him before all others. Make it your daily business to endeavor to bring sin-ners to His feet; He is worthy of every effort you can make.

> Jesus is worthy to receive
> Honor and power divine,
> And blessings more than we can give,
> Be, Lord, forever thine.

APRIL 7.

One thing is needful. Luke x 42.

THE things of time are transient, the things of eternity are permanent. The world passeth away. The body must die ; earthly connections must be dissolved ; but the soul must live forever. The welfare of the soul is the one thing needful. If the soul is in a sanctified and healthy state, it will be found at the feet of Jesus ; it will relish His words ; and enjoy His communications more than the richest feast. We shall be seeking to know Him, love Him, believe Him, obey Him, and enjoy Him. Fellowship with Jesus is needful as an evidence of interest in Him, and as a source of satisfaction and comfort. He that finds a home at the feet of Jesus, will enjoy an eternal heaven in the presence of Jesus. Let not then the *many* trifles of time affect, distract, and bewilder you ; but let the *one thing needful* be the constant object of pursuit and desire. Live at the feet of Jesus, and you are safe. Seek above all things to enjoy Jesus, and you will be happy. Aim in all things to glorify Jesus, and you will be holy. Look daily for the coming of Jesus, and you will be consistent. O Jesus ! manifest thyself to me ; draw me to thy feet, and keep me there !

Engage this roving, treacherous heart
To fix on Mary's better part ,
To scorn the trifles of a day,
For joys that none can take away.

APRIL 8.

He will save. Zeph iii 17.

Whom?—the lost, the wretched, the unworthy. Every applicant, for "Whomsoever shall call on the name of the Lord, shall be saved." "Him that cometh to me, I will in NO WISE cast out." How?—freely, without money and without price; fully, by His blood, power, and providence; eternally, all who flee to Him for refuge, all who build on Him for pardon, peace, and life; shall be saved with an everlasting salvation, they shall not be ashamed nor confounded, world without end. WHY?—because it is His Father's will; because He delighteth in mercy; because it will eternally glorify His name From what?— from sin, in its guilt, filth, and power; from the present evil world; from Satan; from the wrath of God; from every evil work; and from all the evil designs of men. He has saved us, by receiving grace for us and dying in our stead. He does save us, by His presence, word, providence, and the renewing of the Holy Ghost.—He will save in every trouble, from every foe, even unto the end. Look to Him then, and to Him alone, to deliver, direct, relieve, and preserve. He says, " Look unto me, and be ye saved, all ye ends of the earth; for I am God, and there is no other."

> Dear dying Lamb! thy precious blood
> Shall never lose its power,
> Till all the ransomed church of God
> Be saved, to sin no more.

APRIL 9.

Lord, increase our faith Luke xvii 5.

THE believer is as his faith is If faith is weak, he is fearful, fretful, and troubled; if faith is strong and rightly placed, he is courageous, active, and happy. Faith comes from Jesus, He is its author; it leads to Jesus, He is its object. Faith is like a grain of mustard-seed, it grows and increases; but Jesus alone can increase our faith. Let us apply to Him this morning, and let this be our prayer, ".LORD, INCREASE MY FAITH." Strong faith will believe without feeling, yea, against feelings or appearances. It will trust God where it cannot trace Him; it assures the soul that what He has promised He is able to perform, and will assuredly do so. Great faith will have great trials; for God never gives faith without trying it; and the heat of the furnace is in proportion to the strength of our faith Little faith lays hold on Christ, and brings salvation; strong faith receives much and often from Christ, and brings great consolation. Go to Jesus with the faith thou hast, and plead with him for the faith He requires. He gives freely to every importunate pleader; and He will assuredly give to thee. •

> O Jesus, now thyself impart,
> And fix thy presence in my heart,
>   Give strong and living faith!
> Then will I throw off every load,
> And walk delightfully with God,
>   Observing all He saith

104

APRIL 10.

He shall glorify me John xvi. 14. *my life purpose*

IF Jesus is to be glorified, our pride must be mortified, and our spirits humbled. It is the Spirit's office and work to glorify Jesus; this He does, by discovering to us our wretched and ruined state, and leading us to Him to crave salvation as a favor at His hands. By daily emptying us and leading us to Him for all we need. By giving us to see, that all God has created cannot satisfy an immortal spirit for one moment of time, but that there is enough in Jesus to satisfy it throughout eternity. Jesus is glorified when we mourn over sin, and wash in the fountain of His blood; when we renounce our own doings and feelings, and desire to be found in His righteousness alone; when we refuse to look to any other quarter for help, relief, or comfort, but to Him; when His dear name fills all our songs; and when we long to have a crown to cast at His feet, and a harp that will worthily sound forth His praise. "He shall glorify Me." This decrees the death of pride, self, and creature excellence Beloved, whatsoever you do in word or deed, do all to the glory of Jesus; He is the Lord of all.

Lord, draw my heart from earth away,
And make it only know thy call,
Speak to my inmost soul, and say,
"I am thy Saviour, God, thine all!"
Oh, dwell in me, and fill my soul,
And all my powers by thine control.

105

→ *And she went to inquire of the Lord.*
Gen xxv. 22

EXCELLENT example! Let us imitate Rebek-
ah, for God commands us to do so. In all thy
ways, acknowledge Him, and He shall direct
thy steps. Commit thy way unto the Lord
trust also in Him, and He shall bring it to
pass. Are you in trouble? Go and inquire of
the Lord—What is the cause? Unite with
holy Job in praying, "Show me wherefore thou
contendest with me." Are you in perplexity?
Go and inquire,—What is the design? He
will instruct thee and teach thee in the way
thou shouldest go, He will guide thee with His
eye. Go in an inquiring spirit. Go persuaded,
whatever thy circumstances or trials may be,
that as a believer in Jesus, wrath and curse can
have nothing to do with thee; they were exhausted when Jesus died in thy stead. Be
assured that whatever comes from God is a
blessing, a benefit, a favor, a proof of love; however painful, perplexing, or distressing it may be.
Do not reason, but believe in the promise of
thy God; do not despond, grieve, or complain;
but go and INQUIRE OF THE LORD; at His
throne, of His word. He says, "I will be in-
quired of."·

Prayer was appointed to convey
The blessings God designs to give;
Long as they live should Christians pray,
For only while they pray they live.

106

4/16

APRIL 12.

He cannot deny Himself. 2 Tim. ii. 13

GOD has opened His heart to us in His word. He has told us all His mind. He intends every word He has spoken, and will fulfil every promise He has made. He cannot deny Himself or falsify His word; He can have no temptation to do so. Man may be fickle, he is but a bruised reed; Jehovah is always the same, He is the rock of ages. He will have compassion on the miserable, who seek His face; and show mercy to all who plead with Him in Jesus' name. He cannot cast out a coming sinner, or refuse to receive a confessing backslider. He cannot turn a deaf ear to our cries, or refuse to deliver us when we call on His name. He will take His own time, but will never dishonor His faithful word. He will be rigidly faithful, both to His threatenings and promises. Let us take courage and trust in Him; we have His word, it is true from the beginning; we have this assurance, that HE CANNOT DENY HIMSELF. Let us then stay ourselves on the word of our God; let us trust Him though the night be dark and the burden be heavy. He exhorts, "Trust ye in JEHOVAH forever, for in JAH, JEHOVAH, there is everlasting strength."

God is love, and will not leave you,
  When you most his kindness need,
God is true—nor can deceive you,—
  Though your faith be weak indeed.

107

APRIL 13.

Why are ye troubled? Luke xxiv 38

CONSIDER what Jesus has done for you, promised to you, and is gone to prepare for you
Consider what He is to you, your loving Bride
groom, faithful Friend, and gracious Saviour
What troubles you ? Is it sin ?—He will pardon
subdue, and destroy it. The world ?—He has
overcome it, redeemed you from it, and is lead
ing you through it Satan ?—he is conquered
condemned, and will soon be imprisoned. The
cares and troubles of life ?—Jesus says, "Bring
them to Me by prayer, cast them on Me in
faith, leave them with Me ; I know what you
want, I have provided of my goodness, I will
supply all your needs ; your bread shall be
given you, and your water shall be sure.
will make a way in the wilderness of trouble
and a path in the desert of perplexity. Le
not your hearts be troubled, ye believe in
God, believe also in Me Try Me. Trust Me
In all your ways acknowledge Me, and I will
direct your paths I have wisdom, power, and
love ; and all that I have is yours : to be em
ployed for your good." Commit thy way unto
the Lord, trust also in Him, and He will bring
it to pass.

> Yield to the Lord, with simple heart,
> All that thou hast, and all thou art ;
> Renounce all strength, but strength divine
> And peace shall be forever thine
> Behold the path the saints have trod,
> The path which led them home to God.

108

APRIL 14.

Ye are complete in Him. Col. ii. 10.

Look not too much at thyself, there is nothing but vanity, weakness, sin, and misery there; *true* but thy God hath united thee to His beloved Son. Jesus is one with thee, and all that He has is thine. Thou art unholy, but He is made unto thee sanctification; and He will sanctify *Amen.* thee wholly, body, soul, and spirit. Thou art foolish, but He is made unto thee wisdom; and He will make thee wise unto salvation. Thou art weak, but he is thy strength; and thou canst do all things through His strengthening thee. Thou art unrighteous; but He is made unto thee righteousness; and thou art not only righteous, but the righteousness of God in Him. Thou art lost, but He is made unto thee redemption; He has redeemed thee from the curse of God, and from the present evil world, and He will redeem thee from death. In thyself thou art not only incomplete, but wretched, miserable, poor, blind, and naked; but in Jesus thou art holy, wise, strong, righteous, rich, happy; in a word, COMPLETE. View thyself, then, at least occasionally, as COMPLETE IN CHRIST, who is the head of all principality and power.

Still onward urge your heavenly way,
Dependant on Him day by day,
  His presence still entreat;
His precious name forever bless,
Your glory, strength, and righteousness,
  In Him you are complete.

Set your affections on things above. Col. iii. 2

WE are apt to be much affected by earthly things, but our affections should be permanently fixed on things above. Let us lift up our eyes and hearts to heaven this morning; there are the proper objects of our love, desire, and esteem. There is Jehovah our heavenly Father, dwelling in an approachable light. There is Jesus, our dear and adorable Saviour, exalted, dignified, and glorified at the right hand of the Father. There is the Holy Spirit, our divine, gracious, and condescending Comforter. There the love, favor, and presence of God are fully enjoyed. There peace, rest, and happiness are eternally realized. There is the crown of righteousness, the throne of glory, and the rivers of pleasure, which our God has promised, and set before us. There are our brethren who have gone home before us, and there our affections should be. What is earth? Whatever it is we are leaving it. What is time? We shall soon have done with it. Oh, let us then SET OUR AFFECTIONS ON THINGS ABOVE, AND NOT ON THINGS OF THE EARTH.

Why should my heart descend so low,
To brood on earth—a world of woe,
While heaven, where endless pleasures **roll,**
Waits to entrance my new-born soul?
Saviour! let thine attractions be
But felt in all their force by me;
Then shall I mount on wings of love,
And feast my soul on things above.

APRIL 16.

He will subdue our iniquities. Micah vii.

Sɪɴ must not only be pardoned, but corruption must be subdued; the one is freely promised as well as the other. The grace of God pardons, the power of God subdues; but grace and power always go together in the salvation of a sinner. Pardon comes first, and sanctification follows. Light shining upon the understanding, discovers corruption working in the soul; holiness seated in the heart, produces hatred and opposition to it; prayer ascends to God for deliverance from it, and power descends and subdues it. But like fire apparently quenched, it will break out again and again; like rebels in a state, it will seize every opportunity of disturbing the peace and happiness of the soul. Hear, then, what the Lord says to you this morning, "I ᴡɪʟʟ ꜱᴜʙᴅᴜᴇ ʏᴏᴜʀ ɪɴɪQᴜɪᴛɪᴇꜱ." Carry your complaint to His throne, plead His faithful word, and expect His promised power to subdue your iniquities. Sin shall not have dominion over you, for you are not under the law, but under grace. Grace reigns, and will conquer every rival lust.

Jesus, thy boundless love to me
No thought can reach, no tongue declare;
O knit my thankful heart to thee.
And reign without a rival there.
O grant that nothing in my soul
May dwell, but thy pure love alone:
O may thy love possess me whole,
My joy, my treasure, and my crown.

1

APRIL 17.

Th· forerunner is for us entered.
Heb. vi. 20.

WHATEVER Jesus did was for His people. He is gone into heaven as our forerunner; as the PIONEER goes before the army to remove obstacles, clear the road, and render the march more easy, so did Jesus go before us. As an interested and kind FRIEND, He shows the practicability of the way; as a wise GUIDE, He marks out the road for us; as our EXAMPLE, He is gone before, and says to us, "FOLLOW ME." We have now an ADVOCATE with the Father, a HUSBAND preparing our mansions, a SAVIOUR waiting to receive us. We have one in heaven to whom in our addresses to His throne we can say, "Lord, thou knowest from Thy own experience what I feel in my present situation, for Thou wast once tried in all points like as I am." We have one in heaven who will welcome us home, and who when He sees us enter will be glad in his heart. We know Him below, and we shall know, and enjoy, and love Him forever above. He is gone into heaven FOR us, nor shall we know until we arrive there, how much we are indebted to His intercession and pleading above. O my soul, look at Jesus as thy Forerunner, and follow in His steps!

Before His heavenly Father's face,
For every saint He intercedes :
For mercy and abounding grace
There Jesus, our Forerunner, pleads.

APRIL 18.

Our sufficiency is of God 2 Cor iii. 5.

LET us think of this, whenever we are cast down on account of our weakness, or the difficulties we meet with in our way. We are weak, but Jesus is strong; and His strength is made perfect in our weakness. He has given us His word, that He will work in us to will and to do, of His own good pleasure. He speaks and it is done. The word of the Lord knows no obstacles or difficulties; all things must obey Him. When He sent Moses to Pharaoh, He said, "Certainly I will be with thee:" and the Lord's presence was his strength. He acts just so with us: His fulness is our sufficiency; it is opened to us in Jesus, and we receive from it according to our wants, weakness, and faith. "Through God," said David, "I shall do valiantly." "I can do all things," said Paul, "through Christ strengthening me." Look not then at your own emptiness, or weakness; but look at what God is to His people, and what He has promised to give them, and sing, "OUR SUFFICIENCY IS OF GOD." "God is our refuge and strength; and as our days so shall our strength be." "His grace is sufficient for us; His strength is made perfect in weakness."

When we cannot see our way,
We should trust, and still obey;
He who bids us forward go,
Will instruct the way to know.

113

APRIL 19.

Quicken thou me in thy way. Psalm cxix 37.

WHAT poor, dull, lifeless creatures we often feel ourselves to be ; and how needful is this prayer. It is our duty to RUN in the way of God's commandments ; it is our misery that through sin, weakness, and temptation, we scarcely creep. We are dependant upon the Spirit for quickening. He only can strengthen, animate and enliven us. Let us sow unto the Spirit this morning. He is gracious, and a grace-giving Spirit. He delights to exalt and honor Jesus. Let us therefore beseech Him in Jesus' name, for His sake, that we may bring honor unto His cause, to quicken our souls. Let us pray Him to bring us near to God ; for the nearer to God the happier, and holier, and live- lier, we shall be. Let us ask Him to shed abroad the love of Jesus in our hearts; for the love of Christ will make us live well, bear the cross well, perform duties well, and die well. The command furnishes us with a rule, and the promise finds us strength ; but it is only the Spirit that can put us in possession of the latter, and without that we cannot attend to the former, in a gospel spirit. The presence of Jesus, and the communications of His grace, are daily neces- sary to keep us lively, devoted, and working for God.

> I need the influence of Thy grace
> To speed me in Thy way,
> Lest I should loiter in my race,
> Or turn my feet astray.

114

APRIL 20.

Christ hath made us free. Gal. v. 1.

WE were once the slaves of sin, Satan, and the world; we were under the law as a covenant of life; but Jesus has made us free. We are now delivered from the law, and are under grace. We are dead to sin, and are justified from it. We are delivered from Satan, and are at war with Him. We overcome the world, and are hastening out of it. We are at liberty to serve God, and walk with Him in friendship and holy love. The price of our freedom was the life and death of Jesus; the efficient cause of our freedom was the power and operation of the Holy Spirit; the grand moving cause, was the infinite and everlasting love of God our Father; the instrument by which we are made acquainted with our freedom, is the holy gospel; the grace which puts us in possession of our freedom is faith; and the end of our freedom is, that we may serve God in righteousness and holiness all the days of our life, and then be glorified with Him forever. We are freed from sin, that we may be holy; and are introduced to and accepted of God, that we may be happy. Let us stand fast in the liberty wherewith Christ hath made us free.

Sweet is the freedom Christ bestows,
With which He makes His people free;
A liberty no mortal knows,
Till they His great salvation see:
Freedom from wants, and fears, and cares,
From worldly lusts, and dangerous snares.

APRIL 21.

Walk humbly with thy God. Micah vi. 8.

PRIDE is one of our greatest evils; to indulge it is to nourish a serpent in the bosom. The grace of God always humbles us; and it is only as we are humble that we can be happy. God condescends to walk with the humble man, but He keeps the proud at a distance. Consider what you were by nature, what now lurks in your heart, what you would have been but for the grace of God, and be humble. All you have is the gift of free grace; all you do that is good, is the effect of God's working in you What have you to be proud of? What reason to boast? Oh, lie low in the dust of self-abasement; cherish humbling thoughts of yourself; admire the mercy, condescension, and infinite compassion of God in noticing so vile, so unworthy a worm! Study the character and conduct of the humble Jesus, learn of Him, and endeavor to walk as He also walked. Serve the Lord in all humility of mind. But beware of spurious humility; that is not humility which rests contented without seeking for the utmost God has promised, or aiming at the highest duties God has commanded.

By faith in Christ I walk with God,
With heaven, my journey's end, in view;
Supported by His staff and rod,
My road is safe and pleasant too.
Though earth and Hell my course withstand,
JEHOVAH guards me by His hand.

APRIL 22.

I will surely do thee good Gen xxxii 12.

THOUGH this promise was given to Jacob, it was not confined to him, but is intended for all his spiritual seed. It is thus God speaks to us this morning How gracious! We know not what a day may bring forth, but we know our God, who superintends every event, will do us good. We may mistake as to what will be for our good, but He is infinite in wisdom and goodness, and therefore cannot We may look at afflictions, losses, and crosses, and cry out, "All these things are against me!" But read the history of David, what a train of troubles attended him: hear his acknowledgment. "It is GOOD for me that I have been afflicted" Thy God will do thee good, therefore He will try thee, sift thee, humble thee, and prove thee. He will give thee medicine as well as food He will consider nothing too expensive, or too painful, if necessary for thy soul's welfare. Look at your trials and say, "This also shall turn to my salvation." Look on the past and acknowledge, "Goodness and mercy have followed me all the days of my life." Look to the future and rejoice, "The Lord will give that which is GOOD." Look in every direction, and say, "I will trust and not be afraid."

I cannot doubt His bounteous love,
So full, so free, so kind ;
To His unerring, gracious will,
Be every wish resigned

117

APRIL 23.

Have faith in God. Mark xi 22

You have His word, believe it; plead it; expect the fulfilment of it. He cannot deceive you. His ear is open to you. Try Him What do you want? Why do you want it? If you really need, if your motives are good, plead with God for it; expect Him to bestow it; and receive it as coming from him. In every trial, for all you need, have faith in God. He will be gracious unto you. He is ever with you. He is ready to help you. He rejoices over you to do you good. His word is true from the beginning. He is the faithful God. He keepeth covenant and mercy. Believe in God for all your circumstances require. Patiently wait His time for your supplies. Never give over praying or expecting because He delays; never doubt Him, but trust in Him with all thy heart. He is a God: He is thy God: He is able to do exceeding abundantly above all that we can ask or think. This is thy direction—thy duty—thy privilege: HAVE FAITH IN GOD. Walk with God. Talk with God. Expect from God Use all for God. Be entirely devoted to God. "Casting all your cares upon Him, for He careth for you." "Therefore will I look unto the Lord."

Begone, unbelief! my Saviour is near,
And for my relief will surely appear:
By prayer let me wrestle, and He will perform,
With Christ in the vessel, I smile at the storm.

118

APRIL 24.

I am the bread of life. John vi 35.

JESUS proposeth Himself to be our daily sus
tenance ;—we need bread for the soul as wel
as the body. In Jesus is all we need to refresh
strengthen, and satisfy us; but He must b
received by faith. He must be daily received
Feeding upon Jesus yesterday will not do fo
to-day. We must go to him afresh this morn
ing. He presents Himself; He says, "Eat, C
friends; yea, satisfy yourselves, O my beloved.'
If the Holy Spirit has given us a spiritual ap
petite, if we are hungering after righteousness
Jesus, and Jesus only will satisfy us; and w
are heartily welcome to live upon Him Le
us set him before us many times in the day
let us endeavor to feed upon Him; and if w
feel weak, faint, or weary, let us make use of
this life-giving bread; and let us ever retail
the sweet assurance, that if we feed on Jesu
we shall live by Him, and have eternal life
Beloved, if you can make a living of anything
but Jesus; or if Jesus is not enough in you
estimation, you are either in a carnal, or ar
unhealthy state of soul. Jesus only is THI
BREAD OF LIFE: THE BREAD WHICH CAME DOW?
FROM HEAVEN ! •

Jesus, Thou art the living bread
By which our needy souls are fed ;
In Thee alone thy children find
Enough to fill the empty mind .
Oh, let me evermore be fed
With this divine celestial bread !

APRIL 25.

Who maketh thee to differ from another ?
1 Cor iv. 7

THERE is a wide difference between a Christian
and a worldling ; the one is dead in trespasses
and sins, the other is alive unto God, by Jesus
Christ our Lord. He has been quickened by
the Son of God, is born of the Spirit, and
taught by the eternal Father. He is a new
creature, being created anew in Christ Jesus
unto good works, which God had before ordained that we should walk in them Who made
this difference? You are at once ready to
answer, if really taught of God, " By the grace
of God I am what I am." "Of HIS OWN WILL
begat He me by the word of truth." Yes, it
was the rich, free, and sovereign grace of God,
and that alone, that made you to differ Grace
was given you in Christ before the world
began ; and the Spirit was given you in time,
that you might know and enjoy the things
which are freely given unto you of God Oh,
beloved, view yourself as an infinite debtor to
grace ; be humble before God who has thus
made you to differ ; and pity, pray for, and
strive to benefit those who are still without.
" Look unto the rock whence you were hewn, and
to the hole of the pit whence you were digged."

What was there in you that could merit esteem,
  Or give the Creator delight?
'Twas " Even so, Father !" you ever must sing,
  " Because it seem'd good in Thy sight."

APRIL 26.

Behold the Man. John xix 5.

JESUS is presented before thee crowned with thorns, scourged, with His face so marred more than any man's. His blood is flowing. His heart is breaking, and He is a man of sorrows. Behold Him, then, for in this man, under these circumstances, dwelt all the fulness of the godhead bodily; all the treasures of wisdom and knowledge. In Him the love of God centered and shone forth. He is the only foundation of His church's hopes, the only source of eternal salvation. He is Jehovah's first-born, His only-begotten Son, the express image of His person. He is thy Substitute, Surety, and Redeemer. He is the holy, harmless, and undefiled Lamb of God; taking away the sin of the world. Behold Him, for He here discloses the depth of His love; and teaches thee patience, meekness, and resignation under insult, suffering, and disgrace. Oh, behold Jesus, and be ashamed of complaining, of repining, or indulging any revengeful feelings. Behold and imitate! Behold and love! Behold and adore!

> Wounded head! back ploughed with furrows!
>   Visage marr'd! behold the Man!
> Eyes how dim, how full of sorrows!
>   Sunk with grief, behold the Man!
> Lamb of God, led to the slaughter,
> Melted, poured out like water:
>   Should not love my heart inflame,
>   Viewing Thee, thou slaughter'd Lamb!

I am He that comforteth you Isa. li. 12.

THE Lord's people are often low and despond
ing; they do not live up to their privileges; the
things of time make too deep an impression,
because they do not sufficiently realize eternal
things. But Jehovah is their COMFORTER: as
such He presents Himself unto us this morning. He is the God of all comfort. He
comforteth those who are cast down. To Him
alone we must look for comfort. Looking to
creatures for what God promises, dishonors
Him; and at such times the creature may well
ask, " AM I IN GOD'S STEAD ?" Our God comforts us by His Son, whom He hath given to
us; by the Spirit, which He pours out upon
us; by His word, in which He speaks to us;
by His ordinances, in which He meets with us;
and by His providence, when He appears for us.
Let us look unto God as the author and giver
of all comfort, let us plead with Him to comfort us according to His word, and let us be suspicious of all comfort which does not come from
Him, and lead to Him. He must be the centre
to which we always tend, and the circumference
within which we move.

Jesus, all our consolations
    Flow from Thee, the sovereign good;
Love, and faith, and hope, and patience,
    All are purchased by Thy blood:
Now thy richest grace impart,
Sanctify and fill my heart.

APRIL 28.

Though I be nothing. 2 Cor xii 1

THIS was Paul's estimate of himsef; less than
the least of all saints, and the chief of sinners.
The more we know of ourselves and of Jesus,
the more shall we be humbled in the dust
before God; and the lower we lie before God,
the happier and holier we shall be. Man will,
MUST be something; this is his pride and his
misery: the Christian is willing to be nothing,
that Christ may be all in all. If we daily felt
that we are nothing, how many mortifications
we should be spared; what admiring views
of the grace of God would fill and sanctify our
souls. Apart from Christ we are less than
nothing, but in Christ we are something. We
are empty, but He fills us ; naked, but He
clothes us ; helpless, but He strengthens us ;
lost, but He finds us ; ruined, but He saves
us ; poor, but He supplies us. All we are,
is by Christ; all we have, is from Christ; all
we shall be, is through Christ. Believer, thou
art nothing: therefore beware of thinking too
highly of thyself, or fancying that you deserve
more than you receive, either from God
or men.

Oh, could I lose myself in Thee,
  Thy depth of mercy prove,
Thou vast unfathomable sea
  Of unexhausted love !
I loathe myself when God I see,
Content if Christ exalted be.

But thou art rich. Rev. ii. 9

REAL saints always feel themselves to be poor sinners. Many of God's people are really poor in reference to the things of time, for God hath chosen the poor of this world, rich in faith, and heirs of the kingdom which He hath promised to them that love Him. They are often persecuted, tried, tempted, and cast down; so was the church in Smyrna; but Jesus says to her, "THOU ART RICH." So are all the Lord's people. Rich by RELATION—God is their Father, and Jesus their elder Brother. Rich by DONATION—Jesus has bequeathed unsearchable riches to them. Rich by PROMISE —the Lord has promised all good things. Rich by FAITH—for he that believeth shall inherit all things. Rich in EXPECTATION—for they look for a city which hath foundations, whose builder and maker is God. Believer, thou art rich; Jesus has willed to thee His righteousness, to justify thee; His blood, to cleanse thee; His Spirit, to sanctify thee; His name, to procure for thee; His angels, to minister unto thee; and His heaven, to be thy everlasting habitation. Precious Saviour! I would admire and adore thy love! O teach me to live out of self on Thy fulness.

Called by grace, the sinner see,
Rich, though sunk in poverty;
Rich in faith that God has given,
He's a legal heir of heaven

That which I see not teach Thou me.
Job xxxiv. 32

WE were once blind, but now our eyes are open : but still we are absolutely dependant on divine teaching, or we shall never become truly wise. If God teach us, self will become vile; the world vanity; sin bitter; the blood of Christ most precious; His righteousness glorious; His name our only hope; His love our joy; His Spirit our strength; His glory our aim; and "Teach Thou me," our daily prayer. We see but little of what Christ is in Himself; of what He hath done for His people, of what He possesses, and will give to all who call upon Him in truth; of what He has promised to work in us, and bestow upon us. Beloved, let us daily plead with God to teach us, that we may know Christ, and the power of His resurrection, and the fellowship of His sufferings, and be made conformable to His death. Let us beg the Spirit of wisdom and revelation in the knowledge of Christ, that we may know what is the hope of His calling, and what is the riches of the glory of His inheritance in the saints. Jehovah alone can teach us to profit.

O Jesus, teach my soul to know
Thyself, the truth, the life, the way:
May I in grace and knowledge grow,
Till I arrive in perfect day:
From Satan, self, and sin set free,
And what I know not teach Thou me.

MAY 1.

I will be a Father unto you. 2 Cor. vi. 18. ✓ TY Lord

No man can be a loser by adhering to God's holy word, for he is promised a hundred-fold in the present life, and in the world to come life everlasting. Carnal connections must be broken off. Decision of character must be manifested. The world must be forsaken. Christ and the world will not unite. Carnality and spirituality cannot be reconciled. Our God says, "Come out from among them, and be ye separate: touch not the unclean thing; and I will receive you, and will be a FATHER unto you." What can we need more to encourage, embolden, and produce decision? Suppose men reject me, despise me, and persecute me; God will receive me. Suppose they injure me and try to starve me, God will be a Father to me. He will care for me—protect me—dwell with me—comfort me—supply me—and fill a Father's place. I cannot be friendless. I should not be fearful. Beloved, God says, "PROVE ME." Are you called upon to forsake friends, to break off connections, lose trade, or endure persecutions? Fear not, act for God—look to God—He will receive you, and be a Father to you.

> And wilt thou, Lord, a Father be,
> To those who leave the world for Thee?
> Wilt Thou provide for every want,
> And tokens of Thy favor grant?
> Then, Lord, I bid the world farewell,
> And now Thy word in me fulfil.

MAY 2.

But grow in grace. 2 Pet. iii 18.

NEVER rest satisfied with present attainments
God has much to bestow, and we are capable of
receiving, enjoying, and using to His glory. As
the tree planted in good soil grows both in the
root and the branches, so should the Christian;
he should be rooted in the love of God and grow
up in conformity to Jesus. If we grow in grace,
we shall discover more of our own wretchedness,
misery, and weakness; and more of the preciousness, fulness, and glory of Christ. We
shall be humble before God, and active before
men. We shall trust in Jesus more simply,
having no confidence in the flesh. Grace always leads out of self to Jesus, and puts the
crown of crowns upon His head. Grace is spiritual beauty; it is the very glory of God. To
grow in grace is to grow like Jesus, meek and
lowly in heart; active and devoted in life;
blameless and harmless as the sons of God.
Let us have grace, for God loves to bestow it;
let us grow in grace, for God commands it;
let us look forward for the grace that is to be
brought unto us at the coming of Jesus, for God
has promised it. Look for that blessed hope,
even the glorious appearing of Jesus.

> Though holy deeds and fruits of grace
> Are in believers found,
> 'Tis Christ's command that they increase,
> And more and more abound·
> O Saviour ! may I grow in grace,
> Till I behold Thee face to face.

MAY 3.

Is thy Counsellor perished ? Micah iv 9.

THE Lord's people need counsel, and Jesus is
given to them as a COUNSELLOR He is exactly
suited to their needs, being possessed of infinite
wisdom, unbounded benevolence, great experience, and high honor. He never lost a cause.
He counsels freely, cheerfully, and successfully.
He turns the counsel of all our foes into foolish-
ness. But though we ·have this wonderful
Counsellor, we neglect to consult, employ, or
trust Him; and it may often be demanded of us,
" Is thy Counsellor perished ?" If not, why this
perplexity ? Why these mistakes ? why those
fears, and groans, and forebodings ? Why this
running to creatures for advice and succor ?
Beloved, let us stand reproved; we have walked
in our own counsels, we have not *waited* for
His counsel, we have neglected and forgotten
Jesus in this office. Let us in future never act
without His counsel, never employ men to His
dishonor, never listen to Satan when He would
persuade us not to apply to, trust in, and expect
advice from Jesus as our COUNSELLOR. He says,
"I will counsel thee, mine eye shall be upon
thee."

> Lord, be my counsellor,
> My Pattern and my Guide;
> And through this desert land,
> Still keep me near Thy side;
> Oh, let my feet ne'er run astray,
> Nor rove, nor seek the crooked way.

128

MAY 4.

Sin brings sickness. The believer can only be healthful as he walks with God, lives above the world, and looks for the coming of our Lord Jesus Christ. At the feet of Jesus we are safe, and shall be healthy; but if we wander from Him, spiritual disease will seize upon us. The backslider feels too weak, to run in the way of God's commands; too confused, to read His interest in God's promises; too guilty, to call God Father; too wretched, to rejoice in hope. He has no liberty in prayer; no enjoyment of his Bible; no peace in his conscience; no delight in God's ways. But the Lord says, "Return, ye backsliding children; I WILL HEAL YOUR BACKSLID-INGS." This is a message from the Great Physician, an invitation from our Father's throne, a promise of our Saviour's love. Oh, let us return unto Him with weeping and supplication, adopting David's prayer as our own, "Heal my soul, for I have sinned against thee." Let us take up the determination of the church, "Behold, we come unto thee, for thou art the Lord our God." He will receive us graciously, and love us freely.

> Give me Thy pardoning love to feel,
> And freely my backslidings heal,
> Repair my faith's decay;
> Restore the sweetness of Thy grace,
> Reveal the glories of Thy face,
> And take my sins away.

I

MAY 5.

BELOVED, let us visit Gethsemane this morning,
and see this strange sight. Here is our SURETY;
the only-begotten Son of God; the brightness
of Jehovah's glory, and the express image of His
person; groaning on the cold ground, and baptized in blood. He is sore amazed; His heart is
filled with horror, and His mind with dread; His
soul is troubled, tossed with tempests and not
comforted; He is exceeding sorrowful, even unto
death. The sorrows of death encompass Him,
and the pains of hell have gotten hold upon
Him. His heart like wax is melted in the midst
of His bowels. His whole nature is convulsed;
He sweats blood; He cries aloud, with an exceeding bitter cry, and His heart faileth Him.
No human hand toucheth Him; but it is the
hour and power of darkness. Our sins meet
upon Him; His soul is made an offering for our
sins; and it hath pleased Jehovah to bruise Him.
Was ever sorrow like unto His sorrow? HE IS
IN AN AGONY. Here our sins are punished, our
iniquities are expiated, and our justification
is procured. Oh, to love Jesus even to an
agony!

> Go to dark Gethsemane,
> Ye that feel the tempter's power;
> Your Redeemer's conflict see,
> Watch with Him one bitter hour:
> Turn not from His griefs away,—
> Learn of Jesus Christ to pray.

130

MAY 6.

Pray without ceasing. 1 Thess. v. 17.

In prayer we must approach God as a Father, ask of Him what we really need, and expect to receive according to His wisdom and word. Our wants are constantly returning, therefore our prayers should be constantly ascending. The ear of God is always open; He is ever ready to listen to us; He invites, exhorts, and commands us to pray always in everything. Every object that meets the eye, every circumstance that occurs, every employment in which we engage, would afford matter for prayer if properly viewed. The believer should acquire the HABIT of prayer. He should look up to His God for all He needs, through all he sees, whenever he has a moment to spare. The prayers of a Christian are pleasant to his God; He says, "Let me hear thy voice, let me see thy countenance; for sweet is thy voice, and thy countenance is comely." The believer should pray as naturally and as constantly as he breathes; for prayer is the breath of the soul. Beloved, if prayer dwindle into a mere duty, is but occasionally offered, or becomes burdensome, it is clear that you are in a most unhealthy state.

> Through the skies when the thunder is hurl'd,
> The child to its parent will flee ·
> Thus, amid the rebukes of the world,
> I turn, O my Father to thee:
> The spirit of prayer in thy mercy impart,
> And take up thy constant abode in my heart.

√131

MAY 7.

O Israel, thou shalt not be forgotten of me.
Isaiah xliv. 21.

WHAT tenderness, mercy, and love are here! Friends forget us, relatives are careless about us, and we sometimes fear our God has forgotten us; but here He assures us that we shall never be forgotten of Him. Our names are in His book; our Representative is always before His throne, and we are the objects of His constant care. He cannot forget us while Jesus pleads for us; and if He does not forget, He will never neglect. There is only one thing He is ever said to forget, and that is our sins; but He is always mindful of His covenant. He will not forget the circumstances in which we are placed, the wants by which we are pained, or the prayers we put up at His throne. But though we are assured our God will never forget us, yet we can find no satisfaction, but as the Holy Spirit humbles us, empties us, and exalts Christ before us; showing us our pardon, peace, and salvation in His life, death, and intercession. Beloved, let us mind the things of the Spirit, and daily seek humbling, quickening, and sanctifying grace.

O Lord, my God! whose sovereign love
Is still the same, nor e'er can move,
Look to the covenant, and see,
Has not Thy love been shown to me?
Remember me, my glorious Friend,
And love me always to the end.

MAY 8.

BELOVED, it is your privilege in every perplexity and trial to go to the Lord, to spread your case before Him, to plead His precious promises, and to wait expecting Him to appear for you. Wait on Him for light to discover the nature and design of your trouble; for wisdom that you may act honorably, and endure scripturally; for power to sustain you under, and bring you through it; and for consolation to make you happy and resigned under it. Wait upon the Lord in earnest, simple, persevering prayer; in searching, reading, and meditating upon His holy word; in self-examination as to your views, motives, and designs. Wait upon the Lord, believing that He will fulfil His word, answer your prayers, and send you deliverance; patiently enduring until He shall see good to appear on your behalf. Waiting on the Lord you engage Him on your side; you put His mercy and faithfulness to the trial; you are assured your strength shall be renewed; and God has promised that you shall not be ashamed. Beloved, let us look to, trust in, and wait upon our God continually.

Oh, teach me, Lord, to wait thy will,
To be content with all thou dost;
For me thy grace sufficient still,
With most supplied when needing most:
O Saviour ! give me grace to wait,
And daily watch before thy gate.

133

MAY 9.

The glory of His grace.   Ephes. i. 6.

THE glory of grace is its FREENESS: it fixes upon objects that are most unworthy; bestows upon them the richest blessings; raises them to the highest honor; promises them the greatest happiness; and all for its own glory. Nothing can be freer than grace. The glory of grace is its POWER; it conquers the stubbornest sinners; subdues the hardest hearts; tames the wildest wills; enlightens the darkest understandings; breaks off the strongest fetters; and invariably conquers its objects. Grace is omnipotent. The glory of grace is its BENEVOLENCE; it never injured one; it has delivered, supplied, conducted, supported, and glorified thousands; it brings the inexhaustible fulness of God to supply the creature's wants; it opens the treasury of heaven, to enrich poor, miserable, and wretched creatures on earth. Grace gives away all it has, reserving nothing for itself but the praise and glory of its acts. Jesus is grace personified; in Him it may be seen, in all its beauty, excellence, and loveliness; by Him it is displayed in all its native dignity. O Jesus! glorify thy free, powerful, and benevolent grace in me!

O Jesus! full of truth and grace,
　More full of grace than I of sin,—
Yet once again I seek thy face,
　Open thine arms and take me in;
Oh! freely my backslidings heal,
And love the dying sinner still.

MAY 10.

He doth not afflict willingly. Lam. iii. 33.

Our afflictions do not flow from sovereignty, but from our Father's wisdom, holiness, and love. He finds no pleasure in our pains, groans, and sighs. He is never hasty in using the rod: mercy flies to help us, but He is slow to anger and of great kindness. He never afflicts us without a sufficient cause; either sin has been committed; duties neglected; mercies slighted; lukewarmness discovered; worldly-mindedness tolerated; privileges abused; warnings despised; temptations trifled with; or danger is near. He never afflicts without a good and gracious intention, to make us fear, loathe, and flee from sin; to show His disapprobation of our unholy course; to quicken us in His ways: to make us long for, seek, and partake of His holiness; to produce contrition and godly sorrow; or to prove that His authority is not surrendered because His love is great. He only afflicts partially, occasionally, and sparingly. He always strikes in love, and aims at our spiritual welfare; and we are often more benefited by afflictions, than we are by comforts and joys. O Saviour, sanctify to me every afflicting stroke!

In the floods of tribulation
While the billows o'er me roll,
Jesus whispers consolation,
And supports my fainting soul:
Sweet affliction,
Thus to bring my Saviour near.

135

MAY 11.

Rejoice in the Lord alway. Phil. iv 4.

THIS is a very difficult precept; sometimes the Lord hides His face; we fear and doubt our interest in His love; we are almost bewildered through the powerful workings of corruption within us: we are bowed down by Satan's sore temptations; and the dispensations of providence are so perplexing, that we are ready to cry out, "All things are against us." But we are not bidden to rejoice in frames and feelings, or in the dispensations of providence, but in the Lord. He has loved us with an everlasting love, and His love is immutably the same; He is our God in Jesus, and has promised to be unto us, to do for us, and freely give us, all that our circumstances require, or that will be for our good and His glory. In weakness we may rejoice in His power; in darkness we may rejoice that He knoweth our path; in sickness and sorrow, that He careth for us; and under any circumstances, in His covenant relations; for He is always our Father, Friend, and God. We should rejoice in His free grace, rich mercy, omnipotent power, faithful promises, special providence, and unchangeable love.

Rejoice in glorious hope !
Jesus the Judge shall come,
And take His servants up
To their eternal home:
We soon shall hear the archangel's voice,—
The trump of God shall sound, REJOICE.

136

MAY 12.

Their righteousness is of me, saith the Lord.
Isaiah liv. 17.

THE longer the Christian lives, the more he learns; and the more the Spirit teaches him, the more he loathes himself, and renounces his own righteousness as filthy rags. He hoped sensibly to grow in holiness, to feel his corruptions subdued, and to enjoy without interruption the presence of his God; but instead of this, he seems to grow more like Satan, corruption appears to get stronger and stronger, and the depravity of his nature appears so dreadful, that he enjoys scarcely anything. He thinks himself a monster of iniquity, and wonders how God can possibly love him, or show any favor unto him. This experience endears free grace, renders Christ unspeakably precious, and the gift of righteousness invaluable. How can such a man be just before God? Where is his righteousness to come from? Jehovah answers, "HIS RIGHTEOUSNESS IS OF ME." Jesus wrought it; the Father imputes it to us, the gospel reveals it; and faith receives it, puts it on, and pleads it before God. O Jesus! in Thee have I righteousness and strength.

My hope is built on nothing less
Than Jesus' blood and righteousness;
I dare not trust the sweetest flame,
But wholly lean on Jesus' name:
On Christ the solid Rock I stand;
All other ground is sinking sand.

137

MAY 13.

The Lord hath blessed me hitherto.
Josh. xvii. 14.

BELIEVER, cannot you join with the children of Joseph this morning, and bear a similar testimony? Thy God hath blessed thee in Jesus and through Jesus; look back to the rock whence you were hewn, and to the hole of the pit whence you were digged; call to mind the time and place, when and where thy God first led thee to cry for mercy, and seek for salvation; remember the distress and bondage felt before mercy was manifested; and then remember how your soul was delivered, and the comforts of the Holy Ghost imparted. Think of thy difficulties and dangers, thy trials and fears, and the deliverances the Lord has wrought, the favor He hath shown, and the comforts He has imparted: and surely you will gratefully acknowledge, "HE HATH BLESSED ME HITHERTO." He promised to bless, and you have found Him faithful. He has manifested a Father's love, and a Mother's tenderness in dealing with you. But what have been your returns? Oh, be humble, for you have been ungrateful! But cleave to Jesus, for God gives no blessing but by and through Him.

Jesus found me vile and guilty,
  I had broken all His laws;
When He look'd He saw me filthy;
  All corrupt my nature was:
Mine appear'd a hopeless case,
Such it had been but for grace.

MAY 14.

They shall be mine, saith the Lord of Hosts.
Mal. iii. 17.

WHO? They that fear the Lord and think upon His name. They who fear to offend Him because they love Him. Who desire above all things to obey Him, be conformed unto Him, and glorify Him. They who think upon His name, "OUR FATHER;" and believe Him to be gracious, merciful, long-suffering, abundant in goodness and truth. Who approach Him as children; who walk before Him, desiring to do everything as under His eye; who are jealous of His honor, and concerned for His glory. Who speak of His goodness, talk of His power, and adore the riches of His grace. "THEY SHALL BE MINE, SAITH THE LORD OF HOSTS." He will treat them as children, prize them as His jewels, and acknowledge them before assembled angels. He will put a difference between them and others, and will manifest Himself unto them as He does not unto the world. Beloved, are we entitled to claim this precious promise? Do we fear God? Are we grieved at sin, because it dishonors him? Do we think upon His name with love and reverence? If so, He will spare us, preserve us, and place us among His jewels forever.

Hail, sacred day! that shall declare
The jewels of the Son of God,
Design'd to deck His crown they were,
Chosen of old and bought with blood.

MAY 15.

We walk by faith. 2 Cor v. 7.

THE Christian's path is often very rough; thorns and briers grow on either side, dark clouds hang over it, and no cheering prospects appear to animate the heart. But if he acts consistently, he still believes it is the right path; that trials are mercies in disguise, and that the path of tribulation ends in the kingdom of God. He believes it is all needful, it is the very best way his Father could select; that the design of God is gracious, and his present trials are to end in His eternal welfare. He believes his God is with Him, though He does not enjoy His presence, and that all needful supplies will be sent, though he cannot tell from whence. He rests on the faithful word, trusts in an immutable God, and says, when surrounded by trials, "None of these things move me; I know that it is through much tribulation that I must enter the kingdom; my God will support me, His hand will defend me, and His grace shall be glorified in my present and eternal salvation. I know not the way, but my God knows, and He will lead me; He will never leave me, but will be my guide, even unto death."

Oh may I daily walk by faith,
  Believing what my God has spoke;
Rely on His unchanging love,
  And cease to grasp at fleeting smoke;
On His eternal truth depend,
And know Him as my God and Friend.

140

MAY 16.

Blessed are ye that hunger now. Luke vi. 21.

APPETITE supposes life, and is regulated by nature; the carnal appetite is satisfied with carnal things; but a Christian can only be satisfied with spiritual things. He hungers to enjoy an interest in Christ; for righteousness wrought in him by the Spirit, and given to him by Jesus; to be conformed to the image of Christ; to know Him extensively, experimentally, and practically; to enjoy God as his portion; and that Christ may be magnified in him by life or by death. His appetite is fixed on its object; no substitute can be found; it is only as he feeds upon Christ that he enjoys satisfaction. Beloved, how is it with you this morning? Are you hungering for Jesus? He filleth the hungry with good things; He pronounces them blessed. They are blessed with spiritual life; with an interest in the things for which they hunger; and with the operations of the Holy Spirit. None but God can produce this hunger, and only God can satisfy it; and He will; for He has said, THEY SHALL BE FILLED. This is plain; positive; unconditional; and certain. Believe it and be happy.

> Bless'd are the souls that thirst for grace,
> Hunger and long for righteousness;
> They shall be well supplied, and fed
> With living streams, and living bread:
> Oh, may my hungry soul receive
> The food on which Thy people live.

MAY 17.

He will rest in His love. Zeph. iii. 17.

MAN's love is changeable, being a passion; God's love is unchangeable, being a perfection. Having loved, He always will love. Nothing can occur in time but what He knew from eternity; consequently there can be no reason to-day, why God should not love me, but what He knew would be before He set His heart upon me. He fixed His love upon us in the fore-view of all that would be done by us, or felt within us: and connected us with Jesus, that He might never withdraw His love from us. Oh, to be able to say with holy John, "We have known and believed the love that God hath to us! God is love!" The love of God is from everlasting to everlasting; without variableness, or the shadow of a turn. Here God resteth, and here we should rest. Herein is love, that God should take such poor, vile, ungrateful, wretched creatures, and make them the bride of His Son, the delight of His soul, and His portion for evermore. Oh, the riches of divine love! Admire it, trust it, rejoice in it; and make it the subject of your daily meditation. HE WILL REST IN HIS LOVE. On this rock we may rest with confidence; on this pillow we may repose in peace.

The cov'nant of grace all blessings secures;
Believer, rejoice, for all things are yours;
And God from His purpose shall never remove,
But love thee, and bless thee, and rest in His love.

MAY 18.

And went and told Jesus   Matt. xiv 12.

WHEN Herod beheaded John, his disciples took up his body and buried it, and went and told Jesus.   Let us imitate their example, and carry all to Jesus.   He loves to listen to the tale of human woe.   He can and will sympathize with us in all our trials and troubles.   He is our Father, and to whom should the child tell his troubles, but to his kind and tender parent? He will direct our steps, avenge our wrongs, and turn all things to our advantage.   Does business go wrong?   Are enemies active?   Is corruption strong?   Does faith flag?   Are you tried in your family?   Go and tell Jesus.   It will ease your mind; prevent sin; insure supplies; manifest relation; and frustrate the designs of Satan. Do not sit poring over your miseries; go not to creatures; neither murmur, complain, nor fret; but go to Jesus; go with speed; go in hope; go and tell Him all, without reserve.   Go this morning, with all thy complaints, desires, and fears; lay them all before Him, and beseech Him to undertake for you   He loves to hear you, has promised to help you, and will certainly bless you. It is your duty, and your privilege, to pour out your heart before Him, and find Him a refuge for you.

> Our sorrows and our tears we pour
>   Into the bosom of our God,
> He hears us in the mournful hour,
>   And helps to bear the heavy load.

MAY 19.

It shall be well 2 Kings iv 28.

THIS was the language of a believer, in trouble; and it should be our language under similar circumstances. Our trials, troubles, and difficulties may be great; but it shall be well with them that fear God. Are you alarmed at the powerful working of corruption within you? It shall be well, for sin shall not have dominion over you; for you are not under the law, but under grace Are you distressed by the evil suggestions and powerful temptations of Satan? It shall be well, for the God of peace will bruise Satan under your feet shortly. Is your soul cast down by the vexations, difficulties, and trials of the way? It shall be well, for all things shall work together for good, to them that love God, to those that are the called according to His purpose. Do you conclude your case is singular, and therefore fear? It shall be well, for no temptation hath taken you but such as is common to man; and God is faithful, who will not suffer you to be tempted above that ye are able; but will also with the temptation make a way to escape, that ye may be able to bear it. Oh, precious promise of a gracious God! Lord, help me to believe, rely, and rejoice.

> What cheering words are these,
> Their sweetness who can tell!
> In time, and to eternal days,
> 'Tis with the righteous well

144

MAY 20.

IT is impossible to be more welcome at the throne of grace than we are, or for God to be more willing to bestow. We are as welcome to the throne of grace, as angels are to the throne of glory. Our God has provided on purpose to give. He invites us to come that we may receive. He gives grace upon grace. He is never weary of bestowing, though we are of asking. We dishonor Him when we ask doubtfully, when we ask for small matters; He bids us ask in faith, nothing doubting; to open our mouths wide that He may fill them. Grace comprises all we need, to pardon our sins, sanctify our natures, conquer our foes, bear our trials, or perform our duties. If we have not, it is because we ask not; or because we ask amiss, to consume it on our lusts. There is grace for us this morning; let us apply for it, expect to receive it, and determine to use it for God's glory and the good of souls. He will give grace and glory, and no good thing will He withhold from them that walk uprightly. They that seek the Lord shall not want any good thing. Ask, and you shall receive; seek, and you shall find. He giveth liberally and upbraideth not.

> Transporting truth—amazing word!
> What! grace and glory from the Lord!
> Oh, may I feel the promise true,
> Fulfill'd in grace and glory too!

MAY 21.

Take heed to your spirit. Mal. ii 15.

THE spirit of the believer should be character-
ized by forbearance, humility, and love ; he is
exhorted to put away all anger, wrath, clamor,
evil-speaking, and malice ; and to put on bowels
of mercy, kindness, humbleness of mind, meekness, long-suffering, and to be ready to forgive.
A bitter, contentious, censorious spirit, is just
the opposite of the Spirit of Christ ; and an un-
forgiving person cannot be a Christian, for Jesus
has said, "Except ye forgive men their trespasses, neither will my heavenly Father forgive
you." Take heed then to your spirit ; lest it be
said, "Ye know not what manner of spirit ye
are of." Learn of Jesus ; He was meek and
lowly ; patient and forbearing ; kind to His enemies, and ready to forgive. A proud, contentious, overbearing disciple, cannot expect to have
fellowship with a humble, lowly, and broken-
hearted Master. Beloved, let us watch over our
spirits ; he that rules his own spirit, does more
than he that conquers a city ; and a spirit, that
is not under control, is like a city with the walls
and gates broken down ; open to the enemy on
every side.

Come, blessed Spirit, heavenly Dove
Descend on balmy wings ;
Come, tune my passions all to love,
And strike the peaceful strings :
Let every action, thought, and word,
Bring honor to my holy Lord,

MAY 22.

If ye shall ask anything in my name, I will do it.
John xiv. 14.

THIS is the word of Jesus to us this morning; it is intended to encourage and embolden us at the throne of grace, and to comfort us under all our privations and wants. Jesus has all power in heaven and in earth; all things are delivered unto Him by the Father. He has a large store, and a kind and tender heart. Let us therefore go to Him with our wants, that He may supply them; with our fears, that He may quell them; with our sins, that He may pardon and subdue them; with everything that troubles us, or is likely to harm us. Let us go to Him with confidence. He says, " What wilt thou that I shall do for thee? If ye ask anything that will do you good, promote my cause, or glorify my name, I WILL DO IT. Be not afraid to ask, for I am omnipotent; do not doubt, for I give you my word; I WILL DO IT." Oh, believer, what a friend is Jesus! how kind! how gracious! Never complain, never despond, never be cast down, while Jesus is thy FRIEND. He is, and will be thy friend forever. Oh, make a friend of Him; visit Him daily; trust Him implicitly; and follow Him fully. Make Him your all in all. He is worthy. He will not deceive.

Jesus, my Lord, I look to Thee;
Where else can helpless sinners go!
Thy boundless love shall set me free
From all my wretchedness and woe.

147

We look for the Saviour. Phil. iii. 20.

Our beloved Saviour is now at the right hand of God. He waits, expecting His enemies to be made His footstool. He will come again; the time is hastening on, and we should be living in expectation of His appearing. The Christian posture is that of waiting, looking, hasting to the coming of the day of God. He will come the second time, as certainly as He did the first. He will come as a thief in the night. He will come in His glory, and all the holy angels with Him. He will come to reign, to reward His people, and to punish His foes. Let us not be slothful, careless, or indifferent about the coming of our Lord; He comes for our salvation. Let us look for Him daily, with earnest desire, ardent hope, fervent love, importunate prayer, and diligent preparation. When He comes, the earth will be delivered from the bondage of corruption, into the glorious liberty of the children of God; the groans of creation will be silenced, the prayers of the Lord's people be answered, and crowns of righteousness bestowed. Let us abide in Him, that we may have confidence, and not be ashamed before Him at His coming.

Lo! He comes, with clouds descending
Once for favor'd sinners slain;
Thousand thousand saints attending,
Swell the triumph of His train.
Hallelujah!
Jesus comes, and comes to reign.

MAY 24.

The enemy. Luke x. 18.

THE Christian has many foes, but there is cne who is emphatically called, " THE ENEMY." He is the god of this world; all worship him, except those whom Jesus has delivered from him. He is the prince of the power of the air, he rules over and works in all unbelievers. He is a subtle serpent, endeavoring to deceive; a roaring lion, seeking to devour. He has the power of death. He gains access to our hearts, and is always attempting to lead us astray. He is well versed in Scripture, and will often quote it, in order to misapply it; he will use one part to fill us with terror, another to lead us to make light of sin. He is always planning how he shall injure us, and is incessantly trying to draw us from God. Beloved, there is no safety for us but at the feet of Jesus; it is only as we abide in Him, and walk with Him, that we can overcome Satan. Our weapons are the blood of the Lamb, and the word of the divine testimony; faith seizes the perfect work of Christ as its shield, and the word of God as its sword, and thus overcomes the infernal foe. Let us put on the WHOLE ARMOR of God.

Jesus hath died for you;
  What can His love withstand!
Believe, hold fast your shield, and who
  Shall pluck you from His hand !
You shall o'ercome through Jesus' blood,
And stand complete before your God.

MAY 25.

Certainly I will be with thee   Exod iii 12.

It is a great honor to be favored with the presence of Jehovah: but in every enterprise for His glory, in every duty required in His word, in every dangerous part of the pilgrim's path, in every trouble in this land of strangers, He has promised to be with us. His presence is to encourage, strengthen, protect, and prosper us. This promise should arm us against fear, nerve the mind against opposition, and embolden us in a good cause. Beloved, has God promised to be with us? Let us then seek to realize His presence; never let us be satisfied with any religion, without the Lord's presence.— If God be with us we shall be successful; all He requires He will provide; and display in our experience the exceeding riches of His grace. His presence is sure to His people; He is not always perceived by sense, but certainly He is present; for though heaven and earth may pass away, one jot or tittle of His word shall in no wise pass away; all must be fulfilled. Let us then seek and expect the presence of Jehovah this day; and rejoice that He has said, "I will never leave thee, nor forsake thee."

Then rest, my soul, upon the Lord,
Believe and plead His faithful word,
He will be with thee, He will guide,
And for thy every want provide:
Then trust His faithful love and power,
In every gloomy trying hour.

10/24

MAY 26.

Let a man examine himself. 1 Cor xi 28

This is necessary, that we may know upon what we are resting; and whether we are growing or declining. Let us examine this morning upon what foundation are we building for eternal life; and from what does our hope arise? What is the source of our satisfaction, pleasure, and peace? What do we possess to prove the reality of our religion? Have we been quickened by the Holy Spirit? Is Christ our life, and is He living in us? Are we enlightened to see sin, in its nature, character, and actings? Have we living faith, which receives Christ; believes His word; and lives to Him? Have we a good hope through grace? Is the love of God shed abroad in our hearts by the Holy Ghost? Do we love God because He first loved us, and walk with Him in peace and holiness? Have we the earnest and witness of the Spirit in our hearts? Are we conflicting with sin, and praying to be delivered from it, as from a tyrant, a plague, the most fearful evil? Let us examine carefully, deliberately, prayerfully; taking God's word for our rule and guide. Let us prove our own work, so shall we have rejoicing in ourselves alone.

> Searcher of hearts! oh, search me still;
> The secrets of my soul reveal;
> My fears remove: let me appear
> To God and my own conscience, clear:
> Each evidence of grace impart,
> And deeply sanctify my heart!

MAY 27.

And He blessed him there. Gen. xxxii. 9.

Poor Jacob, full of fear and alarm, retired to plead with his God; he wept and made supplication, he had power with God and prevailed. "And he blessed him there." Our God delights to bless us; therefore He began so early, for He blessed us with all spiritual blessings in Jesus, before the foundation of the world; He gave us grace in His Son, before He gave us a being: but yet He will have us plead with Him, and weep before Him. He is "The blessing God." There never was a want that ever pierced the heart of fallen humanity, or met the omniscient eye of Jehovah, but that want was anticipated, and provided for, in the person and fulness of Christ. And however great our conflicts and trials may be, we can have no reason to despond, for grace is given us; and grace always goes hand in hand with omnipotence. Our heavenly Father's love cannot fail, our divine Saviour's fulness cannot be exhausted, the faithful promise cannot be broken; let us therefore plead in the valley of Achor, wrestle on the battle-plain, and it shall again be said, "He blessed him there." Oh for the Spirit of Prayer.

Lord, let me know the grace below,
To all believers given:
Oh, bid me feel thy love, and go
In perfect peace to heaven!

MAY 28.

In all thy ways acknowledge Him Prov. iii. 6.

BELOVED, we are the Lord's, the creatures of His power, the purchase of His blood, the subjects of His grace. He has set His love upon us, employed His wisdom for us, and is deeply interested in all that concerns us. Everything we do, should be done with a view to His glory; and in everything by prayer and supplication with thanksgiving, we should let our requests be made known unto Him. Everything should be mentioned at His throne; His presence, direction, and blessing, should be sought in reference to every circumstance of our lives. Our misery can never exceed His mercy, or our application at his throne find His ear pre-occupied. He is our Father, and as such ought to be consulted; He is our God, and ought to be honored. We should ask of Him, and ask with the whole heart; for He that withdraws his heart in asking, will find God withdraw His hand in giving. Acknowledging God in all things, will produce a steady peace of mind; preserve us from many temptations; and strengthen our faith in Him. He that always acknowledges God, will find that God always acknowledges him.

Stretch o'er my head Thy guardian wings,
Secure my soul, O King of kings!
  My shield and refuge be:
Thy grace and mercy, Lord, display,
Through Christ the Life, the Truth, the Way
  That I may come to Thee!

MAY 29.

And be found in Him. Phil. iii. 9.

To be in Christ, is to be united to Him by faith and love; and is of the utmost importance. Apart from Christ we are wretched, miserable, poor, blind, and naked; united to Christ we are immensely rich; immutably safe; exalted to the highest honor; and shall appear without a fault before the throne of God. If we are in Christ, or one with Christ, we are justified by His obedience, as the debtor is cleared by the payment made by his surety; we are sanctified through Him, as the vessel is cleansed in the fountain; we are protected by Him, as Noah was in the ark; we are preserved from judicial proceedings, as the manslayer in the city of refuge; and are exalted to honor as the BRIDE of the KING ETERNAL, Immortal, the only wise God. Well may the Apostle desire "TO BE FOUND IN HIM." No mind can conceive, no tongue can declare the blessedness that flows from being ONE WITH CHRIST. Let us therefore, beloved, ask, this morning, "Am I in Christ at present? Am I living with Him as His faithful bride; for Him as His devoted servant; upon Him as His dependant child? Do I renounce all for Christ? Can I say, I am crucified with Christ? The world is crucified unto me, and I unto the world?"

Yes, yes, I must and will esteem
All things but loss for Jesus' sake,
Oh, may my soul be found in Him,
And of His righteousness partake.

154

MAY 30.

JESUS is the fountain of living waters; the wells
of salvation are found in His person, work, and
word; He says, "If any man thirst, let him
come unto me and drink." · The springs of
comfort, peace, and salvation, are all in Him;
and in Him for us; therefore called our springs.
The waters cleanse from all defilement; refresh
the faint and weary; and satisfy the longing
soul.   The springs bespeak plenitude—whosoever will may come and take; for they are
never dry.   We are absolutely dependant on
Jesus, this is our mercy; we are not absolutely
dependant on any besides, this is our happiness.
Our desires should concentrate in Him; our
affections should be fixed upon Him; and our
expectations should be only from Him   In
Jesus is all possible variety; He can do, and
bestow all we can possibly want; for it hath
pleased the Father that in Him should ALL fulness dwell   If all our springs are in Jesus, let
us not then look to any other; but let us with
joy draw water out of the fountains of the Saviour.   Let us ask, and He will give us LIVING
WATER; that we may thirst no more.

> To whom, dear Jesus, oh, to whom
>   Shall needy sinners flee,
> But to Thyself, who bid'st us come ?
>   Our springs are all in Thee.
> Now fill my soul with Thy pure love,
> And raise my thoughts and hopes above.

MAY 31.

THE Lord's people are justified by grace, through faith, in the righteousness of Jesus; and all who are thus justified are created anew, have immortal principles of holiness and justice implanted in their hearts, so that they hate sin, follow holiness, and walk uprightly. Sin has not dominion over them, nor will they be slaves to lust. They meet with many troubles, they have to pass through fire and water, but they shall come out into a wealthy place. They shall not perish in their affliction, for the Lord upholdeth them with His hand. Beloved, look beyond your present trials; remember if you suffer as a Christian, you suffer with Christ; and if you suffer you shall also reign with Him. Your God is able to deliver; He has promised to do so; trust in Him without wavering; yield not to temptation; avoid the appearance of evil; and your God will bring you out of trouble. He will bring forth your righteousness as the light, and your judgment as the noonday. You shall also forget your misery, or remember it as waters that pass away. Present troubles will end in everlasting peace.

Millions who now His throne surround,
Here sought relief, here mercy found;
The Lord dispell'd their gloomy fears,
Heal'd all their wounds, and dried their tears.
And thou shalt also mercy find,
For God is faithful, just, and kind.

JUNE 1.

JESUS is Jehovah, the self-existent, eternal, and immutable God. He is our righteousness. To this end He assumed our nature; came into our place; labored, suffered, bled, and died in our stead. We have no righteousness by nature, but we have the righteousness of God by grace. "Their righteousness is of me, saith the Lord." Jesus completed for us all that was necessary to justify us; He made an end of sin; He magnified the law and made it honorable; He brought in everlasting righteousness; and now He clothes us with the garments of salvation, and covers us with the robe of righteousness. In Him we possess all justice can demand, or God require, for our full and eternal justification. This portion is not necessary merely for one day, but every day; it silences an accusing conscience, confounds Satan, strengthens the soul, and glorifies God. Let us look to-day, all the day, and every day to Jesus, as "THE LORD OUR RIGHTEOUSNESS." Let us go to duty, to conflict, to trials, in the strength of the Lord; making mention of His righteousness, even of His only. This is our plea at the throne of grace, our song in the house of our pilgrimage, and our confidence in the prospect of death. -

Saviour divine, we know thy name,
And in that name we trust;
Thou art the Lord our Righteousness,
Thou art our joy and boast.

157

JUNE 2.

I will deal well with thee. Gen xxxii 9.

So the Lord promised Jacob, and the promises made unto our fathers, He will fulfil unto us their children But such a promise does not exclude great trials, sore temptations, deep personal afflictions, fiery persecutions, poverty, disappointments, and perplexity; all these things may happen unto us, and yet the Lord deal well with us The promise secures the sanctification of our troubles, the communication of grace, deliverance from real evils, the supply of all wants, and the satisfying of our best desires. Is not this enough, to know that Jehovah will deal well with us, in sickness and health; in life and in death; in time and through eternity? This promise is Jehovah's bond, the believer's plea, the ground of the Christian's confidence, a reason for contentment and gratitude, and the cause of our enemies' confusion. Jacob, though tried, found the Lord faithful, and so shall we. Let us therefore rejoice that our God has said, "I will deal well with thee. I will make all my goodness pass before thee. I will save thee with an everlasting salvation. I will be thy God and thy glory."

Jesus ! in whom but Thee above,
Can I repose my trust, my love ,
Thy counsels and upholding care,
My safety and my comfort are ;
And Thou shalt guide me all my days,
Till glory crown the work of grace.

158

JUNE 3.

The exceeding riches of His grace. Eph. ii. 7.

JEHOVAH glories in His grace. It is His riches
—His wealth. All its riches are intended for
us, to be expended upon us. They are all treasured up in Jesus to be received by us. They
are promised and presented to us. They exceed our thoughts, our expectations, our faith,
we do not believe that God has provided and
promised so much for our good as He has; and
therefore we do not ask for, and expect so much.
Let us this day think of THE EXCEEDING RICHES
OF GRACE. Jesus was the gift of grace, so was
the Holy Spirit, and so are all spiritual blessings. Grace includes, and is the source from
which flows all the church has received, is receiving, and will receive throughout eternity.
Grace freely gives, but never sells. It has a
bountiful eye, a tender heart, and a liberal hand.
We are not straitened in God, but in our own
hearts. Oh, that we did but believe what God
has revealed in reference to the riches of
grace, and expect to receive according to His
most liberal promises! There is an abundance
of grace, and it is for us; for us this morning,
for us whenever we apply. Let us therefore
have grace, whereby we may serve God acceptably, with reverence and godly fear.

> Amazing grace! how sweet the sound!
> That saved a wretch like me!
> I once was lost, but now am found;
> Was blind, but now I see

JUNE 4.

His kindness towards us. Eph. ii. 7.

WHAT a subject is the kindness of God towards us! Let us think of it, as it appears in the place and circumstances of our birth; in happy Britain, not in a heathen land. In our education and preservation. Especially in our regeneration, that we were born again, not of the will of the flesh, nor of blood, but of God. How many, born in the same place, about the same time, and educated in the same school, have been allowed to pass out of time into eternity, carnal, and under the curse of God; or are living in that state! Why were we distinguished? Called by grace? Justified from all things in the righteousness of Jesus? Kept by the power of God? Supplied according to the promises? Walking with God? Looking for the coming of Jesus with hope, holy longing, and steady faith? Having the promise of the life that now is, and of that which is to come? Warranted to say, "All things are mine, for I am Christ's, and Christ is God's?" Oh, how great is the goodness of our God! How unsearchable His grace! His kindness to us is wonderful!

Who can have greater cause to sing,
　　Who greater cause to bless,
Than we, the children of a King,
　　Than we who Christ possess?
Our all we to His kindness owe,
And grateful praise should ever flow.

JUNE 5.

Lord, what wilt thou have me to do? Acts ix. 6.

A VERY proper inquiry to bring to the Lord's throne, for all the Lord's people should be employed in the Lamb's vineyard, for the Lord's glory. There is something for each of us to do, and something for us to do to-day. JESUS is our MASTER, He has a right to reign over us, and employ us as He will. He should be obeyed. We especially who are so deeply indebted, should obey Him willingly—cheerfully—habitually. Is our enmity subdued? How can we manifest it, but by seeking to be in His employment? Have we faith, love, hope, humility, peace, gratitude? Are we not then desirous of obeying Him, who gave us all these blessings? We ought to be employed—always employed— and so employed as if every day were our last. That is the best employment, which we can look at with satisfaction on a death-bed; of which we shall not be ashamed at the day of judgment. Are you doing for Jesus? Are you doing in the spirit of Jesus? Beware lest you put your doings in the place of Jesus; do all you can, and then lay all you do at the feet of Jesus.

Never did men by faith divine
To selfishness or sloth incline,
The Christian works with all his power,
And grieves that he can work no more:
Commits his works to God alone,
And seeks His will before his own.

L

JUNE 6.

He hath done all things well. Mark vii. 37.

THIS was the testimony of the multitude concerning Jesus. He did many things, but He did everything well. Cannot we bear the same testimony this morning? He called us by His grace; and when we reflect upon the means, the manner, and the period, must we not say, "He did it well?" He has tried us in many ways; but when we think of His design, the mercies He mingled with the afflictions, and the deliverance He granted us out of them, must we not say, "He hath done all things well? If we look back, and see Him standing forward as our SURETY with the Father in eternity; or if we behold Him taking our nature, bearing our sins, procuring our righteousness, and sending His Holy Spirit to sanctify and save us; must we not say, "He hath done all things well?" And when our mansions are prepared, our bodies raised from the grave, and our persons are perfectly conformed to His image; when we hear Him say, "Come, inherit the kingdom;" oh, with what rapture, gratitude, and love shall we shout, "HE HATH DONE ALL THINGS WELL!"

How sovereign, wonderful, and free,
Is all His love to sinful me;
He pluck'd me as a brand from hell!—
My Jesus hath done all things well:
And since my soul has known His love,
What mercies has He made me prove;
Mercies which all my praise excel—
My Jesus hath done all things well.

162

JUNE 7.

Ye are my witnesses, saith the Lord
Isaiah xliii 12.

WE are to witness to the truth, power, and
sweetness of religion ; to the goodness, holiness,
and faithfulness of God. We are to witness to
the world, by our spirit, testimony, and conduct ; we are to witness to poor, doubting,
fearful souls Our witness should be unequivo-
cal, and should be borne with courage, constancy, and love. Our testimony should be from
experience. Do we know the Lord? Do we
daily experience the power of truth in our
hearts? Does it free us from slavish fear, the
love of the world, and the dominion of sin?
Can we say. We have known and believed the
love which God hath to us—God is love? Are
we saying to those around us, Oh, TASTE and
see that the Lord is good ; there is no want to
them that fear Him? Suppose we should be
called to bear witness before judges, or kings ;
in the prison or at the stake ; how would it be
with us then? Could we witness that God is
good and gracious ; that He is enough to make
us happy ; if He were to strip us as He did Job,
or try us as He did Paul? He says, " YE ARE
MY WITNESSES."

Give me to bear Thy easy yoke,
And every moment watch and pray ;
And still to things eternal look,
And hasten to Thy glorious day !
I would Thy daily witness be,
And prove that I am one with Thee.

163

JUNE 8.

If God be for us, who can be against us.
Romans viii. 31.

BELOVED, if we are believers in Jesus, all the perfections of Jehovah's nature are arrayed for our defence and safety. He is engaged by covenant, by promise, and by oath, to support, supply, and befriend us. He is for us. Engaged in our cause. Opposed to our enemies. Pledged to deliver us in six troubles, and not forsake us in the seventh. We may challenge our foes, for God is with us; what then is man? What devils? We may admire our safety, happiness, and honor; God, the Lord God omnipotent, is our ally. We should be grateful, for what is our desert? What do we possess? What were our expectations? What has God promised? We may triumph in Christ, but only in Christ. If God be for us, then supplies shall certainly be sent us. If God be for us, men or devils shall never prevail over us. If God be for us we shall overcome the world, conquer death, and eternally inherit glory. But God is for us, who then shall harm us? What shall alarm or terrify us? God is ours; we are God's This is our honor, our happiness, our boast and glory.

Yes, God is above men, devils, and sin,
My Jesus's love the battle shall win:
On His mighty power I'll daily rely,
All evil before His presence shall fly:
I fear no denial, no danger I fear,
Nor start from a trial, while Jesus is near.

164

JUNE 9.

Let Israel hope in the Lord. **Psalm cxxx. 7.**

THIS title is applied to all the Lord's people; it sets forth their dignity,—they are PRINCES; it refers to their experience—they wrestle with God in prayer, and they prevail. Despondency does not become a prince, much less a Christian. Our God is "THE GOD OF HOPE:" and we should hope in Him. Israel should hope in His mercy—in His patience—in His provision—in His plenteous redemption. They should hope for light in darkness; for strength in weakness; for direction in perplexity; for deliverance in danger; for victory in conflict; and for triumph in death. They should hope in God confidently, because He has promised; prayerfully, for He loves to hear from us; obediently, for His precepts are to be observed by us; and constantly, for He is always the same. Beloved, let not your hope rest on frames, or duties, or men, or anything; but hope in the Lord, in the Lord only. Israel's God is at all times Israel's hope. The hope of Israel shall never be disappointed. Therefore hope in God, for it is good that a man should both hope, and quietly wait for the salvation of the Lord.

The gospel bears my spirit up;
A faithful and unchanging God
Lays the foundation for my hope,
In oaths, and promises, and blood;
Then, O my soul, still hope in God,
And plead thy Saviou's precious blood.

JUNE 10.

I am Alpha and Omega. Rev. xxii. 13.

JESUS is the first and the last. He began, He carries on, and He will complete the great work of our eternal salvation. He was the first object to which we were directed to look, and He will be the last we shall wish to see. He was the first subject we began to learn, and we shall be learning Him to all eternity. He is first with us in every trial and trouble, and will never leave us nor forsake us. He is the foundation on which we build, and He will be for a covering. We should look to Him first in every trouble, and go to Him first with every want. He includes all that is good, great, and glorious. He that hath Jesus hath all things. Let us begin with Jesus, and then go on with Jesus, so shall we end with Jesus : and a blessed ending it will be. He is our great lesson, and we have learned nothing to purpose until we know Him. Oh, to know Him, and the power of His resurrection, and the fellowship of His sufferings, and to be made conformable to His death! Let us endeavor to learn the happy art of looking to Jesus, expecting from Jesus, and glorifying Jesus as our ALPHA and OMEGA from day to day.

Christ is my hope, my strength, my guide,
For me He groan'd, and bled, and died;
Christ is the source of all my bliss,
My wisdom and my righteousness:
My Saviour, Brother, faithful Friend,
On Him alone I now depend.

166

JUNE 11.

The Lord is my portion. Lam. iii. 24.

How poor is the worldling's possession, if compared with the Christian's portion; it is but for a few days; it cannot satisfy, it cannot bless. But, beloved, Jehovah hath given us Himself; He says, "I AM YOUR INHERITANCE." We are ever with Him, and all He has is ours. His power is ours to support us, His wisdom to guide us, His love to comfort us, His mercy to relieve us, His goodness to supply us, His justice to defend us, His covenant to secure us, and His heaven to receive us. He is a suitable, sufficient, and immutable portion. We are to live upon Him, draw from Him, rejoice in Him, and look to Him for all we need. For Him we must renounce all other; to His glory all our efforts must be directed, and with Him we must daily walk. Men cannot deprive us of our portion, fire cannot consume it, nor rust corrupt it; let us not therefore be much affected by anything that occurs below; if the streams are dried, the fountain remains; if creatures fail or deceive us, our God is the portion of our inheritance and of our cup; He maintains our lot, He is our strength and OUR PORTION FOR-EVER.

> Begone, ye gilded vanities;
>   I seek the only GOOD;
> To real bliss my wishes rise,
>   The FAVOR OF MY GOD:
> Thy love, my God, my portion be,
> And let me find my all in Thee.

JUNE 12.

The Lord God is a Sun and Shield.   Psalm lxxxiv. 11.

To Him we must look for light, comfort, and fruitfulness. He is our light and our salvation. He will not leave us comfortless. From Him is our fruit found. The people who know Him, believe Him, and walk with Him, are blessed; He giveth light in darkness, joy in sorrow, and life in death. He is our defence; from Him we must expect protection. His salvation is our shield; faith lays hold of it, and employs it against all our foes. He will enlighten and protect us; He will never fail us, or leave us to want or perish. He communicates His favors as freely, as easily, and as plentifully as the sun shines; there is enough in Him, and He will cheerfully bestow; let us therefore wait upon Him this day, and walk in the light of His countenance. Who is among you that feareth the Lord, and obeyeth the voice of His servant, that walketh in darkness and hath no light? Let him trust in the name of the Lord, and stay upon His God. His heart is evermore towards us, His promises shall be fulfilled to us, and He will glorify every perfection of His nature in us.

> Lord, be my safety and defence,
>   My light, my joy, my bliss,
> My portion in the world to come,
>   My confidence in this : —
> Be thou, O Lord, my Shield and Sun,
> As I the path of duty run.

168

3/17/24

JUNE .3.

The angel of the Lord stood by   Zech. iii. 5.

WHO was it that thus stood by Joshua, when
Satan accused and resisted him; when his filthy
garments bore testimony against him, and he
was cited to appear before God? Surely it was
Jesus. Jesus, the messenger of the covenant;
the minister of the true tabernacle, which God
pitched, and not man; the angel of Jehovah's
presence. This same Jesus stands by all His
people; He stands by us. He stands on our
side in prayer—in trouble—in temptation—in
all our efforts to glorify His name. He stands
by to instruct us in the will of God; to help us
in the work of God; to enrich us with the
wealth of God; and to watch over us for good.
Beloved, whoever leaves us, Jesus still stands
by us. Our eyes should always be fixed upon
Him. We ought never to forget, there is one
witness to every action; Jesus stands by observing. We should therefore be circumspect—
grateful—and courageous. He stands at the
right hand of the poor, to save him from those
who condemn his soul. He stands ready to
help, waiting to give, determined to bless. May
we always realize that Jesus stands by.

Look up, my soul, with cheerful eye,
See where the great Redeemer stands,
The glorious Advocate on high,
With precious incense in His hands!
On Him alone thy hopes recline:
His power and love are all divine.

169

JUNE 14.

No man can possibly tell what is before him; but our God knoweth, and He has promised His people strength proportioned to their trials. We should not be anxious, for with the trial comes the strength Our troubles are very generally to be numbered amongst our mercies. Temporal prosperity, without a special blessing from God, will prove to be a curse; and it always brings a solemn responsibility with it. We always have found our God faithful; He always has given strength according to the day; and why should we now doubt? We may look forward and suppose the worst, and then say, "I will trust and not be afraid; for the Lord Jehovah is my STRENGTH and my song; He also is become my salvation." We go from strength to strength, and every true believer shall appear in Zion before God He will perfect that which concerneth us, but will never forsake the work of His own hands. Let us then expect the Lord to give WHEN we want, AS we want, and ALL we want; let us believe that our strength will be equal to our burden, to our day. The promise is plain, it is positive, it is sure, and our God is faithful.

God is love, and will not leave you,
    When you most his kindness need;
God is true, nor can deceive you,
    Though your faith be weak indeed.

JUNE 15.

Let not your heart be troubled. John **xiv. 1.**

JESUS does not approve of your being in an agitated, perplexed, uncomfortable state. He wishes to see you steady, holy, and happy. He forbids your fear; He commands your faith. As He is with you, as He is engaged for you, you should leave your concerns very much with Him But how can we attend to this exhortation? Get the mind assured of a covenant interest in God, as your God. Live under the impression, God is with me; He minutely observes everything that takes place within and around me; He is watching for an opportunity to do me good; He will not allow anything to hurt me; He will glorify Himself in me, and me in Himself; He bids me trust Him; I will trust and not be afraid. What will follow? He will keep them in perfect peace, whose minds are stayed on Him; because they trust in Him. Trust then in the Lord forever; for in the Lord Jehovah is everlasting strength. Let nothing trouble you, for your souls are in the hands of Jesus; your life is hid with Christ in God; your times are at God's disposal; and all things are working together for your good.

O my soul ! what means this sadness ?
Wherefore art thou thus cast down ?
Let thy grief be turned to gladness,
Bid thy restless fear begone ,
Look to Jesus,
And rejoice in his dear name.

171

JUNE 16.

I go to prepare a place for you.   John **xiv. 2.**

SEE, beloved, what Jesus is doing. He is engaged for us; He did all He could for us on earth, and then ascended to heaven to carry on His work   The place He prepares will be worthy of Himself; "His rest will be glorious." It will just suit us; there the wicked cease from troubling, sin shall no more annoy, troubles shall no more beset, but the weary shall be at rest.   He is preparing us for it, as well as it for us; therefore we are so tried and afflicted. Our light afflictions which are but for a moment, are working out for us a far more exceeding and eternal weight of glory.   Let us daily think of Jesus as employed for us; let us consider death as going to take possession of the place He has prepared for us; and under all that tries us or casts us down, let us remember, Jesus will come again and receive us unto Himself, that where He is we may be also.   Our present cottage may be incommodious and uncomfortable: but our mansion will be spacious, magnificent, and worthy of a God.   He that overcometh shall inherit all things, and Jehovah will be His God.

And art Thou, gracious Saviour, gone,
A mansion to prepare for me?
Shall I behold Thee on Thy throne.
And there forever sit with Thee ?
Then let the world approve or blame,
I'll triumph in Thy gracious name.

JUNE 17.

Salvation is of the Lord. Jonah ii. 9.

THE love of the Father, the work of the Son, and the operations of the Holy Ghost, save the soul. The Father devised the scheme, the Son gave the ransom, and the Holy Spirit puts us in possession of the blessing. It is of God. It is by grace. It is through faith. Deliverance from dangers, trials, and wants, is of the Lord. He delivered Jonah when he cried, though he was a poor, proud, obstinate, peevish, fretful sinner: and He will deliver us. He says, "Look unto me and be delivered, for I am God. Look, for I bid you. Look, for I will attend to you. Look, for I will deliver you." He will deliver in six troubles, and in seven He will not forsake us. He will deliver our souls from death, our eyes from tears, and our feet from falling. He will deliver the needy when he crieth, the poor also, and him that hath no helper. Are you looking to others? Are you drooping, fearing, or desponding? Your God takes it unkindly; He asks, "Is my hand shortened at all, that it cannot redeem? Or have I no power to deliver? Is anything too hard for me?" He says, "I WILL WORK." He asks, "WHO SHALL LET IT?"

Of all the crowns JEHOVAH bears,
Salvation is His dearest claim,
That gracious sound well pleased He hears,
And owns IMMANUEL for His name
He saves us by His precious blood,
And proves Himself the MIGHTY GOD.

JUNE 18.

BELIEVERS when in darkness, often fear that Jesus has forsaken them: this is natural; but it is unscriptural · for He has said, "I will never leave thee, I will never forsake thee." His offices require His presence with us, His love secures His presence to us. He will not leave us orphans. We are absolutely dependant upon Him, our comfort is His gift, and the continuance of comfort depends on His presence and grace. He is the great source of comfort to His people; His presence and His comforts are generally connected; He may withhold them for a time to reprove—instruct—or correct us; but we may calculate upon His comforts returning, for His promise is plain; it stands unrepealed in His word; and His nature and love are the same. His precious word of promise should be believed—pleaded—firmly trusted. We never shall be orphans, for our Father ever lives; our home waits to receive us; and our hope is imperishable. Oh, beloved, plead this precious word of Jesus; expect Him to make it good; aim at His glory, and your comforts are sure.

Most Holy Spirit, give me faith,
To rest on what my Saviour saith:
May I the sweetest comforts prove
Of His divine eternal love:
And daily trust His faithfulness,
Who will not leave me comfortless.

All His saints are in Thy hand. Deut. **xxxiii. 3.**

EVERY believer is a saint, separated by the purpose of God; sanctified by the operations of the
Holy Spirit; set apart for God, and devoted to
His service. Every saint is in the hand of Jesus; in the hand of His mercy—in the hand of
His power—and in the hand of His providence.
The hand of Jesus is large enough to hold all;
strong enough to defend all. They are in His
hand as His property, purchased by His blood;
as His charge, committed to Him by His Father;
at His disposal, to do with them as seemeth
good in His sight; under His protection, to be
kept from Satan, death, and hell; to be guided
through this desert world, to our Father's house
above; to be moulded by His skill, and conformed to His own lovely image; to be covered
from the storm, and preserved from the furious
blast; to be used for His praise, and be lifted
up to His eternal throne. They are HIS SAINTS;
He chose them for HIS BRIDE; He rescued them
from the hand of the enemy; He claims them
as His right; He made them what they are;
and He will glorify them forever.

Blessed are the saints of God;
They are bought with Jesus' blood,
They are ransom'd from the grave,
Life eternal they shall have.
With them number'd may I be,
Now, and through eternity!

JUNE 20.

It is God that justifieth. Rom. viii. 33.

To be justified is to be acquitted, a J pro-
nounced righteous. Every believer in Jesus,
however ungodly he may have been, or however
vile and unworthy he may feel, is justified by
Jehovah. The perfect work of Jesus is imputed to him, free grace is glorified in him, and
he is passed from death to life. To him there
is no condemnation, no one can lay anything to
his charge, he is accepted in the Beloved, Christ
lived and died for him; and now he liveth, and
shall be glorified through and with Jesus. All
trespasses are freely forgiven and eternally forgotten. God has cast all our sins behind His
back, and now He pronounces us just. Let us
approach God believing that He has justified
us; and let us look forward and rejoice that the
Judge of all the earth will declare us righteous.
Who shall lay anything to our charge It is
God that justifieth. Who is he that condemn-
eth? It is Christ that died, yea, rather that is
risen again, who is even at the right hand of
God, who also maketh intercession for us. My
soul look to Jesus, to His perfect work, and
prevalent intercession; there see thy salvation
and find peace.

> They are justified by grace;
> They enjoy the Saviour's peace;
> All their sins are washed away;
> They shall stand in God's great day.
> With them numbered may we be,
> Here, and in eternity.

JUNE 21.

How is it that ye have no faith? Mark iv. 40.

WHERE there is little faith there are many fears. The disciples were filled with alarm, and Jesus inquires, "How is it that ye have no faith?" May not our heavenly Father often address us in the same language? How is it that ye give no credit to my word? "How is it that ye place no dependence on my relation—character—and veracity? How is it that ye have no confidence in my presence—power—and love? How is that ye do not expect my interference, and look for my supplies? Have I not made promises which are plain—positive—and sure? Have I not fulfilled my promises again and again? Have I not summoned witnesses to attest the truth of my work? Have I not promised you my Holy Spirit? Have I not pledged my holiness? Have I not given my Son for you, and to you? Have I not appeared for you in every past difficulty? How is it then that ye have no faith?" Beloved, let us humble ourselves before God. Let us plead guilty of indulging in unbelief, and plead for faith. Let us look for God in every place and in everything.

Why should my soul indulge complaints,
　And yield to dark despair?
The meanest of my Father's saints
　Are safe beneath His care:
Dear Lord, increase my faith in Thee,
Till I Thy full salvation s⁚e.

JUNE 22.

God is faithful. 1 Cor. x. 13.

THIS is the believer's sheet anchor; without this his comforts would droop, and hope would give up the ghost. We are at times shaken to pieces by unbelief, and filled with tormenting doubts. We feel nothing of the presence, power, or comforts of the Holy Ghost; faith, hope, and love seem to be quite extinguished. We have no power and scarcely any inclination to pray; and we only feel hardness, fretfulness, and misery. We are tempted by Satan, and harassed with tormenting thoughts, so that we feel tired of this miserable life. But God is faithful; He never fails us; but appears again and again, restoring us to peace, joy, and satisfaction; and our most miserable times are often succeeded by peculiar joys. The scriptures are opened up to our understandings, the promises are applied to our souls, and we are filled with the comforts of the Holy Ghost. Then our souls melt before God in contrition, and holy penitence; we feel crumbled into dust before Him; and can only admire and adore the riches of free and sovereign grace. Beloved, in the darkest night, remember, "GOD IS FAITHFUL."

He will not His great self deny;
A God all truth can never lie:
True to His word, God gave His Son
To die for crimes which men had done
Blest pledge ! He never will revoke
A single promise He has spoke.

178

JUNE 23.

What do these Hebrews here? 1 Sam **xxix. 3.**

DAVID's host wanted to mingle with the Philis-
tines' army; this was decidedly wrong: and it
is as wrong, when God's people unite with the
world contrary to His word. We may ask,
"What do these Christians here?" What do
they joining with the world? Their Master has
told them to "come out and be separate."
What do they seeking a settlement below? He
has said, "Arise ye, and depart, this is not
your rest." What do they out of the path of
duty, or by their presence sanctioning sin?
He has said, "Be ye holy, for I am holy."
What do they on Satan's ground? In the
enemy's ranks? Do they intend to leave Jesus,
and join the world? Are they tired of His
company, set against His word, and determined to throw off His yoke? Do they intend
to share in what they have proclaimed as the
sinner's doom; the frown of Jesus, the wrath of
God, and the slavery of Satan? WHAT DO
THEY HERE? Their conduct is unnatural—
degrading—traitorous. Beloved, you should
keep the company of Jesus, walk with spiritual
persons, and keep yourselves unspotted from the
world.

Ye tempting sweets forbear,
Ye dearest idols fall;
My love ye must not share,
Jesus shall have it all :
Aid me, dear Saviour, set me froo,
And I will all resign for Thee.

JUNE 24.

Ye are a chosen generation. 1 Pet ii. 9

RELIGION does not originate in chance, but in the purpose of God; it flows not from the nature of man, but from the unalterable decree of the Most High. Every believer is a chosen vessel. The church had its origin in Jehovah's eternal election. Election flows from love; it is the exercise of sovereignty; it secures man's salvation and God's glory. It injures none, but it pours incalculable blessings upon thousands. It was the act of God before time. He chose us in Christ as our head; it was of pure grace; it was to holiness. We were chosen to be redeemed from death; purified from sin; separated from the world; devoted to God; and raised to a state of oneness with Jehovah. Being chosen of God, we choose God in return; He chose us to be His people, we choose Him to be our God. He chose us to be the beloved Bride of Jesus, and we choose Jesus to be our beloved Bridegroom. His election is the cause, our choice is the effect. His choice prevented ours; or else we had chosen death, in the error of our ways. Beloved, if we are the elect of God we are holy; we are in union with Jesus

All the elected train
Were chosen in their Head,
To all eternal good,
Before the worlds were made;
Chosen to know the Prince of peace,
And taste the riches of His grace.

180

JUNE 25.

What manner of persons ought ye to be? 2 Pet. iii. 11.

THE people of God are expected to be different
from the world; they profess to have another
Spirit in them; and to be the sons of God.
They believe the present frame of things is to
be dissolved; they look for a new heaven and
a new earth, wherein dwelleth righteousness;
they are strangers and pilgrims here. What
manner of persons then ought we to be? Surely
we ought to set light by the things of time, and
aim at the things which are eternal. We ought
to be watchful—prayerful—diligent—holy—patient—thankful—and expectant. We ought
to be contented with such things as we have;
to give all diligence to prove our title, make
sure our election, and rejoice in our destination.
We ought to walk as Jesus walked. To live
as Paul lived, dying daily. Let us ask this
morning, Do we habitually believe that present
things will soon be dissolved? If so, are we
acting according to the same? Are we laying
up for ourselves treasures in heaven? Are we
doing good, that we may be rich in good **works**
and an honor to religion?

Then let us wait the sound,
That shall our souls release;
And labor to be found
Of Him in spotless peace,
In perfect holiness renew'd,
Adorn'd with Christ, and meet for God.

JUNE 26.

My grace is sufficient for thee. 2 Cor. xii. 9.

You need look to no other quarter for help, relief, or comfort. Jesus assures you that His grace is sufficient. You are welcome to it. You are exhorted to have it. To be strong in the grace which is in Christ Jesus. It is sufficient to support you under every privation, to help you over every difficulty, to strengthen you for every duty, to mortify every lust, and fill you with all joy and peace in believing. His grace is almighty—it is free—it is durable—it brings salvation. Look not at difficulties—dangers—or thy own weakness; but look to the free, powerful, promised grace of Jesus. Go to His throne of grace this morning, on purpose to receive grace for this day; go every day; and whenever you feel weak, timid, or cast down. His grace was found sufficient for Paul, for the martyrs and saints, in the deepest trials, and it shall be found sufficient for thee. He says, "I am the Lord thy God, open thy mouth wide and I will fill it. Come boldly to the throne of grace, that ye may obtain mercy and find grace to help you in time of need. Every one that asketh receiveth." O Jesus, make good Thy word in me!

Thy strength in weakness is display'd;
My soul this truth can relish now·
A worm upon Thy power is stay'd;
The weaker he, the stronger Thou:
My hope, my joy, is this alone—
My strength is Christ, THE MIGHTY ONE.

great reminder

JUNE 27.

Remember Lot's wife. Luke xvii. 32.

SHE received the angels, and hospitably enter-
tained them; she believed their message, and
prepared to act upon it; she obeyed their command, and left Sodom and her children behind
her. She forsook the ungodly, and went in company with the saints; yet her heart was left
in the city, and she looked back. She was de-
prived of life for too highly prizing its comforts. She was cut off by a visible display of
God's judgment. The situation in which she
died was instructive; it was not in Sodom, but
on the plain; she escaped one judgment, but
was overtaken by another. She was left as a
sad example of God's jealousy, and displeasure
against sin. Here is a warning to the covetous,
whose hearts are set on things below: to the
self-willed, who trifle with God's commands;
to the undecided, who stand between Sodom
and Zoar. God will be honored by our obedience, or by our sufferings. It is dangerous
to trifle with the smallest of God's commands.
We may overcome one temptation, and yet fall
by another. Let us examine—are our hearts
detached from the world? Be not high-minded,
but fear.

Waiting for our Lord's returning,
  Be it ours His word to keep,
Let our lamps be always burning;
  Let us watch while others sleep:
We're no longer of the night:
We are children of the light.

183

trifle = to act w/o seriousness, gravity.
to indulge in trivial amusements

JUNE 28.

The Lord will be the hope of His people.   Joel iii. 16.

WE know not what a day may bring forth; we are born to trouble; many unexpected trials may befall us; but our God will be our hope. He is the REFUGE, to which we may always repair, and find safety: the Fulness, from which we shall receive a plentiful supply. His oath, His promises, His covenant character, and the blood of Jesus, lay a firm foundation for our hope; and His gospel warrants us to hope in Him at all times, for all things. Therefore let what will come, we can have no reason to be disconsolate; we can have no cause to fear; our God is our hope. May the God of hope fill us with all joy and peace in believing, that we may abound in hope by the power of the Holy Ghost. Let us gird up the loins of our minds, be sober, and hope to the end for the grace that is to be brought unto us at the appearing of the Lord Jesus. Let us look for that blessed hope, even the glorious appearing of the great God, even our Saviour Jesus Christ, who gave Himself for us, that He might redeem us from all iniquity, and purify unto Himself a peculiar people, zealous of good works.

In Him I hope, in Him I trust,
His bleeding cross is all my boast:
Through troops of foes He'll lead me on
To victory, and the victor's crown.

JUNE 29.

My Son, give me thine heart. Prov. xxiii. 26.

BELOVED, the Most High presents Himself as a Suitor this morning; He asks for thy heart. It is His workmanship, He wants it to be His habitation; He made it by His power, He wants to rule it by His grace. He will not be satisfied with anything else; if He have the heart, He has all; if He has not the heart, He has nothing. Let us surrender our hearts to Him this morning, and every morning; let us ask Him to sanctify them by His grace, to fill them with His Spirit, to engrave on them His image, to keep them by His power, and to fill them with the fruits of holiness. If the heart is given to God, the life will be according to His word; if He rule in us, we shall walk as Jesus walked; and if our walk is not holy, our religion is but a form. "He that saith, I know Him, and keepeth not His commandments, is a liar, and the truth is not in him." Oh, how awful, to think and profess that we are the Lord's, and yet to have the heart under the influence of sin, Satan, and the world! Jesus says, "MY SON, GIVE ME THINE HEART." Let our reply be, "Lord, take my heart, reign and rule in it forever."

O Jesus! wounded Lamb of God,
Come, wash me in thy cleansing blood;
Take my poor heart, and let it be
Forever closed to all but Thee:
Unloose my stammering tongue, to tell
Thy love immense, unsearchable.

I am Thine, save me. Ps cxix. 94.

WE profess to be the Lord's. We are not our own. We belong not to the world. We are no longer the servants of sin. We are solely and entirely the Lord's; having willingly given up ourselves into His hands, to be saved by His grace, devoted to His service, and employed for His glory. We are His children by grace and adoption; His servants by voluntary engagement; His soldiers by public profession; and His spouse by affection and union. Being the Lord's, we may expect His interference on our behalf; and we should call on Him and plead with Him in all straits and difficulties. He will save. He will deliver us. Let us therefore lay our case before Him; and then ardently expect Him to glorify His grace in us. Let us walk worthy of God as beloved children: and live under the impression that He will make all grace abound toward us, so that we, having all sufficiency in all things, may abound in every good work. His mercy is great unto the heavens, and His faithfulness unto the clouds; and He never said to the seed of Jacob, " SEEK YE ME," in vain. But He saith, " SEEK YE ME, AND YE SHALL LIVE."

Jesus, my Saviour, and my God,
Thou hast redeem'd me with Thy blood;
By ties both natural and divine,
I am, and ever will be Thine:
Save me from sin, and Satan's power,
Guide me and guard me every hour.

JULY 1.

The Lord thy God is a merciful God. Deut. iv 81.

IT is no uncommon thing to mistake the true character of our God, and conceive of Him so as to dishonor His name, and distress our own souls. It is plainly and plentifully asserted in the divine word, that our God is merciful, and the same is satisfactorily proved in nature, providence, and redemption. It is to be firmly believed and constantly remembered, especially when burdened with guilt, or at the throne confessing sin; when enduring trials, or pleading with God for blessings; when performing duties, or suffering privations; when witnessing misery, or comforting mourners. "OUR GOD IS A MERCIFUL GOD." But mercy and holiness are united in His nature—word—and ways. He is not implacable or difficult to please, but He should be daily loved and constantly trusted. His mercy is the sun that enlightens, the ocean that supplies, and the army that guards us. But for His mercy we should soon sink into despair, or run into desperation; but now we may trust and not be afraid, walk with Him in peace, and rejoice in Him day by day.

Merciful God, Thyself proclaim
  In my polluted breast;
Mercy is Thy distinguish'd name,
  Which suits a sinner best
Thy mighty mercy now make known
In me, and claim me for Thy son

JULY 2.

He that toucheth you, toucheth the apple of His eye.
Zech. ii. 8.

How infinitely tender is Jehovah of His people! They had lately been visited with sore
judgments; reduced to great straits; appeared
to be neglected of God; were generally despised; had only just escaped from the enemy's
land; and returned with weeping and supplication, like brands plucked from the burning, to
their own country. And now the Lord says, "He
that toucheth you, toucheth the apple of His eye."
How wonderful the ways of God! As the wise
physician, He will touch to cure; but He will not
allow others to touch to hurt. Like the tender
mother, He can correct His children Himself;
but will not allow others to do so. How close
the union! How peculiar the affection! How
tender the sympathy! How kind the care!
How constant the attention! How merciful
the provision! How safe and how happy they
are! Beloved, take encouragement under all
your persecutions and trials; be comforted in
all your afflictions; you are as near and as dear
to Jehovah as the apple of His eye; and you
are hid under the shadow of His wings.

No condemnation now I dread;
Jesus, and all in Him, is mine;
Alive in Him, my living Head,
And clothed in righteousness divine,
Bold I approach the eternal throne,
And claim the crown, thro' Christ, my own.

188

JULY 3.

Their heart is divided. Hosea x. 2.

THIS is a very serious charge; for God demands the whole heart, and His people profess to surrender it. But have we not reason to fear that many are guilty on this point? They appear so undecided, that we must think that the heart is divided between God and the world; between sin and holiness; between truth and error; or between Christ and self. What are the symptoms of a divided heart? Habitual cleaving to earth. Being satisfied with a form of godliness. Backwardness to examine ourselves. A dislike to plain, close, soul-searching, rousing preaching. Putting away eternal things to a distance. Beloved, how is it with you? God rejects half the heart, He will have all or none. Do you fear on this point. There is a remedy. Thoroughly examine your heart. Condemn whatever you detect amiss in it. Take it to Jesus, and beseech Him to heal it. Expose it to the keen edge of God's word. Endeavor to keep up a constant sense of the presence of God. Converse much with eternal realities. As the heart is, so will the life be; so will the comfort and peace be. O Lord, unite my heart to fear Thy name!

> Let me, according to Thy word,
> A tender, contrite heart receive,
> Which grieves at having grieved its Lord,
> And never can itself forgive
> A heart Thy joys and griefs to feel,
> A heart where Christ alone may dwell.

JULY 4.

He shall testify of Me   John xv. 26.

It is the office and work of the Holy Spirit to bear testimony of Jesus; He hath done so in the word; there Christ is set forth in His glory and grace. He testifies of Jesus by the preaching of the gospel; for we preach Christ crucified, and are determined (when under Divine teaching) to know nothing else among men. He testifies of Jesus to the heart; and then we see His loveliness, behold His glory, pant for an interest in His salvation, sigh for union to His person; or, trust in His promises, accept His invitations, rejoice in His name, and melt in love and gratitude before Him. We have then no doubt about His divinity, suitability, or love; all we want is to enjoy, possess, and glorify Him. Every idol falls before Him, every grace springs up and is in exercise upon Him; we love Him; believe Him; hope in Him: mourn for Him; are humbled before Him; and are zealous for Him: our language is, "NONE BUT JESUS, NONE BUT CHRIST FOR ME." Oh, for the Spirit, to testify of Jesus to our hearts and consciences, this day and every day, especially our last day; and to bear witness with our hearts that we are sons of God.

Saviour, I Thy word believe,
   My unbelief remove;
Thy testifying Spirit give,
   The unction from above:
Show me, O Lord, how good Thou art,
And fix Thy witness in my heart.

JULY 5.

I know their sorrows. Exod iii 7

THE Lord is acquainted with all the sorrows of His people; they do not suffer unnoticed; He sympathizes with them, and will sanctify sorrow to them. Israel suffered, but Jesus sympathized. "In all their affliction He was afflicted; and the angel of His presence saved them; in His love and in His pity He redeemed them; and He bare them, and carried them all the days of old." Beloved, He knows our sorrows, and He will be our Comforter. Let us lay them before Him; let us plead with Him; He will be very gracious unto us at the voice of our cry; when He heareth He will answer. He is touched with the feeling of our infirmities. He once suffered; He was "THE MAN OF SORROWS;" and He is able to succor us who now suffer. His sorrows are ended, and so will ours be soon; weeping may endure for a night, but joy cometh in the morning. Light is sown for the righteous, and joy for the upright in heart. We shall obtain joy and gladness, and sorrow and sighing shall flee away. We shall enter into His joy, be filled with His love, and so be forever with Him. O Jesus! suffer me not to dwell on my sorrows, but by Thy Spirit direct my heart into Thy love!

Away with our sorrow and fear,
We soon shall recover our home ·
The city of saints shall appear,
The day of eternity come,

191

JULY 6.

God is with us. Isaiah viii. 10.

THE Lord's people are never alone, therefore they should not feel lonely. God is with them as an OBSERVER; He notices every thought, word, and action; every trial, every foe, and every danger. He is with them as a FATHER, loving and holding communion with them. He is with them as the LORD OF HOSTS, having all the armies of earth and heaven under His direction to befriend them. He is with them as a GUIDE, to lead them; as a COUNSELLOR, to plead their cause; as a FRIEND, to supply and comfort them; as a SAVIOUR, to deliver and exalt them; and as a holy, sin-hating God. He is present with them to try them—to reprove them—to humble them—to preserve them—to comfort them—and to save them with an ever-lasting salvation. Beloved, let us remember that God is with us, everywhere and always; this will check levity; prevent impatience; make us honest; encourage prayerfulness; inspire with fortitude; and produce diligence. If God is with us thus, He is for us; and if God be for us, who can be against us? But do we so walk, as by our conduct to say, "GOD IS WITH US?"

> Be it my only wisdom here,
> To serve the Lord with filial fear,
>   With loving gratitude;
> Superior sense may I display,
> By shunning every evil way,
>   And walking in the good.

192

JULY 7.

I will not remember thy sins. Isa. xliii 25.

WE need fear nothing but sin; and we have no reason to fear whether God will pardon that, and save us from it, if we believe in Jesus, confess and forsake it. He has promised, "I will be merciful to their unrighteousness, and their sins and their iniquities WILL I REMEMBER NO MORE." He will not impute sin unto us; but He will impute righteousness, even the righteousness of Jesus without works. He has made up His mind thus to glorify the riches of His grace, thus to display the wonders of His love. No one sin shall be charged upon us, He will blot them all completely out of His book, and banish them eternally from His mind. He will treat us as though we had not sinned, or rather as having received full satisfaction for all we have done amiss, and being infinitely delighted with our persons. If one sin were remembered, and laid to our charge, we were undone; but believing in Jesus, we are justified from ALL SIN, we are saved from wrath, and are made "THE RIGHTEOUSNESS OF GOD IN HIM." This is godlike, glorious, divine !

Crimes of such horror to forgive,
Such guilty daring worms to spare ;
This is Thy grand prerogative,
And none shall in the honor share.
Who is a pardoning God like Thee ?
Or who has grace so rich and free ?

JULY 8.

Follow after charity 1 Cor xiv 1

CHARITY is love: and what can be so worthy of the Christian's thought, care, and anxious desire, as LOVE ? Love to God, the centre and source of all excellence ; to Jesus, the Mediator of the new covenant, the personification of everything that is lovely ; to believers, for His sake and because they are His children and representatives ; and to sinners, because He commands us. The law requires it, and the gospel, when applied by the power of the Holy Ghost, produces it. It is not in our hearts by nature ; we are ENMITY. It is not to be produced by human effort. It flows from grace. It is produced by the Holy Ghost. It is connected with evangelical sentiment. Its exercise is our happiness and our holiness. There is no real religion without love ; and only so much true godliness as there is love. LET US FOLLOW AFTER CHARITY Let us cultivate love to the Lord's people, for the Lord's sake ; not merely those who see as we see, attend the place of worship we attend, and are our personal friends ; this is love of party ; but let us love all who love Jesus, though in some things they differ from us.

'Tis love that makes our cheerful feet
　In swift obedience move ,
'Tis love shall tune our joyful songs,
　In the sweet realms above
Jesus, to me this love be given ;
Fill me with love, for love is heaven.

194

JULY 9.

I will do all my pleasure. Isaiah xlvi. 18.

THE purpose of God cannot be frustrated. His holy mind can never be disappointed. His will is law. His counsel must stand. He is in one mind, and none can turn Him. He takes pleasure in them that fear Him, and in them that hope in His mercy. He chose them to salvation in Jesus, according to the good pleasure of His will. He works in us to will, and to do, of His good pleasure. He will fulfil in us all the good pleasure of His goodness, and the work of faith with power. He is PLEASED to save His people with an everlasting salvation. He is PLEASED with our obedience to His precepts. It is our Father's good pleasure that gives us the kingdom. He accomplishes the purposes of His will by angels—they are His ministers, which do His pleasure; by men, good and bad; by devils; by Jesus Christ; the pleasure of the Lord prospers in His hand. For His pleasure all things are and were created; and He worketh all things after the counsel of His own will. Let us seek to be like-minded with our God; let us acquiesce in all that pleases Him, and let us take pleasure in glorifying Him.

agree, consent

God moves in a mysterious way,
 His wonders to perform;
He plants His footsteps in the sea,
 And rides upon the storm:
His power and wisdom will fulfil
The utmost counsel of His will.

JULY 10.

He that waiteth on his master shall be honored.
Prov. xxvii. 18.

AND who is our master but JESUS? **One is**
your master, even CHRIST. We have chosen to
serve Him, because He chose to save us. He
has given us the knowledge of salvation by the
remission of our sins, that we may serve Him
without fear, in righteousness and holiness all
the days of our life. Our happiness is found in
obeying our Master's word, and studying our
Master's will. Let us wait on Him for the word
of command, nor dare to proceed without it.
Let us wait on Him for ability, to do and suffer all His righteous will. Let us wait His
time for every promised blessing, and continue
looking in faith until we receive it. Let us
expect to live at His table, and wait on Him for
a supply of all our needs, both spiritual and
temporal. Let us wait on Him in private, and
in public always form a part of His retinue. He
will honor us, for He has said, "If any man
serve me, let Him follow me; and where I am,
there shall also my servant be; if any man
serve me, him will my Father honor." We
shall know the truth, and the truth shall make
us free; and all such are free indeed.

That wisdom, Lord, on me bestow,
From every evil to depart;
To stop the mouth of every foe,
While upright both in life and heart,
The proofs of godly fear I give,
And show them how true Christians live.

196

JULY 11.

HOWEVER hot the war, or sore the trial, we may be sure of this, that " as our day, so shall our strength be." God has promised, and He will give. He gives because they are His people, as the father to his children ; because He has covenanted to do so, and He is faithful; lest their foes should triumph over them, whereas He has said, " They shall overcome at the last." He has raised their expectations, and He will not disappoint them ; He has commanded them to pray, and He will not refuse. He will give strength sufficient—enough, but perhaps none to spare—suitable to their circumstances and wants. Has the Lord pledged Himself to give strength to His people ; yea, to be Himself their strength ? Then let us fight courageously ; look forward joyfully ; bear every cross patiently ; pray fervently ; praise daily ; and believe confidently. God hath spoken—saints in every age have found Him a truth-telling, promise-performing God—Satan is a liar, a deceiver, a false witness against God—let us therefore resist him, and he will flee from us.

Give me Thy strength, Q God of power;
Then let winds blow, or thunders roar,
Thy faithful witness will I be.
'Tis fix'd ; I can do all through Thee:
Fulfil Thy sovereign counsel, Lord,
Thy will be done, Thy name adored !

JULY 12.

Happy is the man that feareth alway. Prov xxviii 1*

GODLY fear flows from grace, and is always connected with spiritual knowledge. It is the fear of a tender child, who would not on any account grieve a kind and loving parent. It is a covenant blessing. Our God bestows it on all whom he loves; and they consequently fear to offend Him, their Father; dishonor their gracious Saviour; or grieve the Holy Comforter. They fear lest they should be led astray from God, by their own hearts; by Satan; by professors; by the world; or any of the dispensations of providence. They fear to trust their own judgments; they reverence God's word; and dread a lukewarm state. Happy is the man who THUS feareth alway; he happily preserves a tender conscience; a humble mind; and a consistent walk. He proves his interest in all new-covenant blessings; has much to do with the blood of atonement; and enjoys a solid peace. He is in a happy state, standing high in the favor of God, walking in the comforts of the Holy Ghost, and keeping himself unspotted from the world. Oh, for godly fear to rule my heart, and preserve my goings!

Fear him, ye saints! and ye will then
Have nothing else to fear;
Make ye his service your delight,—
He'll make your wants his care.

198

.JULY 13.

Behold, I have given Him for a Leader to the people.
Isaiah lv. 4.

THIS was in consideration of our ignorance. We know not the way to our heavenly Father's house, but Jesus is sent to lead the blind by a way which they knew not. On account of the difficulties of the way, they are many and great, but Jesus comes as our Leader, saying, "I have made, and I will bear; even I will carry, and will deliver you." It manifests our heavenly Father's concern for our safety, comfort, and confidence. He sent His only Son, because He could trust us in His hands; He being infinitely wise, gracious, forbearing, and powerful. He came to lead us from the world to the church, from the law to the gospel, from sin to holiness, from wrath to love. He leads all His people to the throne of mercy, the house of prayer, the pastures of Jehovah's love, and the mansions of endless glory. He leads us against Satan, and we overcome; against lust, and we conquer. He leads us in the way He went Himself; in the footsteps of His flock: as we are able to bear; so as to cross and crucify the old man, and revive and strengthen the new.

Lead me on, Almighty victor,
Scatter every hostile band:
Be my guide and my protector,
Till on Canaan's shores I stand:
Shouts of victory
Then shall fill the promised land

JULY 14.

My people doth not consider. Isa. i. 3.

THIS is a complaint preferred against us by our infinitely gracious God; let us attend to it a little this morning. What should we consider? Surely, how great things the Lord hath done for us; He hath delivered our souls from death, our eyes from tears, and our feet from falling, that we may walk before God in the land of the living. How God provides for all His creatures, even the meanest, and therefore will certainly provide for us; being engaged to do so as our Creator, Preserver, covenant God, and gracious Father. That He is the supreme and universal Governor; arranging, managing, and directing every event; so that accident can never happen, chance can have no place, but all is directed by infinite wisdom and omnipresent love. Why do we not consider? Because our hearts are fickle, false, and worldly; our minds are influenced by unscriptural notions; and we endeavor to walk by sight instead of faith. What are the consequences of our not considering? Our God is dishonored and displeased; our souls are alarmed and misled; and Satan gains an advantage over us.

Jesus, mighty to renew,
Work in me to will and do;
Stem my nature's rapid tide,
Slay my vile self-righteous pride!
All thy power in me be shown,
Take away the heart of stone!

JULY 15.

What time I am afraid, I will trust in Thee. **Ps. lvi. 3.**

It is no unusual thing for the Lord's people to be cast down, and filled with tormenting fears. They fear their faith is presumption, their hope delusion, and that they shall one day disgrace that holy name by which they are called. They fear to rely on a naked promise, and want comfortable feelings to underprop their faith. But they should take up the Psalmist's resolution, "What time I am afraid, I will trust in Thee." Jehovah in Jesus is the only proper object of trust, and He should be trusted at all times. Beloved, it is well when we can say, "I will depend upon the faithful promise of my gracious God; I will rely on the free grace of my adorable Saviour; I will hope in covenant mercy for evermore; I will fly to my Father's bosom; and venture all in my Saviour's hands." Let us trust in God, in opposition to frames and feelings. Let us trust in covenant love, though providence appears to frown. Our God has said, "Trust ye in the Lord forever." Here is our warrant, let us seek grace to say with Job, "Though He slay me, yet will I trust in Him."

Oh, let me then at length be taught
What I am still so slow to learn,
That God is love, and changes not,
Nor knows the shadow of a turn:
To cast on Him my anxious cares,
And triumph o'er my doubts and fears.

201

Be clothed with humility. 1 Pet v 5

IT is of great importance, to have and to cher
ish right views of our own littleness and insig-
nificance; of our own vileness and unworthiness; and of our absolute and constant dependence on the mercy of our God. To possess a
meek and quiet spirit, which is in the sight of
God of great price; that so we may be humble
under cross providences, *considering* our sin and
ill-deservings, how we have requited the Lord;
seeing the hand of God working all in all; *acknowledging* Divine providence, let who or
what will be the instruments; to be *contented*
with our lot, with such things as we have,
uniting godliness with contentment; to be habitually *looking* at the Lord Jesus, what He was
in His ancient glory—what He became for us—
what He now is—and what we shall soon be
with Him. Humility is the best garment for
a justified sinner to wear, for God has said He
will look to and dwell with the humble. He
giveth grace unto the humble. He that humbleth himself shall be exalted. He will hear
the cry, grant the desire, and save the humble
person.

Jesus, from my proud heart remove
The bane of self-admiring love !
Oh, make me feel and own with shame,
I less and worse than nothing am !
The least of saints with pity see,
The chief of sinners save, in me !

JULY 17.

The faithful Witness. Rev. i. 5

THIS is one of the titles of our adorable Saviour. His Father gave Him to be a witness, to testify unto us of His love, and His testimony is: "God so loved the world, that He gave His only-begotten Son, that whosoever believeth in Him should not perish, but have everlasting life." To testify of His will in reference to sinners, and this is His witness: "This is the will of Him that sent me, that every one that seeth the Son, (perceiveth His divinity, His authority, and office,) and believeth on Him, may have everlasting life, and I will raise him up at the last day." To testify of His delight in making His people happy; and this is the record: "Fear not, little flock, for it is your Father's good pleasure to give you the kingdom." He bare witness that our God and Father will do for us, and give unto us, all that our circumstances require; and we know that His witness is true Let us therefore believe it, simply on the ground of His divinity, knowledge, integrity, veracity, and the interest He takes in our happiness and His Father's glory. Jesus is the faithful Witness, and our glorious Friend.

Great Witness from above,
My tongue would bless Thy name:
By Thee the joyful news
Of my salvation came;
The joyful news of sin forgiven,
Of hell subdued, and peace with heaven.

203

JULY 18.

Blessed are the pure in heart : for they shall see God.
Matt. v 18.

Iт is faith that purifies the heart; it brings home the atonement, and we enjoy pardon, peace, and reconciliation ; it purges the conscience from dead works, and delivers us from all condemnation. It receives the truth of God, and Jesus through the truth ; and we receive power to become the sons of God. We realize our relationship to God, read the gracious promises God has made, and anticipate the glorious kingdom He has prepared ; hope rules in the heart, and every one that has this hope in Him purifies himself, even as Christ is pure. His conscience is made tender, his intentions are honest, and his heart is sound in God's statutes He groans under a body of sin and death, proclaims eternal war with the flesh, and loathes himself on account of filthiness in the spirit He would give a world to be free from sin, for holiness is the element of his soul. He is blessed. He shall see God. and enjoy Him as his Father, Portion,·and everlasting all. He shall be with his God ; and be like Him, in purity, happiness, and glory.

Jesus, the crowning grace impart ;
Bless me with purity of heart,
  That now beholding Thee,
I soon may view Thy open face,
On all thy glorious beauties gaze,
  And God forever see !

204

JULY 19.

Whom having not seen ye love 1 Pet i 8

WE have never seen the glorified body of Jesus, but we have believed what His word declares of Him, and believing we love Him. As the only-begotten Son of God, who was exalted, dignified, and glorified from everlasting: as the voluntary Saviour of poor lost sinners, who became incarnate, suffered, bled and died for them. We love His adorable person—His countenance is majesty—His heart is love—His hand is omnipotence—His eye is bountifulness—His bowels are compassion—and His presence and smile are heaven We love His precious salvation—in its freeness—completeness—and glory. We love His delightful promises, which anticipate our wants—meet all our wishes—and fill our souls with peace. We love His throne, where He meets us—attends to our requests—and blesses us indeed. We love His holy precepts, which exhibit His authority—display His love—and call us to holiness. We love His heaven-born family, who wear His likeness—are the excellent of the earth—and resemble the children of a king. Oh to love Him more! To love Him with all our hearts, minds, souls, and strength! To manifest our love to Him by holy actions, and a useful life!

A bleeding Saviour, seen by faith;
A sense of pardoning love,
A hope that triumphs over death,
Give joys like those above.

205

Pray that ye enter not into temptation.
Luke xxii. 40.

TEMPTATIONS are trials; but by temptations very generally we understand solicitations to evil. Satan is the arch-tempter; he uses every possible variety of instruments, to draw us into sin and folly; consequently we are always in danger from him. But we are liable to be led astray by his temptations often, because they are sudden—powerful—importunate—deceptive—so timed as to fall in with our peculiar circumstances. Also because our hearts are weak—changeable—prone to evil—open to seduction. How many eminent saints have fallen! Let us beware! Falling into temptation dishonors God, disgraces religion, and distresses the soul. God is able to preserve and deliver us. He has promised. But prayer is implied in every promise. Beloved, daily remember you have a malicious and designing foe; he is present with you; he will use saints and sinners as instruments to lead you astray. Pray without ceasing. Pray in simplicity—in sincerity—with importunity. God is faithful, and will make a way for your escape. ♡

Jesus, Redeemer, Saviour, Lord,
 The weary sinner's Friend,
Come to my help, pronounce the word,
 And bid my troubles end
Wisdom and strength to me impart,
To quench each flaming fiery dart.

JULY 21.

Abide in Me. John xv. 1.

By nature we are without Christ and are far from Him; by grace we accept His invitation, and come to Him feeling our need of Him. We are brought to see that nothing but union to Jesus can make us safe and happy; and to give up ourselves to Him, praying to be one with Him; He receives us, sheds abroad His love in our hearts, and we become members of His body, of His flesh, and of His bones. He then bids us to abide in Him, which we do by living in absolute dependence upon Him; by cleaving to Him in love as our beloved Saviour, God, and Friend; by openly professing our attachment to Him, and expectations from Him; by walking in daily fellowship and communion with Him; and by identifying our cause with His. Beloved, we must abide in Jesus if we would get sin mortified; our graces nourished; our lusts subdued; obtain victory over the world; prove a match for Satan; and obtain all necessary supplies. Abiding in Jesus will give us a single eye; a burning zeal; holy discretion; and enable us to seize all opportunities to glorify His adorable name.

Hail, gracious Saviour, all-divine!
Mysterious, ever-living vine!
To Thee united may I live,
And nourished by Thine influence thrive;
Still may my soul abide in Thee,
From envy, pride, and malice free.

JULY 22.

A just God and a Saviour Isaiah xlv. 21.

GOD cannot part with His justice even to gratify His love; and His justice shines equally with His grace in the present and eternal salvation of our souls. He gave His Son for a Substitute, He appointed Him to be our Surety, and punished Him in our stead. He justly condemned Him to die, though guiltless, because our sins were imputed to Him; and He justly raised Him from the dead, because our sins had been expiated by Him. His work was perfect, therefore His deliverance was just. He is a just God, and therefore never will exact the same debt of the sinner, which was paid by His surety; nor condemn Him for that for which His Substitute atoned. His justice will shine in our eternal acquittal, and be eternally honored in our endless salvation. He drew the plan of salvation, sent His Son to execute it, gives His Spirit to put us in possession of the blessing, and at last receives us to Himself, of purest grace. "He saved us, and called us with an holy calling, not according to our works, but according to His own purpose and grace, which was given us in Christ Jesus before the world began."

Mystery of redemption this—
All my sins on Christ were laid;
Mine offence was reckoned His,
He the great atonement made!
Here His justice He displays,
While He saves my soul by grace. ♡

5|7|24

JULY 23.

Hold Thou me up, and I shall be safe.
Psalm cxix. 117

THIS should be the Christian's daily prayer; his way is rough, the dangers are many, his foes are powerful, and he is liable to fall. If we from the heart present this prayer, it proves that we have a sense of our own weakness; a knowledge of the Lord as our strength; genuine humility working within; and a desire to honor God ruling in the conscience. We are in the world, and unless the Lord hold us up, we shall bring guilt on the conscience, disgrace on the gospel, and dishonor to God. We are in the church, and unless the Lord hold us up, we shall prove roots of bitterness, stumbling-blocks, and grieve the godly. We shall be, if we are not, in affliction, and unless the Lord hold us up, we shall faint, be angry with God, as was Jonah, or be hardened through the deceitfulness of sin. O believer, lean not on earth; trust not in a friend; place no dependence on gifts; but let your daily, yea, hourly prayer be, "HOLD THOU ME UP, AND I SHALL BE SAFE." The ear of thy God is open, the heart of thy God is tender, the arm of thy God is strong.

Son of God! Thy blessing grant;
Still supply my every want;
Unsustained by Thee, I fall;
Send the strength for which I call,
Weaker than a bruised reed,
Help I every moment need.

o   209

The way of peace Rom iii. 17.

PEACE is an invaluable blessing, whether we consider it as reconciliation to God, or tranquillity and comfort of mind. It is not to be obtained by the works of the law, but if we would obtain peace, it must be by receiving the Saviour's word into our hearts; by believing on Him as able and willing to save; by trusting the testimony God hath given of His Son; by renouncing self, as loathsome in the sight of God; by relying simply and always on Jesus for all we need; and by daily making a hearty surrender of all to infinite love. If we would maintain peace, we must confide in the promises; walk by the precepts, be loyal to the King of Zion; commune daily with our heavenly Father; attend upon Him in the ordinances of His own appointment; rely on His special and particular providence; frequent the open fountain for purification; cleave to the saints in love, as the body of Christ; and disentangle our affections from the world, and set them on things above. This is the way, walk ye in it. Let nothing tempt you to leave it. Endeavor by all means to attract others to it.

There is no path to heavenly bliss,
Or solid joy, or lasting peace,
　But Christ, th' appointed road:
Oh may I tread the sacred WAY,
By faith rejoice, and praise, and pray,
　Till I sit down with God.

5/8/24

JULY 25.

Be still, and know that I am God. Ps. xlvi 10.

THE dispensations of divine providence are often very perplexing; our God has His way in the sea, and His path in the deep waters, and His footsteps are not known. Reason is confounded, and faith is staggered; but He hushes our fears, silences our cries, and bids us " BE STILL." We must lie before Him, as the lamb at the shepherd's feet; as the child in the parent's arms. He will not harm us Himself, nor will He let others do so. We must learn that He is God infinitely wise, invariably good, always a Sovereign. He doeth according to His will in heaven, on earth, in the sea, and all deep places. None can stay His hand, or dispute His right to accomplish His will. Let us therefore keep silence before Him. He is our God, and we are His people; His mercy is everlasting, and His truth endureth throughout all generations. Let us not murmur, for He is gracious; let us not complain, for He is a Father unto us; let us not fear, for He is faithful; but let us wait upon Him, submitting in all things to His will, and surrendering ourselves into His hands with " Here am I, do with me as seemeth Thee good."

When I can trust my all with God,
In trial's fearful hour,—
Bow, all resign'd, beneath His rod,
And bless His sparing power,
A joy springs up amidst distress,—
A fountain in the wilderness. ♥

JULY 26.

Receive not the grace of God in vain
2 Cor. vi 1.

By the "grace of God" in this passage, we are
to understand the everlasting gospel; which is
a glorious proclamation of favor manifested to
the vile and unworthy. It proclaims that God
has come down unto us in the person of Christ;
that He has accepted the labors, sufferings, and
death of Jesus, as the ground of our deliverance
from death, and as our title to eternal life; and
He now sends His ambassadors to assure us
that He is our Friend; that He will not impute
our trespasses unto us; that He views us in
Jesus as a NEW CREATION, all former things are
passed away and forgotten; and He will make
all who receive His word, and believe in His
Son, the righteousness of God in Him. Let us
not then receive this glorious message in vain;
we do so if we indulge the thought that God is
angry with us; if we doubt our acceptance of
God in Christ; if we fear that He will be wroth
with us. He informs us of His grace, to encourage us to believe, to quicken us in His
ways, to embolden us at His throne, to produce
love to His name, and to furnish us with an
answer to all objections.

> Oh, what amazing words of grace
> Are in the gospel found!
> Suited to every sinner's case,
> Who knows the joyful sound.
> May I this glorious grace receive,
> And to my Saviour's glory live.

212

JULY 27.

I will wait upon the Lord. Isaiah viii 17.

THE Lord had concealed His face, His favor could not be discovered, but marks of displeasure appeared; yet the church determines not to despond or yield to fear, but to wait upon the Lord who was hiding Himself from the house of Israel, and to look for Him. It is a great trial to a real believer for His God to hide His face; but it is still his privilege to wait daily at His gates, and to watch at the posts of His doors, persuaded that He will turn again, and display His forgiving love. We must not give up hope, nor abandon the Lord's ways, nor restrain prayer before Him; but we must wait in faith, believing His word; in expectation, trusting His faithfulness. Nothing should be allowed to weaken our faith in God's word; or drive our souls from His throne. He waits for the fittest time to be gracious, and we should wait His time to be comforted, or delivered. Wait on the Lord and KEEP HIS WAY. Wait as a servant for his master's return; as a child for his father's blessing; as a bride for the tokens of her bridegroom's love. He says, "Behold, I come quickly; blessed is he that watcheth."

Still nigh me, O my Saviour, stand,
And guard in fierce temptation's hour;
Hide in the hollow of thy hand,
Show forth in me thy saving power;
Still be thine arm my sure defence,
Nor earth nor hell shall pluck me thence.

He will yet deliver us. 2 Cor i. **10.**

How many times has our God delivered **us,** from how many dangers, in how many ways; and He who hath delivered, doth deliver, and in Him we trust that He will yet deliver us. He delivered us from spiritual death, by the operations of His Holy Spirit; and from eternal death, by the sacrifice of His Son. We were dead, but we are now alive unto God, through Jesus Christ our Lord; and He who delivered from the greatest evil, spiritual death, will not refuse to deliver us from any lesser danger. Let us trust in Him, rely upon Him, and expect Him to deliver; it is written, " Many are the afflictions of the righteous, but the Lord delivereth him out of them all. He knoweth how to deliver the godly out of temptation." Let us triumph with Paul, " The Lord stood with me, and strengthened me; and I was delivered out of the mouth of the lion; and the Lord shall deliver me from every evil work, and will preserve me unto His heavenly kingdom; to whom be glory forever and ever. Amen." If He had not intended to carry on the work, He would not have begun it; for He well knew what opposition it would meet with; but He that began will perfect it in the day of Jesus Christ.

> Yet I must fight, if I would reign;
> Increase my courage, Lord!
> I'll bear the toil, endure the pain,
> Supported by Thy word.

JULY 29.

I am a stranger in the earth. Ps. cxix. 9

BELOVED, we are strangers and pilgrims in the earth, as all our fathers were; our days are as a shadow, and there is no abiding. We are born from above and are bound for glory. We are distant from home, where our kindred, our treasure, and our hearts are found. Here we have no fixed residence; nor should we have any fellowship with the unfruitful works of darkness, but rather reprove them. We are called to submit to many inconveniences. The Bible is our light, our food, our joy, and our directory. We want a guide, a guard, a companion, a comforter; but Jesus has engaged to fill each of these offices. We should pray for the peace of the country where we sojourn; we should not be meddlers with its concerns, but keep ourselves detached; we should be thankful for every advantage, but set and keep our affections on things above; we should neither be impatient nor reluctant in reference to going home, but submit to our Father's will; we should consider ill-treatment as permitted to do us good; and contrast the present with our own beloved country and home.

There is my house and portion fair,
My treasure and my heart are there,
  And my abiding home;
For me my elder brethren stay,
And angels beckon me away,
  And Jesus bids me come.

JULY 30.

He that glorieth, let him glory in the Lord.
1 Cor. 1 31.

It is unlawful to glory in ourselves, our descent, our possessions, our connections, or doings; if we glory it must be in the Lord. We must glory in Him as gracious and merciful, exercising loving-kindness and tender mercies in the earth; in what He is to His people, their God, their portion, and their Friend; in what He has for us, has already given to us, and will without doubt bestow upon us. In Christ, as crucified for our sins, raised for our justification, and ascended to heaven in order to plead our cause, and take possession of the kingdom in our names. In our relation to Him, interest in Him, and oneness with Him, this is our glory, that we are one with Christ, and one with the Father through Him. That we are heirs of God, and joint-heirs with Jesus Christ; that all things are for our sakes, that the abundant grace might, through the thanksgiving of many, redound to the glory of God. Beloved, let us glory in the Lord, in His free grace, eternal love, well-ordered covenant, precious promises, splendid mansions, and glorious name.

> In Christ my full salvation stands,
> In Him alone my glorying be:
> Nothing shall pluck me from His hands,
> From condemnation I am free
> Be holiness my costly dress,
> And my best robe His righteousness.

216

JULY 31.

The things that accompany salvation.
Heb. vi. 9.

LET us inquire, What are they? Do we possess them? Spiritual life—evidenced by conviction of sin; hatred to sin; crying to God for deliverance from sin; groaning under the weight of the body of sin and death. A tender conscience, —which trembles at sin, and feels deeply for God's glory. A filial fear of God,—lest we should dishonor His name, disgrace His cause, and grieve His love. An anxiety and deep-rooted concern for holiness,—both in the heart and the life. Contrition or brokenness of heart for sin,—accompanied with holy mourning before God. Fervor in devotion,—earnestly breathing out the desires of the heart before God, or grieving when it is not so. A jealousy of self,—as to our sincerity and uprightness of intention; lest we should be led astray by the corruptions which are within. A chaste conversation coupled with fear. Diligence in the means of grace. Searching the scriptures, to ascertain our real state and condition; what is the Lord's will and our duty. An increasing discovery of our own weakness, imperfection, and misery.

Ye saints! your music bring,
  And swell the rapturous sound,
Strike every trembling string,
  Till earth and heaven resound:
The triumphs of the cross we sing,
Awake, ye saints! each joyful string

217

AUGUST 1.

We trust in the living God. 1 Tim iv. 10.

THE living God is opposed to a dying world, to our dying frames, and to our dying friends; these must not be trusted, or we shall be wretched. Our God may, ought to be trusted, for He is the only suitable object of a Christian's trust; He is able to do exceeding abundantly above all we can ask or think. He is immutable. He never disappointed a sinner's hope, if founded on His word; or refused a believer's petition, for deliverance or relief. If we trust in the living God, it will preserve us from perpetual disappointment; from bitter reflections on self and others; from many dangers; and from the threatened curse. If we trust in the living God we are blessed; we shall be fruitful; we shall be delivered from slavish fears; we shall enjoy perfect peace; we shall be provided for; we shall find a refuge in every storm; have an answer for all who reproach us; experience firmness and stability; and enjoy solid happiness. Let us ascertain, Are we trusting in the living God? Let us seek grace, daily to live in simple, child-like dependence upon Him. Blessed is the man that trusteth in the Lord.

In Thee, O Lord, I put my trust,
Mighty, and merciful, and just,
  Who hides my life above;
Thou canst, Thou wilt my helper be;
My confidence is all in Thee,
  My faithful God of love.

218

My son, despise thou not the chastening of the Lord
Heb xıı 5.

THE Lord speaketh unto us as unto children. He speaks in reference to our afflictions : they are chastisements ; they are sent in love ; when we are chastened we are judged of the Lord, that we may not be condemned with the world. Let us not faint under them, let us not despise them.   We do so when we think there is no occasion for them, and that we could do as well, or better without them.   When we do not seek to ascertain the cause why they are sent; or to learn the lessons they are intended to teach. When we do not acknowledge the Lord's right to chasten; His love in doing it; and His wisdom in the time, nature, and duration of the trial.   When we do not seek grace to submit cheerfully, or at least silently ; and to glorify God in it, and after it.   When we do not seek to be improved in our knowledge, sanctity, and spiritual vigor by it.   When with a carnal, flesh-pleasing view, we seek to be delivered from it   Beloved, let us beware of despising divine chastisement in any of these ways; but let us glorify God in the day of visitation.

Father, if Thou must reprove
  For all that I have done,
Not in anger, but in love,
  Chastise Thy wayward son
Correct with kind severity,
  And bring me home to Thee.

5/13

AUGUST 3.

WHEN we think of the greatness and glory of Jehovah, man appears so worthless and insignificant, that we are ready to ask, " Will the Lord regard us, bless us, and dwell with us ?" Yes —He has promised to do so in His word, and He has informed us that His thoughts are perpetually taken up with us. He thinketh upon us, to supply our need, protect from foes, lead us in His ways, and make us meet for His kingdom and glory. His thoughts are thoughts of peace and not of evil, to give us an expected end. He thinketh upon us by day and by night, when at home or abroad ; and He thinks of us with love as His children ; with pleasure as His friends ; with a purpose to bless us, as His dependants. We think He may perhaps have mercy, He may do a little for us ; but as high as the heavens are above the earth, so are His thoughts above our thoughts ; and His ways above our ways. His thoughts are worthy of a God. What are the promises ? Only His thoughts put into our language. And what do they prove ? Truly that He thought of all our wants, wishes, and desires, and made full provision for them.

> Father, I want a thankful heart,
> I want to taste how good Thou art ;
> To plunge me in Thy mercy's sea,
> And comprehend Thy love to me ;
> The length, and breadth, and depth, and height
> Of love divinely infinite.

AUGUST 4.

Thou shalt know hereafter.   John xiii. 7.

WE are often at a loss to account for many
things in our feelings, in our circumstances, and
in the Lord's dealings with us; but what we
know not now, we shall know hereafter.   This is
our Saviour's promise; let us take the comfort
of it, and expect its fulfilment to our perfect satisfaction by-and-bye.   We shall know some
things before the coming of our Lord, and we
shall know all things after.   Every difficulty
will then be cleared up, and all the trying dispensations of divine providence accounted for.
Let us therefore be patient, and wait the Lord's
time; the coming of our Lord draweth nigh.
Let us silently submit to our Father's will, for
we shall see that it was wise and kind.   Let us
acknowledge the right of God to conceal the
cause of His working, until He has fully accomplished His designs.   Let us praise Him for all
that is past, and trust Him for all that is to
come.   "Now we see through a glass darkly,
but we shall soon see Him face to face; now
we know but in part, then shall we know even
as also we are known."   May the Lord direct
our hearts into His love, and into the patient
waiting for Christ.

Jesus, we own Thy sovereign hand,
    Thy faithful care we own;
Wisdom and love are all Thy ways,
    When most to us unknown:
To Thee we cheerfully resign,
    For Thou art ours, and we are Thine.

AUGUST 5.

He will ever be mindful of His covenant.
Psalm cxi. 5.

THE Lord's people know their God as a covenant God, reconciled to them, at peace with
them, and dwelling among them, through the
work of Jesus. He has made a covenant in
which they are interested, from which all their
blessings flow, and on which their confidence is
founded. Of this covenant, God is ever mindful. He is mindful of the engagements of Jesus
as our Surety ; of the relationship in which He
was pleased to manifest Himself, as our Father ;
of the state in which He viewed us, as poor
wretched sinners ; of the provision He made for
His own glory and our needs ; of the promise
made to Jesus, including all the promises made
to us ; of the oath He swore, that He would
not be wroth with us ; of the blood of his Son,
as the victim slain to confirm and ratify it ; of
the end He had in view in making it, even the
display of all His glorious perfections in our
eternal salvation. He will ever be mindful of
His covenant. He cannot forget it, He will not
act contrary to it, but will confirm it even to
the end. Beloved, let us also be ever mindful
of His covenant. ◁

Firmer than heaven His covenant stands :
Tho' earth should shake, and skies depart.
We're safe in our Redeemer's hands,
Who bears our names upon His heart :
For us He lived, and died, and rose,
And triumphed over all our foes.

AUGUST 6.

Come ye near unto me. Isaiah xlviii. 16

THE believer's happiness and Jehovah's pleasure are united; we are only happy as we are near to Him, and He is only pleased as we cleave unto Him. He has taken us into a near relationship as His children, people, and beloved bride; He has represented our union by the most striking figures, the branch in the vine, the member with the head, and the building with the foundation. He has made His name our strong tower, His Son our fountain of supply, and His secret place our home. In living near to Him, we enjoy the sweetest comforts; possess unutterable peace; realize the fullest liberty; and find safety and rest. Our assurance, light, holiness, and strength come from His presence; our misery, wretchedness, and woe, from living at a distance from Him. He invites us this morning, as Jacob did his beloved son, "Come near unto me." He intends to bless us, as that patriarch did his child; to discover Himself unto us; to show us His covenant and secret; to make us understand His will and word; to preserve us from all evil, fill us with grace, and conform us to His image.

When trials vex my doubting mind,
Jesus, to Thy dear wounds I'll flee;
No shelter can I elsewhere find,
No peace or comfort but in Thee:
To Thee my cause I recommend,
On Thee for future grace depend.

223

AUGUST 7.

Surely I come quickly Rev **xxii** 20.

Who is this proposing to come quickly? Is it an enemy threatening us? Is it a stranger? No—it is Jesus whom we love, speaking to cheer us. It is Immanuel, to whom we are betrothed in righteousness, judgment, loving-kindness, mercies, and faithfulness. It is our Saviour, who saved us by His death, and preserves us by His life. He will come shortly, the period cannot be far distant. He will come gladly, with delight and pleasure to receive us to Himself "Surely," He says, "I come quickly;" and is it not a source of joy to us—does it not excite and draw forth holy expectation? He comes to end our persecutions, to silence our complaints, to conform us to His image, to fill us with His love, to clothe us with His glory, and to bring us grace. Do we say with the church, "Amen, even so, come, Lord Jesus?" Or, are we indifferent about His coming? He says, "Behold, I come quickly; blessed is he that watcheth and keepeth his garments, lest he walk naked and they see his shame." Let us look for, and hasten to the coming of the day of God. He comes for our redemption. His coming completes our salvation.

Fly, ye seasons, fly still faster :
Let the glorious day come on,
When we shall behold our Master
Seated on His heavenly throne !
When the Saviour
Shall descend to claim His own.

AUGUST 8.

Owe no man anything Rom xiii. 8.

RASH speculations are inconsistent with Christianity; and getting in debt is as much a breach
of a divine precept as robbery or murder. Every
believer should live within his income, and not
bring a disgrace on religion, by contracting
debts which he is unable to pay. If he has
done so, he should be very humble; he should
confess his sin before God, and pray to be enabled to fulfil his engagements. It is not necessary that he should make an appearance, as it is
called; but it is necessary that he should adorn
the doctrine of God his Saviour. He that is in
debt, and is not grieved by it, humbled under
it, and striving to extricate himself from it, is a
very suspicious character, whatever profession
he may make. Our God says, and He speaks
to all who profess His name, " OWE NO MAN
ANYTHING BUT LOVE." A Christian's payments
should be prompt and punctual; his word should
be as firm as a bond, and his promise as sacred
as an oath Oh, may our God bring back His
people to primitive simplicity! May they all be
slow to promise, quick to perform, and so fulfil
the law of Christ.

Let those who bear the christian name
  Their holy vows fulfil;
The saints—the followers of the Lamb,
  Are men of honor still.
Their Saviour's precepts they obey,
And hasten to the judgment day.

That He might deliver us from this present evil wo ld.
Gal. ɪ. 4.

THE whole world lieth in the wicked one, as the devoted child in the arms of Moloch; or as the putrid corpse in the grave, over which is written, "HERE LIETH." We were once dead in sin, and buried in corruption, but Jesus Christ interfered for us. "He gave Himself for our sins, that He might deliver us from the present evil world, according to the will of God and our Father." The world is evil, therefore we are delivered from it. Jesus died to deliver us from its *spirit*, by which we are influenced in a state of nature; from the *love* of the world, which is enmity with God; from seeking *satisfaction* in the world, which is idolatry; from its fearful *doom*, which is eternal destruction. He intended to raise us above it, in our desires and pursuits; to lead us through it, and glorify us beyond it. Let us inquire this morning, Are we of the world, or are we delivered from it? Have we another spirit in us? Are we become dead to the world by fellowship with Christ in His death? Is Jesus loved, praised, and obeyed, out of gratitude for delivering us?

> Jesus, I my cross have taken,
>   All to leave and follow Thee;
> Naked, poor, despised, forsaken,
>   Thou from hence my all shalt be:
> Thou hast my Deliverer been,
> I have Thy salvation seen.

226

AUGUST 10.

O Lord, I beseech Thee, deliver my soul.
Psalm cxvi. 4.

THE prayer of faith is generally short, and always to the point. It takes the soul and places it before God, in its real state and true character. It pleads with Him for what is really needed, what must be had. The believer often needs deliverance, and faith cries to God for it. His language is, " O Lord, I beseech thee, deliver my soul from doubts and fears, which continually beset me ; from a spirit of bondage, which would daily entangle me; from Satan who worries, harasses, and hinders me; from THE sin which so easily besets me ; from men who would injure or mislead me ; from my own feelings, which daily burden me." Thus the Lord is acknowledged as the great Deliverer ; our own inability is practically confessed; it is evident our trials and troubles are sanctified ; the legitimate tendency of grace is discovered by the earnestness, simplicity, importunity, and success of our prayers. Be this our daily cry until deliverance be no longer needed; for our God says, " Call upon Me in the day of trouble, I WILL DELIVER THEE."

Oh, for that tenderness of heart
    Which bows before the Lord,
Acknowledges how just Thou art,
    And trembles at Thy word !
Saviour, to me in pity give
The pledge Thou wilt at last receive.

AUGUST 11.

Heirs of the kingdom.   James ii 5.

HE raiseth the poor from the dust, and the beg
gar from the dunghill; such were we by nature,
but through rich grace we shall inherit the
throne of glory. He has prepared for us, promised to us, and will bestow upon us a KINGDOM.
A kingdom in which his glory will be seen, felt,
and enjoyed forever. In which all His riches
of grace, mercy, and glory will be displayed.
In which peace, joy, and pleasure will eternally
reign. A kingdom which cannot be moved, and
will never know a change. But who are the
acknowledged heirs? The poor of this world,
who are poor in spirit. The rich in faith, who
believe in God, in Jesus, who exercise faith
on the precious promises, and whose faith is
proved to be good by the works they produce.
Those who love God, from a knowledge of
His love to them, and as the effect of His
love being shed abroad in their hearts, by the
Holy Ghost. Am I an heir? Are you, my
friend? If so, rejoice and be exceeding glad;
imitate those who through faith and patience
now inherit the promises, and the end will
crown the whole.

There shall your eyes with rapture view
The glorious Friend who died for you;
That died to ransom, died to raise
To crowns of joy, and songs of praise:
Jesus, to Thee I breathe my prayer!
Reveal, confirm my interest there.

228

6|18|24

AUGUST 12.

Thou shalt see greater things than these.
John i. 50.

WHEN the eyes of our understanding are opened by the Eternal Spirit, we begin to see out of
darkness and obscurity ; but our sight is imperfect, we have seen but little yet, there is much
more behind to be revealed by-and-bye. We
shall see greater depths of sin in our nature, and
greater depths of grace in the person of Christ;
we shall have clearer evidences of interest in
Jesus, and see more of His love to us. We
shall experience the cleansing efficacy of His
precious blood to a greater extent; and see the
power of His arm displayed more visibly for our
deliverance. We shall see more of the emptiness, vanity, and deceitfulness of the world ;
and have greater reason to rejoice that we are
delivered from it. We shall see greater things
in our Bibles, and feel ourselves under greater
obligation to the Holy Spirit for His teaching.
We shall see Christ descending, present things
abolished, and the glories of eternity unfolding.
Let us seek greater things, for Jesus has promised them ; and daily pray, " What I know not
teach Thou me."

O Lord, how little do we know;
How little of Thy presence feel ;
While we continue here below,
And in these earthly houses dwell!
When wilt Thou take us up above,
To see Thy face without a cloud ?

AUGUST 13.

Men shall be blessed in Him. Psalm lxxii. 17.

EVERYTHING out of Christ is under the curse; all blessings are treasured up in Him, and can only be received and enjoyed by union to and communion with Him. If in Him, He is made of God unto us, wisdom, righteousness, strength, sanctification, and redemption; if separate from Him, His work will profit us nothing. How important then is union to Jesus! All who are in Him are blessed with the favor of God, which compasses them as a shield; with access to God, by the Spirit, as to a kind and indulgent Father; with the friendship of God; He calls them not servants but friends, and His friendship is a good fortune; with justification before God, as the great Lawgiver and Judge of all; with sanctification by God, to the praise, honor, and glory of his grace; and ultimately they will be glorified with God through eternal ages. All things are theirs, and for them is laid up a crown of righteousness, which fadeth not away; a treasure in heaven which corrupteth not, and where thieves cannot steal. Oh, blessed state! Oh, happy persons! But this honor have all the saints.

> Blessings abound where Jesus reigns:
> The prisoner leaps to lose his chains,
> The weary find eternal rest,
> And all the sons of want are blest:
> In Him the tribes of Adam boast,
> More blessings than their father lost.

230

5/19/24

AUGUST 14.

In the day of adversity, consider. Eccles. vii. 14.

CIRCUMSTANCES sometimes regulate duties.
The Lord's people have to pass through many
changes; they are strangers and pilgrims here.
Sometimes prosperity calls for rejoicing, and
sometimes adversity calls for consideration. If
prayer appears to be shut out, our petitions
seem to be denied, and we cannot enjoy the life
and power of religion; it is the day of adversity.
If providence frowns, and the heart contracts
and becomes hard, it is a day of adversity; now
we should consider, Is there not a CAUSE? What
is it? Has sin been indulged? or mercy slighted?
or duty neglected? or self deified? What is
the INTENTION? Is it to correct, reprove, and
restore us? How should we now ACT? Let us
take shame to ourselves; justify our God; confess
sin; lament over our folly; crave pardon; and
plead for restoration. It is our comfort to know
that the Lord calls us to return, declares He is
ready to forgive, promises a gracious reception,
and assures us He will heal our backslidings and
love us freely. Let us, believing, look for His
blessing.

Of my extreme distresses
  The author is the Lord:
Whate'er His wisdom pleases,
  His name be still adored.
If still He prove my patience,
  And to the utmost prove,
Yet all His dispensations
  Are faithfulness and love.

AUGUST 15.

The expectation of the poor shall not perish forever
Psalm ix 18.

THE promises of God raise the expectation of His people, and His providence tries it; what the promise has engaged to give, providence seems loath to bestow But God is faithful. We may expect the Lord to appear for us in every trouble, if our faith is fixed on His word, and prayer is daily sent up to His throne. We may expect to be supported under all our trials, and to be supplied with all necessary good, if we are making God our portion, and seeking to glorify Him We may expect to be pardoned, justified, and saved; if we believe with the heart, confess with the mouth, and walk according to our profession. God notices our expectations, Jesus pleads that they may be realized; and nothing shall be able to turn away the bountiful hand of our God He will regard the prayer of the destitute, and not despise their prayer. Our fears may be strong, and our doubts may be many; but our security is in the character, word, and work of our God and Saviour. He will not fail us, nor forsake us, until He hath done all which He hath spoken to us of.

Soon the delightful day will come,
When my dear Lord will bring me home,
　And I shall see His face;
Then, with my Saviour, Brother, Friend,
A blest eternity I'll spend,
　Triumphant in His grace.

5/20/24

AUGUST 16.

HE is the great author of your being, and the only proper object of your faith, fear, and worship. Remember the promises He has made, the deliverances He has wrought, the blessings He has conferred, the invitations He has given, and the relations He now fills. Remember Him in calamity, to trust Him; in prosperity, to praise Him; in danger, to call upon Him; in difficulty, to expect His interference. Remember to obey his commands; to attend to His exhortations; to keep His company; to seek His blessing; and to aim at His glory in all you do. Remember Him, for it is your duty; it is your privilege. Remember Him, in order to strengthen your faith; as an antidote to your fears; as a source of encouragement to your souls; and as a preventative to sin. Remember He is holy, just, and good; and He will be glorified in all them that draw nigh unto Him. Whatever or whoever you forget, always " RE-MEMBER THE LORD." He is your life, your strength, your food, your portion, your God, your all. Remember Him, for he never forgets you; cleave to Him, for He will never forsake you.

Oh, may I still from sin depart!
A wise and understanding heart,
Jesus, to me be given!
And let me through Thy Spirit know,
To glorify my God below,
And find my way to heaven.

AUGUST 17.

In quietness and in confidence shall be your strength.
Isaiah xxx. 15.

QUIETNESS is expressive of submission to the
holy will of God, and supposes a waiting upon
Him as directed by His word It is the believer's duty to be silent before God while He is
working, being assured that his best interests are
secured by the promises, and that all things will
be made plain by-and-bye. He should confide
in the Lord's word; and rely on the Lord's wisdom, love, and ability. Our confidence must
arise from God's word, a review of His dealings
with His people, and the relation in which He
stands to us We may be confident, for God
who has spoken is true, and hath confirmed his
word in every generation. Quietly confiding
in God will give us strength; we then put His
love and faithfulness to the trial; we honor Him
by our confidence, and He will honor us by appearing for us Let us endeavor to be STILL,
to be SILENT before Him, when He is raised
up out of His holy habitation. Let us wait for
Him, for it is good that a man should both hope
and quietly wait for the salvation of the Lord.
Beware of complaining or replying against God..

When, my Saviour, shall I be
Totally resigned to Thee!
Poor and vile in my own eyes,
Only in Thy wisdom wise,
Only guided by Thy light,
Only mighty in Thy might!

234

AUGUST 18.

The Lord is nigh unto all them that call upon Him.
Psalm cxlv. 18.

REAL prayer is calling upon God. He is our
Father; we are His children. We have nothing;
He has all things to bestow, and is willing to
give them. From a sense of need, we call on
the Lord for a supply; from a sense of weakness, we call on Him for strength; from a sense
of guilt, we call on Him for pardon. Being
diseased, we cry for health; being troubled, for
comfort and peace; being in distress, for relief
and deliverance. We go out of self to Jesus,
accepting His invitation, to plead His promise,
and find Him faithful. Our God is always near
the praying soul, not merely as the omnipresent
Jehovah, but as our faithful Friend. He is near
us, lovingly to listen to what we have to lay before Him; mercifully to relieve our miseries, be
they what they may; graciously to help in every
difficulty or danger. Beloved, our God is near
us. He is attentive to us this morning; let us
call upon Him in spirit and in truth. Let us
lay all our concerns before Him; He loves to
listen to the often-told tale; He has patience
with us, blessings for us, and will do us good. .

O Lord, each day renew thy strength,
And let me see Thy face at length,
  With all Thy people yonder;
With them in heaven Thy love declare,
And sing Thy praise forever there,
  With gratitude and wonder.

235

AUGUST 19.

My presence shall go with thee. Exod. xxxiii 14.

So the Lord promised Moses, and so He has promised us. Let us never venture anywhere, if we have reason to think the Lord will not favor us with His presence there. The Lord's presence produces holiness, imparts power, fires with zeal, brings into union, and often fills with comfort, joy and peace. His presence is our glory, and it will yield us support under losses, crosses, and bereavements. Let us plead for the Lord's presence to go with us; let us expect it; let us not be satisfied with anything else. He went with Moses, and he persevered; with Joshua, and he conquered; with David, and he reached the throne; with Paul, and he was more than a conqueror. Nothing can be a substitute for the Lord's presence; and as it is so graciously promised, let us not attempt to find a substitute, but daily cry, "IF THY PRESENCE GO NOT WITH ME, CARRY ME NOT UP HENCE." Jesus has said, "If a man love me, he will keep my words; and my Father will love him, and WE will come unto him, and make our abode with him."

O Lord, be ever near us,
  Fix in our hearts Thy home,
By Thine appearing cheer us,
  And let Thy kingdom come:
Fulfil our expectation,
  And give our souls to prove
Thine uttermost salvation,
  Thine everlasting love.

236

AUGUST 20.

The Lord preserveth all them that love Him.
Psalm cxlv 20.

ALL who know the Lord love Him, and none can love Him until taught by His Spirit. If we know God in Christ as our covenant God, and enjoy our interest in Him, we shall love Him supremely, above our tranquillity, natural relations, earthly possessions, gifts, and reputation. We discover in Him, greater glory, more real worth, pre-eminent beauty, and superior excellence. Those who love Him are preserved by Him. He preserves them in trouble, from its natural effects; in the world, from its spirit and doom; from enemies, evils, and wrath. His loving-kindness and truth will continually preserve them; yea, He will preserve them unto His kingdom and glory. But He preserves us in the use of means; let us therefore walk before Him; confide in Him; wait upon Him; and often demand of our hearts, Do we love the Lord? Are we desiring to love Him? Are we preserved from sin, the world, and all evil? If so, we must ascribe it to free and sovereign grace; if not, let us search and try our ways, and turn again to the Lord. He bids, He exhorts us to come.

Infinite grace! almighty charms!
Stand in amaze, ye rolling skies!
Jesus, the God. extends His arms—
Hangs on the cross of love, and dies.
Sure I must love, my passions move:
This heart sha' yield to death or love.

237

AUGUST 21.

Shall not God avenge His own elect?
Luke xviii. 7.

THE Lord's people are often oppressed, they are tempted to be revengeful, but our God says, " Vengeance is mine, I will repay." Under man's wrath, remember you are the objects of the Lord's love ; when men oppress you, rest assured that God will befriend you. Carry your case to Him, spread the whole of the matter before Him ; plead with Him, and then rest assured that He will appear for you The master will interfere for a servant he values ; the parent for the child he loves, and the husband for the bride he has chosen : "and shall not God avenge His own elect ? I tell you He will avenge them speedily." Cry to Him day and night, look to no other quarter for relief or deliverance ; never encourage any unholy feelings, but pray for grace to imitate your insulted, persecuted, and crucified Lord. Consider Him who endured such contradiction of sinners against Himself, lest ye be weary and faint in your minds. He will tread all your enemies under His feet shortly. He is able to avenge you, and His word is passed.

Shall we distrust our faithful God,
Or question His almighty power,
Because He doth not our desires
Accomplish in a little hour ?
He will avenge His own elect,
And evermore His saints protect.

5/23/24

They that seek the Lord shall not want any good thing
Psalm xxxiv. 10.

WHAT a comfortable promise is this to the poor, weak, and timid Christian ; he has not attained to a state of assurance, but He is seeking the Lord, and here his God promises him that he shall not want any good thing. He feels that he has no good thing in him, finds he can do no good thing of himself, fears that good will never be enjoyed by him ; but his God assures him, no good thing shall be withheld from him. His God will pardon his sin, justify his person, strengthen his soul, supply his needs, comfort his heart, conquer his foes, sanctify his trials, and give him victory over death He shall not want long, if God is able to supply ; he cannot be neglected, if our God is true ; he shall receive all that is good, and when, and as it will do him most good Let us therefore seek the Lord, and rest assured that He will withhold from us no good thing The silver and the gold are His, and He says, " If ye, being evil, know how to give good things unto your children, how MUCH MORE shall your heavenly Father give good things to them that ask Him."

If earthly parents hear
Their children when they cry,
If they with love sincere
Their children's wants supply,
Much more will God His love display,
And answer when His children pray.

God, even our own God, shall bless us.
Psalm lxvii 6.

HE has pledged Himself to do so in His word, and He delights to make good His promise. He is our God by covenant; by a spiritual birth; through Christ Jesus; and at our own desire, request, and consent. He is the great God, who fills heaven and earth; the all-sufficient God, who has all resources in Himself; the unchanging God, who is eternally the same. He espouseth the quarrel of His people, He dignifies and ennobles them, and proves Himself gracious and merciful unto them. He blesseth them indeed; and if others curse, He turneth the curse into a blessing. We may rest fully assured of this pleasing fact, " GOD, EVEN OUR OWN GOD, WILL BLESS US." He has done so in Christ before time, He has promised to do so through time, and when time shall be no more. He will bless us in temporals and spirituals, He will bless us wherever we are. Let us believe the fact, and plead for its realization in our experience; this will embolden us in danger, fortify us against fear, and keep us in perfect peace. Let us trust in Him, and He will bless us; and so shall we rejoice in Him.

Rise, my soul, with ardor rise !
Breathe thy wishes to the skies !
Freely pour out all Thy mind,
Seek, and thou art sure to find ;
Ready art thou to receive,
Readier is thy God to give.

AUGUST 24.

A living sacrifice. Rom. xii 1.

WHEN a beast was set apart for sacrifice, it was considered sacred, and was carefully preserved from all injury. The Christian is devoted; he is intended for the ALTAR, his body as well as his soul, and he is required to present it to God holy, acceptable, as a reasonable service. It is not to be defiled by fornication, by intoxication, by gluttony, by filth, by pride; he is to look upon it as the Lord's, bought with the blood of Jesus, consecrated as the temple of the Holy Ghost, set apart to be the habitation of a Holy God. The believer's body should not be united by marriage to an unbeliever; this is SACRILEGE, for the vessel is holy; it is REBELLION, for it is plainly and positively forbidden; it is SINNING WILFULLY, and provoking the eyes of divine holiness. It is offering INSULT to the God of love, and calling upon Him to vindicate His injured mercy. Believer, present thy body daily to God, washed in pure water; that is, cleansed from defilement by observing His word; never call that common which God has consecrated, or debase that which He has devoted to Himself.

Lord, it is but just and right
That I should be wholly thine ;
Only in Thy will delight,
In Thy blessed service join :
Now my sacrifice receive,
Give me grace to Thee to live.

AUGUST 25.

The Spirit helpeth our infirmities. Rom. viii 26.

WE are compassed with infirmities; we know but little of ourselves; we know not what would be best for us; we know not what is coming upon us; we know not Satan's position or design; we know but little of God's provision or intention; we are as weak as we are ignorant; weak to withstand evil; weak to perform good; weak to obtain benefits; our infirmities, many of them are constitutional, arising from our tempers and dispositions; from bodily ailments; and from the smallness of our capacities. But though thus infirm, Jesus is touched with a sympathetic feeling for us; and the Holy Spirit is given to assist us. He teaches us what we want; leads us to the precious promises; furnishes us with the prevailing plea; excites us to pray, and assists us in prayer. He produces the ardent desire; bestows the wrestling power; and warms the affections while pleading; gives us such a keen sense of what we need, and such an ardent desire after it, that unutterable groans are begotten, to which God attends. Let us daily seek the Spirit's power to help.

> Spirit of interceding grace,
>   I know not how or what to pray;
> Relieve my utter helplessness,
>   Thy power into my heart convey;
> That God, acknowledging my groan,
> May answer, in my prayers, His own.

242

AUGUST 26.

The unsearchable riches of Christ. Eph. iii. 8. Rom. vii. 2.

NEVER forget that Jesus is our BROTHER, and
that He has devoted all His riches to us, so
that the riches of Jesus are the Christian's fortune. "Ye know the grace of our Lord Jesus
Christ, that, though He was rich, yet for our
sakes He became poor, that we through His
poverty might be rich." He employed all He
possessed for our redemption, sanctification, and
salvation; and now, at the right hand of the
Majesty on high, He giveth liberally, and upbraideth not. He has riches of grace; riches
of mercy; and riches of glory. The residue of
the Spirit is with Him. He has promised
largely; He has proved His readiness to bestow,
in the most wonderful way, let us therefore expect great things from Him, for He has UN-
SEARCHABLE RICHES. O believer, look not at thy
poverty, at thy wants, or thy circumstances; but
look at Jesus; all things are under His feet, all
blessings are at His disposal, and His heart is
set upon thee to do thee good! He will supply
all thy needs while on earth, and afterwards
receive thee to glory. My soul, thy Jesus has
all thou needest: therefore look to Him, and
Him alone!

> Possessing Christ, I all possess,
> Strength, wisdom, sanctifying grace,
>   And righteousness complete
> Bold, in His name, I dare draw nigh,
> Before the Ruler of the sky,
>   And all His justice meet.

AUGUST 27.

WITHOUT union to Christ, there can be no good works; and until we are dead to the law we cannot be married to Christ. We must see that there is neither help nor hope for us in any law that God has given; that only grace can save us, before we shall be willing to take Christ as God has set Him forth in the everlasting gospel. Being married to Christ, we renounce our own name and take His; we live upon His fulness, walk by His word, and aim to please Him in all things. By His grace we perform good works; and through His merit, and His name, they are accepted as evidences of our love, proofs of our sanctification, and fruits of our oneness with Him. He that is joined to the Lord is one spirit with Him; and it becomes his meat and drink to do the will of God. Without union to Christ we can do nothing acceptable to God; being married to Him, our poor, imperfect, and (in themselves) worthless performances, are acceptable and well-pleasing to God. No UNION NO FRUIT, NO FRUIT NO UNION. Beloved, are we bringing forth fruit unto God? Do we bring forth much fruit? Herein is our Father glorified, that we bear much fruit.

> Blest Jesus, animate my heart;
> Let Thy rich grace abound;
> So, to the honor of Thy name,
> Shall plenteous fruit be found.

5/26

AUGUST 28.

Being justified freely by His grace.
Rom. iii. 24

IT was a solemn question which was proposed
in the days of old, "How can man be just with
God?" Man is without righteousness; he is
chargeable with many crimes; he is brought in
guilty, and condemned by God's holy law; and
he has no excuse to make. His mouth is stop-
ped. We feel this to be our situation by nature.
But the Lord who is our Judge, hath devised a
way by which He can be just and yet justify us.
IT IS BY GRACE. He justifies, or acquits us from
all charges; pronounces us righteous; accepts
us; and introduces us into His favor, friendship,
and fellowship, FREELY; without anything being
done or suffered by us. HE PRESENTS US with
the work of Jesus, by which all our debts are
paid; our righteousness is wrought out; the law
and government of God are honored; and a good
title to eternal life is made out; we RECEIVE
this work by faith, which He also bestows, and
we are " JUSTIFIED FROM ALL THINGS." Not one
charge remains. There is no condemnation.
But we are justified freely by grace without the
works of the law.

Slain in the guilty sinner's stead,
Jesus, Thy righteousness I plead,
  And Thine atoning blood:
That righteousness my robe shall be;
Thy merit shall avail for me,
  And bring me near to God.

They all slumbered and slept. Matt. **xxv. 5.**

W<small>HEN</small> we think of the warnings Jesus has given, the promises He has made, and the precepts He has delivered, we are ready to conclude that His people must be always active and always happy. But when we look around us, or when we look at our own course, we are obliged to lament that this is not the case. Jesus is gone to receive a kingdom and to return; He has given talents to his servants, and TO EVERY MAN HIS WORK, and commanded the porter to watch. But it is said of the wise, as well as the foolish virgins, " THEY ALL SLUMBERED AND SLEPT." Are we awake to our duties, to our privileges, to our expectations? Are we looking, longing, and preparing for the coming of Jesus? Are we sober and vigilant, because our adversary the devil, as a roaring lion, is going about seeking whom he may devour? Are we active for God? Are we hasting home? Do we pass the time of our sojourning here in fear? Is the talent in the NAPKIN, or at the BANK? Let us not sleep as do others, but let us watch and be sober Behold the judge standeth before the door. It is high time to awake out of sleep.

> He comes, He comes to call
> The nations to His bar;
> And take to glory all
> Who meet for glory are:
> Make ready for your full reward;
> Go forth with joy to meet your Lord.

246

5/27

AUGUST 30.

He will not always chide. Psalm ciii. 9.

If we sin, our heavenly Father will correct us, in order to reclaim us; His strokes often fall heavy, and the effects remain for a long time. But He will not always chide; when we repent and confess, He pardons and restores. His anger is but for a moment; but His mercy is everlasting He loves when He frowns, and pities while He reproves. " The Lord is gracious, full of compassion, and plenteous in mercy; He hath not dealt with us after our sins, nor rewarded us according to our iniquities, for as the heaven is high above the earth, so GREAT is His mercy toward them that fear Him." Let us not therefore DESPISE the chastening of the Lord, nor FAINT when we are rebuked of Him; for whom the Lord loveth He chasteneth, and scourgeth every son whom He receiveth. In a little wrath He may hide His face from us for a moment; but with everlasting kindness will He have mercy on us, and prove Himself our Redeemer. His frowns are transient, but His love is everlasting. His strokes are few and light, but He daily loadeth us with benefits; and crowns the year with His bounty.

God will not always chide:
And when His strokes are felt,
His strokes are fewer than our crimes,
And lighter than our guilt.
He chides us with a Father's heart,
That we from Him may not depart

247

AUGUST 31.

The Lord is good unto them that wait for Him.
Lam. iii. 25.

THE Lord is good to all, and His tender mercies are over all His works ; but He is especially
benevolent, kind, and attentive to the praying,
waiting soul. He has prepared of His goodness
for the poor, and His goodness is ever great towards us. He bids us ask, promises to bestow,
makes us wait, and then blesses us indeed.
We have proved Him to be good ; but if we had
more faith in Him, and were more earnest with
Him, we should see and enjoy His goodness in
a much greater degree. He delivered David
from the horrible pit ; Jeremiah from the dun-
geon ; Daniel from the lions ; Peter from the
waves ; and Paul from the forty Jews. "The
Lord is good, a stronghold in the day of trouble ;
and He knoweth them that trust in Him." He
will renew our strength, illumine our path, take
vengeance on our foes, and introduce us into the
glorious liberty of the sons of God. Let us wait
for Him in faith, look for Him in hope, and
plead with Him to work in us all the good
pleasure of His will, and the work of faith with
power. Wait for the Lord, and prove Him good.

Jesus, preserve my soul from sin,
Nor let me faint for want of Thee ;
I'll wait till Thou appear within,
And plant Thy heavenly love in me :
In every soul that waits for Thee,
Thou wilt Thy goodness, Lord, display.

248

5|26

SEPTEMBER 1.

The Deliverer Rom. xi. 26

THE Lord Jesus Christ is anointed and appointed to deliver His people whenever they need His aid; for this purpose all the treasures of wisdom and knowledge are stored in Him, authority over all flesh is given to Him, and every attribute of Deity can be exerted by him. We are not left to the mercy of men, we are not expected to deliver ourselves, but we are to look to Jesus, who is glorified in delivering us from all evil, and preserving us to His eternal kingdom and glory. To Him we are to repair in every trial, from Him we are to expect deliverance in every danger; He is in office on purpose to hear us, appear for us, and bless us. He delivers in temporals as well as in spirituals, from internal and external foes. Let us remember this title of our beloved Lord, and make use of Him as the DELIVERER, in preference to every other; apply to Him first in every difficulty, rely on Him with confidence in every trial, and He will deliver you until deliverance is no longer required. " He will deliver thee in six troubles, and in seven shall no evil touch thee."

Why should His people now be sad?
None have such reason to be glad
  As those redeemed to God;
Jesus the mighty Saviour lives,
To them eternal life He gives,
  The purchase of His blood.

SEPTEMBER 2.

Be not high-minded, but fear. Rom xi. 20.

BELIEVERS are sometimes tempted to think more highly of themselves than they ought to think, they forget that they are indebted to the free, sovereign, and distinguishing grace of God, for all the difference there is between them and the vilest of the vile. They should consider they are still weak, and liable to be overcome; foolish, and prone to wander; sinful, and easily wrought upon; that Satan is strong and determined; subtle and insinuating; malicious and designing; active and persevering; that the world is alluring and ensnaring; treacherous and vain; attracting and deceitful; and this would preserve them from being too secure. A high-minded Christian is sure to be unfruitful, and is generally left to fall. Therefore let him that thinketh he standeth take heed. David fell, Peter fell, and thousands beside have fallen; and they exhort us with groans, sighs, and tears, "BE NOT HIGH-MINDED, BUT FEAR." "Work out your own salvation with fear and trembling." Let us cultivate humility of mind, and habitual dependence upon God; so shall we be safe, holy, and happy.

Jesus, if Thou withdraw Thy hand,
  That moment sees me fall;
Oh, may I ne'er on self depend,
  But look to Thee for all.
Lead me in all Thy righteous ways,
Make plain Thy path before Thy face.

5|29

SEPTEMBER 3.

My God shall supply all our need
Phil. iv. 19.

So Paul assured believers at Philippi, and so He assures us. They had many wants, so have we; they were dependant on God, and so are we. The Lord engaged to supply them, and He is engaged to supply us. The Lord was faithful to them, and He will be faithful to us. His absolute promises are our invaluable treasure; His unchangeability is our immutable security. While Jehovah lives we cannot be friendless, we shall never be left to want; and at last we shall be able to testify, " Not one thing hath failed of all that the Lord our God hath promised." We can this morning rejoice, and say, "The Lord hath blessed me hitherto. Thou hast dealt well with Thy servant, O Lord, according to Thy word." Our wants should remind us of God's promises; the promises should be used to quell our fears, and comfort our hearts. We know not what a day will bring forth; but we know that " our God will supply all our needs according to His riches in glory by Christ Jesus." Let this banish care, and let us rejoice in the Lord as our PROVIDER.

In Jesus is our store,
Grace issues from His throne;
Whoever says, ' I want no more"
Confesses he has none:
But they who come to be supplied,
Will find Jehovah doth provide.

251

SEPTEMBER 4.

The gospel of your salvation   Ephes. i. 18.

OUR salvation is our deliverance from sin, the curse, and the wrath of God; this was impossible to man, but God sent His own Son in our nature, to save us freely, fully, and eternally. The gospel is the "GOOD NEWS OF OUR SALVATION." It is sent to inform us that God is love; that grace reigns; that heaven is opened; that provision is made for our guilt, weakness, and fears; that God waits to receive us, bless us, and glorify us with Himself forever. It sets before us all Christ has done; all he possesses; and invites us to come and receive, to use and be happy. It requires nothing of us to entitle us, it presents all it has, and gives it freely to the poor, the halt, the maimed, and the blind. It has all our misery requires, all our wants demand: we cannot wish for more than it brings; it is full of grace and full of glory. Precious gospel! Glorious news! May we receive it, believe it, act upon it daily, and so be happy. It is intended to FILL US with joy and peace in believing, to lead us to abound in hope; and to make us more than conquerors over despondency, doubt, and fear.

For you the purple current flowed,
In pardons from His wounded side;
Languished for you the eternal God
For you the Prince of Glory died
Believe, and all your sin's forgiven;
Only believe, and yours is heaven

252

SEPTEMBER 5.

I will in no wise cast out   John vi 37.

THE strongest believer is subject to fears, and may at times be strongly tempted to doubt, not only all that God has done for him, but His right and title to every promise in God's Book; at such times it is well to have recourse to those wells, from which we have drawn the choicest consolation in former times; and the words of Jesus which we have chosen for this day's portion stand foremost. Here He tells us, with peculiar tenderness and love, that He has made up His mind, that He will on no account refuse to receive the coming sinner, or allow him to be driven from His throne; neither the nature nor number of his transgressions, his age or circumstances, shall be found sufficient to procure Him a rejection His arms and His heart are open, He stands and calls us to Him, giving us this assurance, "I WILL IN NO WISE CAST OUT." Nearly two thousand years have rolled away since He spake the words; millions of sinners of every clime and character have made application, and all have found Him faithful. Let us not then grieve His love, and distress our own souls, by doubts and fears, but trust His word.

When, gracious Lord, when shall it be,
That I shall find my all in Thee ?
The fulness of Thy promise prove,
The seal of Thine eternal love ?
Ah ! wherefore did I ever doubt !
Thou wilt in no wise cast me out.

SEPTEMBER 6.

I will love them freely. Hosea xiv. 4

THE Lord loves his people naturally, as parents love their children; freely, without any cause whatever in them. He looks for nothing in them to move Him to love; nor will He allow anything in them to prevent His love. He loves them as vessels of mercy; disciples of Jesus; as bearing His image, His name, and His nature. His love to them is infinite, fruitful, and unchangeable. He will love them, though they deserve hatred, merit wrath, and may be justly sentenced to perdition. Beloved, let us never look into ourselves to find out the cause of God's love; it is in Him, not in us; but let us believe Him when He says, "I have loved thee with an everlasting love." Let us plead with Him, encouraged by the words of Jesus, "The Father Himself loveth you." Let us rejoice before Him, and praise Him for distinguishing grace. If He will love, who shall forbid Him? If He will love us, who shall dispute with Him? If He love us, as His word testifies He does, who shall estimate the honor, the advantage, or the happiness, which will eternally flow from His love? All glory to free grace.

O Jesus, full of truth and grace,
  More full of grace than I of sin;
Yet once again I seek Thy face;
  Open thine arms and take me in:
And freely my backslidings heal,
And love the faithless sinner still.

254

SEPTEMBER 7.

Rejoicing in hope Rom. xii. 12.

THE believer cannot always rejoice in possession, for he appears stripped of everything; but he may rejoice in hope even then. He is warranted to hope for eternal life; for righteousness by faith; that God may be magnified in his body, by life or by death; for the resurrection of the body, and its reunion with the soul; for the appearing of his beloved Saviour, and complete salvation through Him. The hope which is laid up for him in heaven, of which the gospel now informs him—a weight of glory, a crown of righteousness, and an eternal inheritance, are in reserve for him, and in hope of these he may rejoice. They are set before him to excite desire, produce courage, prevent despondency, and fill with joy. They are freely given, plainly promised, and carefully preserved; therefore we shall never be ashamed of our hope. Let us not yield to our gloomy feelings or to distressing forebodings; but let us lift up our heads, rejoicing that we shall so soon be made partakers of our hope. Let us hope in God, and daily praise Him more and more; making use of hope as the anchor of the soul, sure and steadfast.

Come, Lord, and help me to rejoice,
In hope that I shall hear Thy voice,
  Shall one day see my God;
Shall cease from all my painful strife,
Handle and taste the word of life,
  And feel the sprinkled blood.

SEPTEMBER 8.

The word of our God shall stand forever.
Isaiah xl. 8. *yes.*

THE word of our God is like His nature, immutably the same; He saith, " My covenant will I not break, nor ALTER the thing that is gone out of my mouth." Believer, this is thy comfort; every promise is confirmed and shall be fulfilled. But what hath He said? He hath said, " Though your sins be as scarlet they shall be white as snow. Many are the afflictions of the righteous, but the Lord delivereth him out of them ALL. No weapon formed against thee shall prosper. I will strengthen thee, I will help thee. I will never leave thee nor forsake thee. No good thing will He withhold from them that walk uprightly." All that He saith cometh surely to pass. Not one jot or tittle can fail. He never spake hastily, insincerely, or unwisely; He has drawn His plan, given His word, and everything shall answer the end He had in view. Man may be disappointed, God cannot. Man may change his mind, or break his word; but God cannot. He abideth faithful, He cannot deny Himself. Trust, and be not afraid.

> The word of God shall still endure,
> Faithful, immutable, and sure :
> This solid rock shall never break,
> Though earth should to her centre shake,
> And while it stands we should not fear,
> For all we need is promised there.

6/1/24

SEPTEMBER 9.

Oh, love the Lord, all ye His saints.
Psalm xxxi 23.

OUR God has revealed Himself as the source, centre, and end of everything lovely. In Jesus He appears as the fairest among ten thousand, and the altogether lovely. The wealth of the universe is His He is worthy of our highest love. He is all we could wish or desire. To possess Him is to be made for eternity. To have Him on our side is to be safe forever. But you may ask, What is His mind towards us? Emphatically, "GRACE." We have found favor in His eyes. He is the Friend of penitent sinners. He loveth us with an infinite love. Do you doubt it? Read His word. Look at Calvary. Ask His people. Prove for yourselves. See what He has already done for us. Have we a being? He gave it. Have we a good hope? He bestowed it. Have we liberty? He bought it. Have we holiness? He wrought it. Consider what we may have been but for His grace. What we certainly should have been but for His salvation. What we are now, and what we shall be, as the effect of His love; and, "Oh, love the Lord, all ye His saints!" It is happiness! It is holiness! It is heaven!

Love all defects supplies,
Makes great obstructions small;
'Tis prayer; 'tis praise; 'tis sacrifice
'Tis holiness; 'tis all!

SEPTEMBER 10.

To comfort all that mourn. Isaiah lxi 2.

THE Lord's people are all mourners; grace sets and keeps them mourning over sin committed—depravity discovered—evidences needed—comforts forfeited and lost—apparent uselessness—the sins of others—the state of the church—or for the salvation of relatives and friends. We mourn after Jesus when we do not enjoy His love, and over Him as suffering when we do. But He has declared, " Blessed are they that mourn, for they shall be comforted." Jesus Himself is anointed and appointed to be our COMFORTER; He has given Him the tongue of the learned, that He may speak a word in season to them that are weary. He comforts us by pardoning our sins—subduing our iniquities—restoring the joys of His salvation—employing us in His service, and making us successful. He comforts us by His word, His servants, and His Spirit. Admire the wisdom of God in the person appointed; the love of God in the work to which He is appointed; and the faithfulness of God in the perpetuity of His office. He ever lives, and lives to comfort us. Sweet view of Jesus, let us dwell upon it.

> Now in the Lord will I be glad,
>   And glory in His love ;
> In Him I'll joy, who will the God
>   Of my salvation prove :
> My Saviour will my comfort be,
>   And set my soul from trouble free.

258

SEPTEMBER 11.

Wilt thou be made whole? John v. 6.

THE great Physician presents Himself to us this morning, and He asks, "WILT THOU BE MADE WHOLE?" This is a searching question. Are you willing to be sanctified throughout? Willing that He should use what means He pleases, to conform you to Himself? Jesus is able to sanctify us wholly; the time of mercy is now; are we desirous of being healed? If so, let us put ourselves into His hands for the purpose; let us submit without hesitation to His terms; He performs the cure and receives all the glory. Let us not fancy that our case is hopeless, but let us look to Jesus, who will heal us, and heal us GRATIS. Open thy whole case to Him, consult Him daily, trust Him implicitly, and expect to shine before the Father's throne as a proof of His skill and kindness. No case can be desperate, while Jesus lives to heal; no sinner can be too poor, for He heals without money and without price. O Jesus! heal us this morning! Soften our hard hearts. Regulate our disorderly wills. Elevate our earthly affections. Fill us with holiness, fill us with love. We lie at Thy feet, and we trust in Thy word.

> Jesus, to Thee for help I call,
> With pitying eye behold me fall,
>   Diseased at Thy throne;
> Oh, heal my soul, remove my sin,
> Now make the filthy leper clean,
>   Remove the heart of stone.

SEPTEMBER 12.

I lay down my life for the sheep.   John x 15.

JESUS has a flock peculiarly His own ; His Father chose them and gave them to Him ; He received them and became their Shepherd ; they wandered and were doomed to die, but He interfered and died for them.   Oh, what an infinite love was the love of Jesus !   He left His Father's bosom, left the songs of angels, left the throne of glory ; and became a man, that He might become a Substitute.   He offered Himself for them His blood for theirs, His life for theirs.   The offer was accepted, and He redeemed them to God by His blood OUT OF every nation, country, people, and tongue.   They are doubly His, for He bought them when they had sold themselves, though before they were given Him by His Father in love.   Herein is love; not that we loved Jesus, but that He loved us ; and gave Himself to be the propitiation for our sins.   Are we among His sheep ?   Are we like them ?   Do we love them, cleave to them, and walk with them ?   His sheep are gentle, harmless, peaceful, humble, dependant upon Him, and devoted to Him.   They hear His voice, love His ways, and follow Him whithersoever He goeth

When the Shepherd's life was needful
  To redeem the sheep from death,
Of their safety ever heedful,
  Jesus yielded up His breath ;
    Faithful Shepherd !
Love like Thine no other hath.

260

SEPTEMBER 13.

Let patience have her perfect work.
James i. 4.

PATIENCE supposes trials, and troubles it sig-
nifies to remain under a burden; it is opposed
to fretfulness, murmuring, haste, and despondency. It produces submission, silence before
God, and satisfaction with His dealings. The
Holy Spirit produces this grace by means of
afflictions; tribulation worketh patience. Every
Christian is supposed to possess it, and is required to exercise it; yea, to let it have ITS
PERFECT WORK. To this end let us study the
examples of suffering and patience set before
us in the Bible; let us take up and plead God's
promises; let us remember that eternal love
appointed every trial and trouble; that Jesus
forewarned us of tribulation; that He has set
us an example which we are required to imitate.
Impatience dishonors our profession, and grieves
the Spirit; patience benefits others, and is of
great advantage to ourselves. Let us watch
against temptations to impatience, and in patience possess our souls. So shall we fill up
our character as Christians; complete the evidence of our sincerity; and prove our principles
divine.

> Dear Lord, though bitter is the cup
> Thy gracious hand deals out to me,
> I cheerfully would drink it up,—
> That cannot hurt which comes from Thee.
> The gift of patience, Lord, impart,
> T' calm and soothe my troubled heart.

261

SEPTEMBER 14.

And Jacob said, I have enough · or, I have all things.
Gen. xxxiii 10, 11.

Poor Jacob left his father's house with only a staff, but he returned with two bands ; so greatly had the Lord prospered him. But it was not his earthly possessions, but the kindness of his brother, and the grace of his God, which led him to exclaim, " I HAVE ENOUGH : or, I HAVE ALL THINGS." Beloved, such language becomes us, as the objects of Jehovah's everlasting love; as interested in the well-ordered covenent ; as entitled to all the promises ; as invited to come to the throne of grace to receive all we need ; as directed to cast all our cares upon God ; as having a warrant to expect every good thing on earth, and glory at the journey's end. Ought we not to rejoice and shout, " I HAVE ENOUGH." Enough to make me happy. Enough to make me holy Enough to fill me with gratitude. Enough to fill angels with wonder, and devils with envy and vexation. O Jesus ! to what a height hast Thou raised us ! With what great, lasting, and glorious blessings hast Thou blessed us ! Everlasting praises to Thy name, and eternal glory to Thy sovereign grace !

> Jesus is all I wish or want!
> For Him I pray, I thirst, I pant:
> Let others after earth aspire :
> Christ is the treasure I desire,
> He is an all-sufficient store;
> Possess'd of Him, I wish no more.

262

SEPTEMBER 15.

The end of all things is at hand. 1 Pet iv. 7.

THE mountains shall depart, and the hills be removed; only Jehovah's word, love, purposes, and perfections remain the same. The world passeth away, and the fashion of it; but he that doeth the will of God abideth forever. The end of all things is at hand; our labors will soon cease; our commerce terminate; our earthly relationships dissolve; our pleasures and sorrows in this world be concluded; the last sermon will soon be preached; and the last opportunity for us to do good will make its appearance. The coming of the Son of God draweth nigh; let us be therefore preparing ourselves for so great, so solemn an event; and whenever tempted to trifle, to loiter, or to sin, let us remember "THE LORD IS AT HAND." Let us be sober, temperate in reference to the body; and let us think soberly of ourselves, of others, of everything around us Let us not be rash or hasty, careless or indifferent; but let us speak and act soberly, as those that MUST GIVE an account. He that shall come will come, and will not tarry; and He bids us be ready to receive Him with gladness, joy, and rejoicing.

When Thou, my righteous Judge! shalt come
To fetch Thy ransom'd people home,
   Shall I among them stand?
Shall such a worthless worm as I,
Who sometimes am afraid to die,
   Be found at Thy right hand?

Even to hoar hairs will I carry you.
Isaiah xlvi. 4

WHAT a sweet portion is this for the aged disciples of the Lord Jesus; heart and flesh may
fail them, but God will not forsake them
Having begun a good work in them, He will
carry it on His gifts and callings are without
repentance He will be as kind, as tender, and
as gracious at last as at the first. HE WILL
CARRY US. The eternal God is our refuge, underneath are the everlasting arms. He will carry
us safely through every danger, over every difficulty, into His presence and glory. Aged pilgrim, lean upon thy God; look unto Him; and
as the nurse carrieth the sucking child, so will
thy God carry thee. He will prove Himself
faithful to His word, and ultimately call you
forth as a witness to the same. Fear not then
in reference to the evening of old age: thy God
will supply thee; He will support thee; and at
last land thee safe where the storms of trouble
never blow, where weakness and fear are never
felt. Take no anxious thought for the morrow;
let the morrow take thought for the things of itself; sufficient unto the day is the evil thereof.
The promise of thy God cannot fail thee; He
will guide thee and carry thee to His kingdom
and glory. He says—

E'en down to old age, all My people shall prove
My sov'reign, eternal, unchangeable love,
And when hoary hairs shall their temples adorn,
Like lambs they shall still in My bosom be borne
264

Fight the good fight of faith 1 Tim vi 12

Faith has to fight with the deep and direful depravity of the heart; with error and superstition; with despondency and early prejudices; with unbelief and carnal reason; with Satan and the world at large. Faith has to fight for victory; for a crown; for God's glory. True, faith fights in God's strength; with certainty, arising from the faithful promise; in holy fear, produced by grace taking advantage of our weakness; with courage; principally on the knees; and looking to the great Captain of our salvation, the end of the conflict, and the design of the combat. Believer, "Fight the good fight of faith" Thy God bids thee. His promises are intended to encourage thee. The example of Jesus should animate thee. The coward's doom should alarm and instruct thee. The connection between conflict and conquest should impel thee. Jesus says, "To him that overcometh will I grant to sit with me in my throne, even as I also overcame, and am set down with my Father in His throne" God is faithful, by whom ye were called unto the fellowship of His Son Jesus Christ our Lord.

Omnipotent Lord, my Saviour and King,
Thy succor afford, Thy righteousness bring;
On Thee, as my power, for strength I rely;
All evil before Thy presence shall fly
Thy love everlasting will never depart,
Thy truth and Thy mercy shall rule in my heart.

He forgetteth not the cry of the humble
Psalm ix. 12.

THE humble grateful soul, may have anything
from the Lord; so great is His love to them
and delight in them. He cries to the Lord to
be kept from every false way; from falling into
sin; and that he may be devoted entirely to the
Lord's glory. He prays for his enemies, that
they may be blessed; and for his friends, that
they may be rewarded. His cry is constant
sincere; and hearty. But he is often tempted
to think that because he is so unworthy, so
insignificant, and so vile, God will not hear
him, and especially when answers are delayed
But the cry of the humble cannot be forgotten
The Lord will not neglect or pass over such an
one's prayer without notice; He will not despise
or contemn their petitions; but He will regard
attend to, and answer them. His wisdom will
shine forth in the time when, and the means by
which He answers their prayers; and He will
get Himself a glorious name by their sanctification, salvation, and glorification. O believer
never harbor the thought that thy God will for
get thy petitions!

> Friend of sinners, King of saints,
> Answer my minutest wants!
> Let my cries Thy throne assail,
> Entering now within the veil;
> Free my soul from guilt and shame,—
> Lord, I ask in Jesus' name.

2F 3

Sin shall not have dominion over you.
Rom vi. 14

WHAT a precious promise. How many of the Lord's people have been cheered and encouraged by it. Sin lives in us, works in us, fights in us, but it shall not reign. It may annoy, it shall not destroy. Its authority is destroyed by the Lord. Its power is weakened by grace. It is warned to quit its old residence, and it will soon be ejected. We are not under the condemning power of the law, it is not our rule of justification; but we are under favor; God dealeth with us as with children. He pardons, pities, and delivers us. He will not allow sin to hold us in perpetual bondage, or to condemn us at the last day; but He will set us at liberty, and justify us fully. The flesh will lust against the Spirit, corruption will rise and fight; but we shall be strengthened, assisted, and counselled until we finally overcome. Grace shall reign through righteousness unto eternal life, by Jesus Christ our Lord. The law will be honored in our endless blessedness, and Jesus will be glorified in us throughout eternity By grace we are saved.

On such love, my soul, still ponder,
Love so great, so rich, so free!
Say, while lost in holy wonder,
Why, O Lord, such love to me?
Hallelujah!
Grace shall reign eternally.

SEPTEMBER 20.

I have gone astray like a lost sheep.
Psalm cxix. 176.

THIS is the humble confession of a man of God
and may not we adopt it as our own this morn
ing? Have not we also gone astray? Does no
this display our *weakness?* How weak to wan
der from so kind a Shepherd, so rich a pasture
so good a fold! Is it not a mark of *inattention.*
Jesus hath warned and cautioned us against it in
His word. Is it not a proof of our *ingratitude:*
Oh, how ungrateful to forsake Him after so
many favors, such rich blessings, such token
of unmerited kindness! Does it not betray ou
folly?—to go from good to bad, from safety to
danger, from plenty to want and wretchedness
Oh, the power of corruption! The deceitfulnes
of the human heart! Lord, seek Thy servants
for we do not forget Thy commandments. W
smart for our folly; we grieve over our sin; w
desire to return; restore us to Thy fold, to th
enjoyment of Thy favor; and enable us to deligh
ourselves in Thy ways. Jesus, Shepherd of th
sheep, bring us back from all our wanderings
and keep us near Thyself; for why should w
turn aside from Thy flock and fold?

Thou know'st the way to bring me back,
  My fallen spirit to restore—
Oh, for Thy truth and mercy's sake,
  Forgive, and bid me sin no more:
The ruins of my soul repair,
And make my heart a house of prayer.

6|7|24

SEPTEMBER 21.

The Lord was ready to save me.
Isaiah xxxviii. 20.

THIS is the testimony of a good man who had been in great danger. His heart was full of fears, and he gave up all for lost; but now he is recovered, and stands forth to acknowledge his mistake, and bear witness to this pleasing fact, that the Lord is ever ready to save His people in every time of trouble. The Lord hath saved us, and He will save us even to the end. He has power, and He will exert it; He has authority, and He will employ it; He has sympathy, and He will manifest it. He is a Saviour at hand and not afar off. He is ready and willing to deliver. Has He not proved Himself so in our past experience, and ought we not to trust Him for the future? Let us in every danger cry unto God to save us; wait upon Him in humble hope for the blessing; banish carnal and unscriptural fears far away; refuse to listen to Satan, sense, or unbelief; persevere in seeking until we obtain and enjoy the blessing. THE LORD IS READY TO SAVE US. Let us believe, hope, prove, and be happy. He will save, He will rest in His love, and joy over us with singing.

> Salvation to God will I publish abroad,
> Jehovah hath saved me through Jesus's blood;
> The Lamb was once slain, but He liveth again,
> And I with my Jesus forever shall reign :
> Then filled with His love, in the regions above,
> I shall never, no never from Jesus remove.

SEPTEMBER 22.

Be ye imitators of God, as dear children.
Eph. v. 1.

THE Lord proposes Himself to us as our pattern, and He gives grace to every one who desires it to imitate Him. He exhorts us as His dear and tenderly beloved children, and in mildest strains proposeth Himself for our imitation. Let us imitate the Lord in the *world,* dealing justly, ever acting from holy principles, and by a righteous rule; adhering strictly to truth, for our God is THE GOD OF TRUTH: choosing our company, being only familiar with them who are familiar with God; and doing good to all, especially unto them who are of the household of faith; for He causeth His sun to shine on the evil and on the good, and sendeth rain on the just and on the unjust. Let us imitate Him in the *church,* cultivating a spirit of love to all saints, notwithstanding their infirmities, exercising forbearance, and pity; being slow to anger and ready to forgive; accepting the will for the deed, and being always ready to help in trouble and distress. Let us imitate our God, for He commands us; our relation to Him requires it; and our peace is involved in it.

This will solve th' important question,
Whether thou art a real Christian,
  Better than each golden dream;
Better far than lip expression,
Towering notions, great profession;
  This will show your love to Him.

Cast thy burden upon the Lord, and He shall sustain thee.
Ps lv. 22

THE Lord's people are often heavy laden, their burdens are heavy and their grief great; but the Lord kindly directs them to cast eveiy burden upon Him, and promises to sustain them. Guilt in the conscience and a sense of sin in the soul, often prove an intolerable burden; but the Lord will remove it by the blood of His Son, and the whisper of His Spirit. The care of a family sinks the spirit, and fills with distress; but Jesus says, "Cast them all on me." Losses, crosses, enemies, temptations, and the inward conflict, often burden the soul; but our God will sanctify them to us, sustain us through them, and deliver us out of them all. Our God has determined that we shall use Him, feel our dependence upon Him, and glory only in Him Believer, He will sustain thee by speaking peace to thy troubled heart; by enabling you to leave your intricate affairs in His hands; by strengthening you with strength in your soul; and by enabling you to contrast the present with the future. Thanks be unto God who giveth us the victory. O Jesus, teach me to bring every burden to Thy feet and to cast every care upon Thee!

Thou, O Lord, in tender love
Wilt all my burdens bear!
Lift my heart to things above,
And fix it ever there!

SEPTEMBER 24.

In the mount of the Lord it shall be seen
Gen. xxii. 14.

JEHOVAH has provided supplies for His people,
He arranges the bestowment of them, and hears
and answers prayer for them. He may allow
them to come into trials, dangers, and troubles;
but "in the mount the Lord will be seen." He
will show Himself as rigidly faithful to His
word; as kind and merciful in all His dealings;
as attentive to the wants and wishes of His people; as ready to supply them, and display His
love and power in delivering them. In the mount
of the Lord it shall be seen that Satan is a liar;
that our fears were all groundless; that unbelief
is a great sin; that prayer shall surely be answered; that faith and hope shall not be disappointed; that Jesus is touched with the feeling
of our infirmities; and that none shall be ashamed who trust in, wait for, and obey the commands
of the Most High God. Beloved, we have seen
the Lord in the mount of trial, we have found it
turned into the mount of mercy, and we shall
see Him on the mount of glory.

'Tis in the mount the Lord is seen;
And all His saints shall surely find,
Though clouds and darkness intervene,
He still is gracious, still is kind
Yes, in the mount, the Lord makes bare
His mighty, His delivering power;
Displays a Father's tender care,
In the most trying, darkest hour.

SEPTEMBER 25.

What th nk ye of Christ ? Matt. xxii 42

BELOVED, let us inquire what do we think of Jesus this morning? What do we think of His divinity, as one with the Father? Of His humanity, as one with us? Of His complex person, as God and man in one Christ? What think we of His one sacrifice for sin? What think we of His grace as displayed in the whole work of our redemption? What think we of His word as the ground of our hope, the source of our comfort, and the rule of our lives? What think we of His kingdom? What think we of His coming? How do we think of Jesus? Do we think of Him frequently, as of a subject full of pleasure? naturally, as we do of refreshing food? pleasantly, as of choice and delightful music? Or, only seldom, and then with gloom, or without love and ardent desire? What does our thinking of Christ produce? Does it produce desire—contrition—love—trust—resolution —prayer—action? What are we willing to suffer for Christ? What are we willing to part with for Christ? What can we cheerfully give to Christ, to feed His poor, or to help His cause?

Oh ! could I speak the matchless worth,—
Oh ! could I sound the glories forth,
  Which in my Saviour shine;
I'd soar and touch the heavenly strings,
And vie with Gabriel while he sings,
  In notes almost divine.

Partakers of the heavenly calling. Heb. iii. 1.

BELOVED, God hath called us by His grace and gospel, into the knowldege of Christ; into the favor of Jesus; to partake of the Spirit of His Son; to enjoy fellowship with Christ; to wear the image of Christ; and to possess and enjoy His righteousness, strength, wisdom, unsearchable riches, and eternal glory. This calling is heavenly in its origin, nature, tendency, and consummation; it is from heaven and to heaven. All believers partake of the same calling; they are called by the same voice; to the same cross and throne; to possess and enjoy the same title and to claim and use the same blessings This calling is the greatest honor that can be conferred upon a sinner; it is altogether a favor, the fruit of free and everlasting love; its enjoyment calls for gratitude and praise. Are we called with an heavenly calling? Then we should come out from the world; walk with God; imitate the Saviour; set our affections upon things above, and prepaie for, and hasten to, our blessed home, our glorious inheritance. Let us make our calling and our election SURE, and then sing—

As Thou wilt, dispose of me,
Only make me one with Thee;
Make me in my life express
All the heights of holiness,
Sweetly in my spirit prove
All the depths of humble love!

274

SEPTEMBER 27.

Is the Spirit of the Lord straitened?
Micah ii. 7.

Why then do you despond? Why are you satisfied to live so far below your privileges? The Holy Spirit is promised, to teach us all things, to testify of Jesus to our hearts; to glorify our precious Saviour in our souls; to help our infirmities, to comfort us by taking of the things of Christ, and showing them to us; and to lead us in the way everlasting. Do we experience His love in these particulars? If not—what is the cause? "Is the Spirit of the Lord straitened?" NO. But do we sow to the Spirit? Do we pray for the Spirit? Do we expect the Father to give Him, in answer to our prayers; that Jesus will send Him according to His promise? Oh, beloved, look at your doubts, your fears, your carnality, your coldness, your want of life, love, and power; and now ask—"Are these His doings?" Is His arm shortened? Is His love changed? Is His word false? Or, rather have you not grieved Him, quenched His operations, and caused Him to withhold His hand? · Oh, pray for the Spirit! You are absolutely dependant upon Him, for without Him you can do nothing.

Come, Holy Ghost, all-quickening fire,
My consecrated heart inspire,
  Sprinkle with the atoning blood:
Still to my soul Thyself reveal,
Thy mighty working may I feel,
  And know that I am one with God.

Be content with such things as ye have.
Heb. xiii 5

WE may not have what we wish, but we certainly have what our God thinks best for us. Every mercy is directed by infinite wisdom and eternal love, and never misses its road, or comes into the possession of any but the persons for whom it is intended. Let us therefore remember, that our God has chosen our inheritance for us, and it becomes us to be content; yea, to be very grateful. We have infinitely more than we deserve, we have more than many of our fellow-believers We have liberty, while the Apostles were shut up in prison; we have a home, while many of the primitive Christians wandered about in dens and caves of the earth; our lives are protected, while the martyrs were burned at the stake; we live in hope of heaven, while many are lifting up their eyes in hell, being in torments. Let us strive to be content with present things, and hope for better; let us endeavor to learn Paul's lesson, "I have learned, in whatsoever state I am, therewith to be content. I know both how to be abased, and I know how to abound." And say—

Take my soul and body's powers,
Take my memory, mind, and will,
All my goods, and all my hours,
All I know, and all I feel
Thine I live, thrice happy I!
Happier still if Thine I die.

Trust ye in the Lord forever. Isa xxvi 2

WE are often discouraged by the difficulties of the way, and cast down through the weakness of our faith ; we look to creatures, instead of looking to the Lord ; and reflect upon our weakness, instead of believing His promises, and trusting His faithfulness. But the Lord our God should be the only and the constant object of our trust ; His word warrants us to look to Him for all we need, both temporal and spiritual ; and His character assures us that we cannot be disappointed. He will appear for us, and make all His goodness pass before us. If we connect prayer to God with trusting in God, and waiting for God, it is impossible that we should be left in trouble, or be neglected in distress. We may trust Him with the fullest confidence, and expect without doubting all He has promised to bestow. Are you at this time tried, tempted, and distressed ? Cast your burden upon the Lord. Commit your way unto Him ; He will bring to pass His largest promises and your best desires. Seek out His promises, confide in them, and plead them with God, and expect their accomplishment. Oh, trust in the Lord forever !

> Trust Him, He's faithful to His word,
>   His promise cannot fail ;
> He'll never leave you nor forsake,
>   Or let your foes prevail :
> Then trust His word, expect His grace,
> Until you see Him face to face.

277

Ye are under grace. Rom vi 14

BELIEVERS are delivered from the law, and are dead to it; they are married to Christ and are alive unto God as a GOD OF LOVE. The curs is removed, sin is atoned for, and we stand a high in the favor of God as we possibly car We should look upon ourselves as the favorite of God; His beloved children, whom He hat reconciled to Himself by the death of His Sor Grace reigns over us, rules in us, provides fo us, and will glorify us. Why then should w fear? Of whom should we be afraid? Sin i pardoned. The law is magnified. Justice i satisfied. God is at peace with us; yea, H delights in us The world is overcome for us and even Satan shall be bruised under our fee shortly. What shall we say to these things As God is for us, and with us, who shall injure or prevail against us? All things MUST work to gether for our good; nothing shall be able to sep arate us from the love of God; we shall be mor than conquerors through Him who loved us and why? Because WE ARE NOT UNDER THI LAW, BUT UNDER GRACE. Because Jesus lives we shall live also.

On Jesus only I depend,
He is my Father, God, and Friend,
My Prophet, King, and Priest;
Had I an angel's holiness,
I'd cast aside that glorious dress,
And wrap me up in Christ

6/12/24

278

OCTOBER 1.

Your heavenly Father. Matt. vi. 32.

WHEN ye pray, say, "OUR FATHER.' When ye are cast down, remember you have a Father in heaven who loves you, cares for you, has given His word to you, and is ever ready to do you good. It is truly blessed to begin this month, and every month, believing that we have a Father in heaven; and that, "like as a father pitieth his children, so the Lord pitieth them that fear Him; for He knoweth our frame, He remembereth that we are dust." Let there be no reserve between us and our heavenly Father, but let us communicate everything to Him; let there be no hard thoughts of our Father encouraged; but let us take His own word, which sets forth His own immutable mind, and rejoice. Our heavenly Father knoweth what we need, He hath provided all we need, He will give all He has provided; but He will be acknowledged and sought unto. Nothing is too hard for Him to effect, nothing is too great for him to produce, nothing is too good for Him to bestow upon His people. What a mercy to have a Father, and such a Father, in this inhospitable world! To Him let us carry, and with Him let us leave all our cares.

> Father, on me the grace bestow,
> To call Thee mine while here below,
> To love Thee as Thy law requires;
> To this my longing soul aspires.
> May every word and action prove,
> My soul is filled with heavenly love

OCTOBER 2.

Who is on the Lord's side? Exo. xxxii. 26.

EVERY believer is ready to answer, I am. Well, the Lord has a cause upon the earth; it is weak, and wants your support; it is opposed, and needs your countenance. If you are on the Lord's side, you are on the side of truth—holiness—charity—of His worship and ordinances—of His people and His ways—and you are jealous of His honor. You unite with His people, go forth to Jesus without the camp, bearing His reproach. If you are on the Lord's side, He will spare you as obedient children, supply you as faithful servants; protect you as loyal subjects; and honor you as brave and courageous soldiers. You will never see any just occasion to change sides; or regret that you decided to serve so good a Master. You will find the Lord to be on your side, supporting you in affliction; comforting you in trouble; giving you victory in death; and pronouncing you just in the judgment. If you are on the Lord's side, avow it openly; prove it daily; and let your whole conduct say, "I AM THE LORD'S. Use all your influence for His glory, consecrate all your energies to His cause, and rejoice to suffer for His name

Shall I for fear of feeble man,
The Spirit's course in me restrain?
Awed by a mortal's frown shall I
Conceal the word of God most high?
How then before thee shall I dare
To stand, or how thine anger bear?

Thou shalt be a blessing. Ge i. xii. 2.

We were by nature cursed of God, and a curse to others; but a God of love interferes for us, pours His blessing upon us, and makes us a blessing. He gives grace to form the character; gifts to fit for usefulness; wisdom to choose the course; strength to do His will; supplies to complete the design; faith to trust His word, patience to persevere and wait His time; and success to crown our efforts. The result of His thus blessing us is, we are a blessing to others; to sinners and to saints. We are a blessing by the spirit we breathe, if it is meek, gentle, and lovely; by the example we set, if it is an imitation of Jesus; by our prayers for the good of souls, and the glory of God; and by our efforts to spread abroad the knowledge of the truth in every place. What a blessing to be the means of the conversion of but one soul! To be used to instruct the ignorant, to strengthen the weak, or to comfort the desponding, or distressed. O Jesus! make us a blessing. Thy grace is sufficient; fulfil to us Thy promise to Abraham. Beloved, let us look to Him, depend upon Him, act for Him, give praise daily unto Him, and WE SHALL BE A BLESSING. .

Lord, make me faithful unto death,
Thy witness with my latest breath,
To tell the glories of the Lamb,
Him whom I serve, and whose I am;
On whom for strength I daily lean,
Whose strength is in my weakness seen.

I will do you no hurt Jer xxv 6.

How is it possible that a God of love, who is full of compassion, plenteous in mercy, ready to forgive, waiting to be gracious, should do His children hurt? It cannot be. His dealings may cause us pain, but nothing shall by any means harm us. We ought rather to argue with Paul. "He that spared not His own Son, but delivered Him up for us all, how shall He not with Him also freely give us all things?" He sent His ancient people as captives to Babylon, but it was for their good; He allowed His children to be cast into the fiery furnace, into the lion's den, to be driven out to wander in sheep-skins and goat-skins, but He did not allow them to be hurt; all was sanctified to them, and the curse was turned into a blessing. If He scourge us with one hand, He will support us with the other; and at last we shall come up before His throne, out of great tribulation, having washed our robes and made them white in the blood of the Lamb. Not one who has arrived safe in heaven will say that his God allowed him to be hurt; notwithstanding the trials endured by the way. Nothing shall by any means hurt you

> Lord, I would my all resign,
> Gladly lose my will in Thine,
> Careless be of things below,
> Thee alone content to know;
> Simple, innocent, and free,
> Seeking all my bliss in Thee.

OCTOBER 5.

Only acknowledge thine iniquity. Jer. iii. 13.

WILL the Lord receive us when we have backslidden from Him, and are desirous of returning to Him? Oh, yes, He invites, He exhorts, He beseeches us to return. Nor does He prescribe any hard conditions, but He says, "ONLY ACKNOWLEDGE THINE INIQUITY." He is so ready to forgive, so infinitely gracious in His nature, that if we confess our sins, He is faithful and just to forgive us our sins, and to cleanse us from all unrighteousness. Have we wandered? Have we left our first love? Let us go and return to our first husband, for then it was better with us than now. His bowels yearn over us, His arms are open to receive us, and He waits to fall upon our neck and kiss us. Let us go to His throne, and there confess our sins, crave His pardon, sigh for the enjoyment of His love, and He will restore unto us the joys of His salvation, and establish us with His free Spirit. Let us daily confess our iniquities unto the Lord, and He will pardon our numerous sins. In His favor is life. In His frown is distress and woe. He delighteth in mercy. He will receive, pardon us, and bless like a God. His mercy endureth forever.

> This glorious news dispels my fears,
> Makes glad my heart, wipes off my tears,
> Displays the riches of His grace,
> Inflames my love, and claims my praise:
> A pardon'd sinner lives to prove
> The height and depth of Jesus' love.

283

OCTOBER 6.

The righteousness which is of God by faith.
Phil iii 9

THE righteousness here intended is that which God requires in His law; provided by the life and death of His Son; presents to sinners in the everlasting gospel: imputes to every believer, of richest grace; accepts when pleaded at the throne of His grace; and honors with a title to eternal life. This righteousness is by faith; it is the office of faith to receive it; plead it; trust it; rejoice in it; embolden the soul through it; and clothe the soul in it. It is not offered to anything but faith, nor can it be received and enjoyed in any other way. Every unbeliever and self-righteous person rejects it, but every man who is taught of God feels that he needs it; discovers the beauty, glory, and value of it; applies for it with ardent desire and earnest longing; embraces it as one of God's greatest favors; enjoys it as a rich and durable treasure; and dies confidently expecting to be accepted in it and admitted to glory through it. Oh, may we be found in Jesus, not having on our own righteousness, which is of the law, but THE RIGHTEOUSNESS WHICH IS OF GOD BY FAITH! And while we pant for holiness with every breath, and aim at it in every action, may each of us devoutly say—

> And even when I feel Thy grace,
> And sin seems most subdued,
> I'll wrap me in thy righteousness,
> And plunge me in Thy blood.

284

OCTOBER 7.

He that loveth me shall be loved of my Fat.er.
John xiv. 21.

Do we love Jesus? Are we cultivating an acquaintance with Him? If we love Him, we desire to know Him more fully; to serve Him more cheerfully; and to enjoy Him continually. If we love Jesus we are willing to part with all things for Him, to renounce whatever He forbids, and pursue whatsoever he commands. If we love Him, we want to love Him more; and to be always with Him. If we love Him, He assures us His Father will love us; for He so delights in His beloved Son, that He visits, revives, and blesses every soul that loves Jesus. If God loves us, what good thing will He withhold from us? Will He suffer any one to hurt us? Oh, no! He will manifest Himself to us. He will appear for us. He will glorify Himself in us. He will be to us all a God can be, and do for us far above our expectations and hopes. To be the object of the love of God is to enjoy the highest honor, and to possess a title to the greatest happiness which it is possible for rational creatures to enjoy. Let us therefore ascertain beyond a doubt, that we love Jesus, ardently, sincerely.

To His meritorious passion
All our happiness we owe,
Pardon, uttermost salvation,
Heaven above and heaven below:
Grace and glory
From that open fountain flow.

285

OCTOBER 8.

We will remember thy love. Sol. Song i. 4.

WHAT subject is so sweet as the love of Jesus? The good-will of His heart towards us, which He fixed on us sovereignly, immutably, and eternally. Let us remember this love of Jesus, for it is sufficient to fill us with joy, peace, and love. Oh, how it condescended to look upon us, come and die for us, and now to dwell with us! What benevolence it has and does display, giving everything that is necessary for life and godliness. How it dignifies its objects, raising them to glory, honor, immortality, and eternal life. Let us remember His love; to comfort our hearts amidst changing friendships; to encourage our souls in seasons of darkness; to produce confidence in times of trial; to inspire with fortitude in times of danger; to beget patience when burdened and oppressed; to reconcile the mind under bereaving dispensations; and to produce zeal and devotedness in the Lord's cause and service. Oh, love of Jesus! be Thou my daily subject and constant theme! Beloved, let us remember His love, if we forget everything beside; there is nothing so sweet, so valuable, so excellent as this!

God only knows the love of God:
Oh, that it now were shed abroad
  In this poor stony heart!
Give me to know this love divine,
This heavenly portion, Lord, be mine;
  Be mine this better part!

OCTOBER 9.

The poor committeth himself to Thee. Psalm x. 14.

THOSE who appear the most friendless, have the best and truest Friend. The Lord's people are poor, but they are not friendless nor forsaken. They have Jehovah for their God, Jesus for their Saviour, and the Holy Spirit for their Comforter and Guide. They know God and commit themselves and their all to Him. But how do they commit themselves to Him? As the debtor does to His Surety. As a sick man does to his Physician. As the client does to his Lawyer or Advocate. As the needy does to his rich and generous Friend. As a sinner to the Saviour. As the loving bride does to her beloved bridegroom. But why do they commit themselves unto Him? They commit themselves to His grace to be saved by it; to His power to be kept by it; to His providence to be fed by it; to His word to be ruled by it; to His care to be preserved by it; and to His arms at death to be safely landed in glory. This flows from grace, and produces peace, safety, satisfaction, and success. Let us, beloved, commit ourselves to the Lord daily, heartily, deliberately, and unreservedly.

My soul shall cry to Thee, O Lord,
To Thee, supreme, incarnate Word,
My rock and fortress, shield and Friend,
Creator, Saviour, source, and end;
And thou wilt hear Thy servant's prayer,
Though death and darkness speak despair.

287

OCTOBER 10.

Who shall lay anything to the charge of God's elect?
Rom viii 33.

God's elect are sinners; they know it, feel it, and deplore it. The world is against them, and Satan tries every means in his power to ruin them. But blessed be God he cannot prevail. The work of the Holy Spirit within them, sets and keeps them panting for holiness; striving against sin; aiming at God's glory; and desiring to be a blessing to all around them. The work of Christ for them, brings forth a sentence of justification from the eternal Father; and believing His word they realize their privilege, and may boldly ask—"WHO SHALL LAY ANYTHING TO THE CHARGE OF GOD'S ELECT?" Will God? No—for He is perfectly satisfied through the death of His Son. Will conscience? No—for it is cleansed by the blood of Jesus, silenced by the word of God, and corroborates Jehovah's testimony. Can Satan? No—for he is cast out, his testimony cannot be received, having long since been proved a liar by the God of truth. Will Jesus as Judge of all? No—for He would rather die for us than condemn us. O beloved, see the perfection of the Saviour's work.

> Complete atonement He has made,
> And to the utmost farthing paid
>   Whate'er His people owed;
> How then can wrath on me take place,
> If shelter'd in His righteousness,
>   And sprinkled with His blood?

6|7

OCTOBER 11.

Keep yourselves in the love of God. Jude 21.

THE love of God to His people is free, unspeakably great, and eternal; our love to God is dependant on His love to us as its source, on faith and fellowship with Him as its fuel; therefore we are exhorted to keep ourselves in the love of God. This implies that we are beloved of God, and that we know it, and love Him in return. That we should endeavor to retain our standing, and keep ourselves sensibly in the love of God, by setting it always before our minds; exercising our faith on it; and seeking the enjoyment of it by prayer and in the Lord's ways We should keep ourselves in the exercise of love to God by avoiding temptations, walking by faith, and living as in His presence. We should keep ourselves in the exercise of love one to another, by exhortation, forbearance, and example. We should preserve ourselves by the love of God, from the temptations of Satan, the snares of the world, and the lusts of the flesh. Beloved, consider how the love of God aggravates our sins; how it should fire us with courage to oppose everything that is unholy or forbidden.

O love divine, how sweet thou art!
When shall I find my longing heart
  All taken up by Thee?
Grant me, O gracious Lord, to prove
The sweetness of redeeming love,
  The love of Christ to me!

OCTOBER 12.

Be sure your sin will find you out
Num. xxxii. 23.

SIN cannot be concealed; it meets the eye and affects the heart of God; and unless we find it out, confess it with sorrow, and forsake it with disgust, it will find us out, and expose us to the rod of God, and the contempt of godly men. It found Achan out, and proved his ruin; it found Noah out, and covered him with disgrace; and it found David out, so that the sword never departed from his house. God cannot be reconciled to sin, nor should we be. However secret the sin, God is a witness; and He will bring it to light. "HE THAT COVERETH HIS SIN SHALL NOT PROSPER; but he that confesseth and forsaketh his sins, shall find mercy." Let us be careful that we give sin no quarter, or vainly fancy that because God loves us He will not expose us; He assures us OUR SIN WILL FIND US OUT. Oh, to hate sin as God hates it, to loathe it as Jesus loathed it, and to become dead to it, and be entirely delivered from it! It is the source of all our miseries, the cause of all our pains, and the occasion of all our troubles. It cannot be hid, it will find us out, and sorely wound us.

O God, our sins have found us out,
   And melted us with grief!
Before Thy throne ourselves we cast,
   And supplicate relief:
To Jesus' feet we now repair,
And seek, and find salvation there.

OCTOBER 13.

Return, ye backsliding children. Jer. iii 22.

WE are prone to wander, and are daily going astray ; our God may justly cast us off, but He lovingly invites us to return. He bids us take words and come to Him, and gives us every encouragement to hasten to His feet. We are CHILDREN, though backsliding ; and it is our FATHER who bids us return. Beloved, let us return to our God this morning, let us confess our sin, deplore our folly, crave His pardon, plead His word, hope in His mercy, and expect the token of reconciliation and love. What an unspeakable mercy to have such a Father ! So ready to forgive ! So willing to receive ! So desirous that we should be happy and blest ! His love is wonderful, His forbearance beyond description. See His arms extended ; hear His word inviting ; and hasten to be blest. Do not dwell on your miseries, or your wretchedness ; they are the effects of your backsliding ; but He says, " I will heal your backslidings." " Come, and let us return unto the Lord ; for He hath torn, and will heal us ; He hath smitten, and He will bind us up." His heart is grieved for us, His word invites us, and His love will make us happy.

Father of mercies, God of love !
  Oh ! hear a humble suppliant's cry
Bend from Thy lofty seat above,
  Thy throne of glorious majesty.
Oh, deign to listen to my voice,
And bid this drooping heart rejoice.

291

OCTOBER 14.

I will restore health unto thee. Jer. xxx 17.

JESUS is a skilful Physician. He heals all the falls, bruises, and dislocations of His people. He brings health to the heart. Believer, is thy heart hard, wandering, unbelieving, or wounded? Jesus can heal it, and to you He says, "COME AND BE HEALED." He restores the fainting, the dying, and the dead. He is a perfect master of every disease. His terms are "No MONEY : NO PRICE !" But He will have an absolute surrender to Him ; you must refuse all other medicines ; take all He prescribes, bitter or sweet. Touch—trust—and be happy. Jesus is JEHOVAH ROPHI, therefore look for health to no other. Lodge in His neighborhood. Consult Him daily. Lay open your whole case to Him. Never despond until His nature changes, His skill fails, or His advertisement is withdrawn from the book of God. Be grateful for healing, and show your gratitude by endeavoring to send others to Him. Recommend this gracious Physician. Trust Him, and remember His question, "Were there not ten cleansed, BUT WHERE ARE THE NINE ? They are not found that return to give glory to God, save this stranger." Beloved, come to Jesus and be healed ; and be sure you render again according to the mercy shown you.

Saviour, I wait Thy healing hand !
Diseases fly at Thy command ,
Now let Thy sovereign touch impart
Life, health, and vigor to my heart.

And He marvelled because of th ir unbelief.
Mark vi. 6.

UNBELIEF is represented as filling Jesus with surprise; and is it any wonder, especially our unbelief? Consider what God hath done to remove doubt. He hath sent His character, "God is love." He hath made a proclamation, "Behold, now is the accepted time; behold, now is the day of salvation" He hath given an invitation, "Look unto me, and be ye saved" He hath employed entreaty, "As though God did beseech you by us, we pray you in Christ's stead, be ye reconciled to God." He hath issued a command, "This is His commandment, that we should believe on the name of His Son Jesus Christ." He hath sworn an oath, "That by two immutable things in which it was impossible for God to lie, we might have strong consolation" He hath given His Son as a pledge, to assure us that "whosoever believeth on Him shall never perish, but have eternal life." He hath added the testimony of all His saints. Well then may He marvel at our unbelief. Never let us attempt to excuse it, but let us plead and pray against it, until we conquer it.

O Lord, fulfil in me Thy word,
Now let me feel Thy pardoning blood,
  Let what I ask be given;
The bar of unbelief remove,
Open the door of faith and love,
  And take me into heaven.

OCTOBER 16.

The Lord shall be thy confidence.
Prov. iii 26.

OUR happiness consists in knowing God and believing Him; if we know His true character, we can believe His precious word; and if we believe His holy word, we enjoy peace and sacred satisfaction. He presents Himself to us in His word, as able and willing to make us holy, happy, and honorable. To him we may communicate all that troubles us, from Him we may receive all that our circumstances require, with Him we may walk and enjoy peace. We may be confident in God, for He has power, love, and faithfulness; He has spoken to us, will appear for us, and will never turn away from us; but will rejoice over us to do us good, with His whole heart and with His whole soul. Let us make Him our confidence, by believing His word, frequenting His throne, and seeking His glory in all things. Are you troubled, fearful, and cast down? Acquaint now thyself with Him and be at peace, thereby shall good come unto thee. They that trust in the Lord shall be as mount Zion, which cannot be removed, but abideth forever.

Thou, Lord, on whom I still depend,
Wilt keep me faithful to the end:
I trust Thy truth, and love, and power,
Shall save me to the latest hour;
And when I lay this body down,
Bestow a bright immortal crown.

294

OCTOBER 17.

My strength is made perfect in weakness.
2 Cor. xii. 9.

THE more the believer feels his weakness, the more should he expect his Saviour to appear for and strengthen him. The strength of Jesus is imparted, enjoyed, and displayed in our sorest trials and most distressing seasons. Never was Abraham so strong, as when offering up his beloved Isaac upon the mount; never were the martyrs so courageous, as when in prison they felt their entire weakness, cried to Jesus for strength; and depending on His faithfulness and love, left all and went to the stake. Then they could exclaim, "None but Christ. None but Christ." "Farewell life, welcome the cross of Christ" Beloved, let us walk by faith, not by feeling; when we feel weakest, the strength of Jesus is nearest, and He magnifies His mercy by giving power to the faint, and increasing the strength of the weak. Let us depend on Him, for we can do all things through Christ who strengtheneth us. He is our strength, a very present help in trouble. The Lord is our strength and song, He also is become our salvation.

Saviour, on earth I covet not
That every woe should cease;
Only, if trouble be my lot,
In Thee let me have peace.
Thy grace and strength display in me,
Till I arrive at perfect day.

OCTOBER 18.

I will look unto the Lord Micah \ i. 7.

LOOKING to creatures always ends in disappointment; therefore it is forbidden by Him who loves us best, and consults our best interests at all times The prophet had been weaned from this, by many and sore trials; and now he determines to look unto the Lord. Let us imitate his example. We cannot do better than look to the Lord, as our Captain, to command; as our Master, to direct; as our Father, to provide; and as our God, to defend. His name is a strong tower, the righteous run into it and are safe. Looking to Jesus, will preserve us from a thousand snares; and prepare us to suffer as Christians and triumph as conquerors. The eyes of the Lord are always upon us; may our eyes be ever towards the Lord. Let us look to Him for all we need; from all we fear; through all that obstructs our progress; and so press on towards the mark for the prize of the high calling, which is of God in Christ Jesus. He says, "Look unto me and be ye saved." It is recorded, "They looked upon Him and were lightened, and their faces were not ashamed." Jesus is the same, yesterday, to-day, and forever.

> Lord, shine on my benighted heart,
>   With beams of mercy shine;
> And let Thy Spirit's voice impart
>   A taste of joys divine
> To Thee I look, to Thee I cry,
>   Oh, bring Thy sweet salvation nigh.

6/23

OCTOBER 19.

I will call upon Thee, for Thou wilt answer me.
Psalm lxxxvi. 7.

Such was David's purpose, and such his assurance; and we have the same warrant for confidence as he had. Our God will answer prayer. Let us inquire what is necessary, in order to the assurance that our God will answer us. We must REALLY MEAN what we say when we pray. We must pray for a definite object. We must pray in accordance with the will of God, as revealed in His promises and precepts. We must pray in submission to the will of God, as to the time when, and the means by which He will answer us. We must heartily desire what we pray for. Our motives must be pure, as that God may be glorified, sin subdued, and Jesus exalted. We must pray with importunity and perseverance. We must offer all our prayers in the name of Jesus, and expect them to be accepted and honored only for His sake. There must be no sin indulged; for if we indulge iniquity in our hearts, GOD WILL NOT HEAR OUR PRAYER. We must pray in faith, believing that God is, and that He is the rewarder of all them who diligently seek Him.

Lord, on me Thy Spirit pour,
Turn the stony heart to flesh;
And begin from this good hour,
To revive Thy work afresh:
Lord, revive me!
All my help must come from Thee.

OCTOBER 20.

Behold, thy salvation cometh.   Isaiah lxii 11.

THE Lord's people may be now sorely tried and often cast down; but the present is the worst state they will ever be in; they are hasting to the day of God, which is to them the day of deliverance. Their salvation is on the road; they will soon be freed from all disease, from which they now suffer; from all sin, under which they now groan; from all foes, of whom they are now afraid; and from all cares and troubles, with which they are now burdened. Beloved, why are you so fearful, and why do desponding thoughts arise in your hearts? Behold, your salvation cometh; behold, His reward is with Him, and His work before Him. He will free you from all that pains you, and raise you above all your fear. The time of deliverance is at hand, the year of release is near; the trumpet of the Jubilee will soon be heard; our Saviour will arrive to lead us to our Father's house, to the mansions which He hath prepared for us, and so shall we be ever with the Lord. Comfort one another with these words. "Behold, the Bridegroom cometh, go ye out to meet Him!"·

Jesus beckons from on high;
Fearless to His presence fly;
Thine the merits of His blood,
Thine the righteousness of God!
Go, His triumphs to adorn,
Made for God, to God return!

298

OCTOBER 21.

Thou shalt guide me with Thy counsel.
Psalm lxxiii. 24.

THIS supposes a knowledge of the Lord as infinitely gracious; inflexibly just; inconceivably wise; and immutably faithful: except we know Him we cannot trust Him. But here is an entire surrender to Him, to be led where He pleases; as He chooses; and by whom He will. This surrender is becoming, prudent, gainful; for godliness with such contentment is great gain. Such a surrender is the effect of faith in the Lord's promise, gracious presence, and covenant character; it exhibits expectation from the Lord. Whom the Lord guides He protects; He preserves; He supplies; and receives. He receives them now at the throne of grace, to be His charge and His care; and He will receive them at the throne of His glory, and introduce them to holiness, happiness, and honor. Beloved, have you thus surrendered? Are you daily surrendering? Can you say to your gracious God, "Thou shalt guide me with Thy counsel, and afterwards receive me to glory?" If so, happy are ye; the Spirit of glory and of God will rest upon you.

Thy word, O Lord, is light and food,
The law of truth, and source of good;
Oh, let it richly dwell within,
To keep me from the snares of sin;
And guide me still to choose my way,
That I no more may go astray.

OCTOBER 22.

After he had patiently endured he obtained the promise.
Heb vi. 15.

ABRAHAM was long tried, but he was richly rewarded. The Lord tried him by delaying to fulfil His promise; Satan tried him by temptations; men tried him by jealousy, distrust, and opposition; Hagar tried him by contemning her mistress; and Sarah tried him by her peevishness. But he patiently endured. He did not question God's veracity; nor limit His power; nor doubt His faithfulness; nor grieve His love: but he bowed to divine sovereignty; submitted to infinite wisdom; and was silent un 'er delays, waiting the Lord's time. And so, having patiently endured, he obtained the promise. God's promises cannot fail of their accomplishment. Patient waiters cannot be disappointed. Believing expectations shall be realized. Beloved, Abraham's conduct condemns a hasty spirit; reproves a murmuring one; commands a patient one; and encourages quiet submission to God's will and way. Remember, Abraham was tried; he patiently waited; he received the promise and was satisfied; imitate His example, and you will share the same blessing.

All anxious cares I fain would leave,
And learn with sweet content to live
  On what the Lord shall send;
Whate'er He sends, He sends in love,
And good or bad things blessings prove
  If blessed by this Friend.

OCTOBER 23.

We should walk in newness of life R m vi 4.

ALL who profess Christ are supposed to possess a new nature; they are brought under new obligations; and are expected to keep new objects in view. Being baptized into the death of Christ, and participating in His resurrection, they should walk as influenced by new principles; the free grace, holy truth, and divine power of God, should lead them to newness of life. They should walk by new rules, no longer following custom, or imitating the world; they should walk according to God's word, the Saviour's golden rule, and bright example. The love of God, gratitude to God, and zeal for His glory, should be the motives from which they act: while to honor God; to enjoy His presence; to exalt Jesus, to benefit others; to prove the power and purity of their principles; to justify their profession; and to evidence their faith and love; should be the ends they have constantly in view. A new life is expected from new creatures; and without it our religion is vain, and our profession a falsehood. Beloved, do we walk in newness of life?

Finish, Lord, thy new creation,
  Pure, unspotted may we be,
Let us see our whole salvation
  Perfectly secured by thee:
Changed from glory into glory,
  Till in heaven we take our place
Till we cast our crowns before thee
  Lost in wonder, love and praise.

301

I am Jesus. Acts ix. 5

IMMANUEL presents Himself this morning, and tells us He is exactly suited to us, whatever may be our circumstances or feelings; He says, "I AM JESUS." Are you seeking the Lord? He is Jesus, the gracious, powerful, tender-hearted, ready and willing SAVIOUR. Are you tried, troubled, and cast down? He is Jesus, the constant, sympathizing, present, wise, and unchangeable FRIEND. Are you a returning backslider, filled with your own ways? He is Jesus, and He says, "I will receive you; I will heal you; I will restore you; I will rejoice over you, as the shepherd over the sheep he had lost." Beloved, Jesus is the Lord our God, our all in all; our God is Jesus the Saviour, merciful, kind, and tender; this proclamation is cheering to the sinner, and delightful to the saint. Let us remember, whoever may change, whatever may change, He is Jesus still; still touched with the feeling of our infirmities; still able and willing to help us; still full of compassion and plenteous in mercy unto all them that call upon Him; still ready to forgive, waiting to be gracious, full of pity, and pledged to receive us.

When darkness veils His lovely face,
I rest on His unchanging grace;
In every high and stormy gale,
My anchor holds within the veil;
On Christ the solid Rock I stand,—
All other ground is sinking sand.

OCTOBER 25.

In everything give thanks. 1 Thess v. 18.

EVERYTHING we enjoy should be viewed as coming from the liberal hand of God; all was forfeited by sin; what we receive is of grace. The providence that supplies us, is the wisdom, benevolence, and power of God in operation for us; as expressive of His infinite love and unmerited grace. Talents to provide supplies, opportunities to obtain, and ability to enjoy, are alike from the Lord. Every mercy increases our obligation and deepens our debt. Thanksgiving is the ordinance that God hath appointed, that we may express our gratitude, and acknowledge our obligation; and our thanksgivings are acceptable and well-pleasing in His sight. Thanksgiving is never out of season, for we have always much to be thankful for. In everything we should give thanks, to that end view all things as arranged by His wisdom, dependant on His will, sanctified by His blessing, according with His promises, and flowing from His love. All our blessings come through Jesus, and all our praises must ascend through Him; for our Father only accepts what is presented in the name of His beloved Son.

Praise Him who by His word
Supplies our every need,
And gives us Christ the Lord,
Our hungry souls to feed:
Thanks be to God for every good,
Eternal thanks for Jesus' blood.

OCTOBER 26.

Am I in God's stead? Gen. xxx. 2.

ALL our mercies are to be traced up to our God, and all our miseries to ourselves. We are constantly making ourselves wretched, by departing from our God, or by putting creatures in His place. We often put persons and things in God's stead in reference to our affections, loving them inordinately; in reference to our dependence, trusting them instead of Him; in reference to our worship, idolizing them instead of adoring Him; and in reference to our expectations, expecting them to relieve, comfort, or deliver instead of Him. But insufficiency is written upon every created object. No creature can fill the place of Jehovah, take the richest—the wisest—the kindest—the nearest relative or friend, and you must exclaim, "Vanity of vanities, all is vanity." But Jehovah can fill the place of all; He can be instead of Father, Husband, Child, Wealth, Health, yea, of all things. Creatures may say, Am I in God's stead? If not, why look to me? why depend on me? why expect from me? why grieve so to part with me? Am I in God's stead? If so, He will remove me, or I shall disappoint you.

Heavenly Adam, life divine,
Change my nature into Thine:
Move and spread throughout my soul,
Actuate and fill the whole;
Now my fainting soul revive;
There forever walk and live.

304

The Lord will give grace and glory Ps. lxxxiv 11.

THIS is good news, for except the Lord give us grace we shall never be sanctified; and unless He give us glory, we shall never be glorified. All must be the free gift of free grace. If anything good was required of us to entitle us, we must sit down in despair; but now all is of divine bounty, we can hope; we need not be afraid. The Lord has given grace to thousands. He has given grace to us; and He will give more grace; grace to fit for duty, grace to support in trial, grace to sanctify the heart; and He will give glory, which is grace in perfection. Brethren, let us endeavor to believe that our God is as kind, bountiful, and beneficent as His word declares. Let us confess our sins before Him, seek grace from Him, and look to be glorified with Him. Our all is in God; our all must come from God; and all the glory should be daily given to God. Whenever we want grace, let us ask it of God; for He giveth liberally and upbraideth not. Let us approach His throne this morning, and be this our prayer, "Lord, give us more grace. Give us grace daily, grace to devote us to Thy service, and fill us with holy love."

> Blest is our lot whate'er befall;
> Who can affright, or who appal?—
> Since on Thy strength, our rock, our all,
> Jesus! we cling to Thee.

U

Son, go work to-day in my vineyard   Matt. xxi. **28.**

SOME are God's sons only by creation; the Jews were so by national adoption, believers are so by regeneration. They are born of God, and adopted by God. Our God never intended that His children should be idle; He says to every child, "SON, GO WORK" This is the command of a Father; it contains affection, it flows from authority. We are to work for His glory, for the good of others, and to lay up for ourselves treasures in heaven. Working for God is creditable—profitable—pleasant. Our work is in His vineyard, the church finds work for all. Some are employed to plant, some to weed, some to water, and some to watch. The command is "WORK TO-DAY." The present is the period. To-day, while you have light, strength, and opportunity. Remember, it is but a day, a short period at longest, but it often proves to be but a short day. Are you standing all the day idle? Go into the vineyard. Are you discouraged? Imitate her who did what she could. Look to the Lord; He will give ability—opportunity—and crown with success.

O give me, Lord, an upright heart,
  Well nurtured with a godly fear,
Which from thy precepts will not start,
  When clouds and threatening storms appear:
But onward press with even pace,
Refresh'd and fortified by grace.

306

6/28

OCTOBER 29.

The love that God hath to us. 1 John iv 16

WHO shall describe it? What tongue or pen can set it forth? It is infinite, and what can finite mortals say? It is eternal, and how can we who are but of yesterday declare it? It is the present heaven of the saints, to know and believe the love that God hath to them. None can reveal it to us, or shed it abroad in our hearts, but the Holy Ghost. He can direct our hearts into the love of God, and into the patience of Jesus Christ. He is in office to show the saints the things of God, and enable them to believe and enjoy them. Let us, beloved, daily pray that we may know and enjoy the love that God hath to us; it will be an antidote to all our miseries, a source of joy under all our sorrows. Our friends and frames may change, but the love of God is unchangeable. Our temporal prospects may be all blighted, but if we know and enjoy the love of God, we cannot be unhappy. WHO, OR WHAT SHALL SEPARATE US FROM THE LOVE OF GOD? Jesus has told us that we shall never perish, neither shall any pluck us out of His hand. The love of our God is the source of our happiness, and the cause of our safety. Oh, to know and believe the love which God hath to us! GOD IS LOVE.

What shall I do my God to love ?
  My loving God to praise ?
The length, and breadth, and height to prove,
  And depth of sovereign grace ?

Take heed, and beware of covetousness. Luke xii. 15.

This is a warning from the lips of our beloved Lord. He knows our weakness and our foes, and He cautions us against them. We want but little here below, for we shall not be here long; and we are going to the land of plenty, rest, and joy. A little with the Lord's blessing is enough. We ought not to be anxious about temporals; only let us be careful that the world is not a loser by us, and we need trouble no further. The Lord will give us enough if we are living by faith upon Him, and walking in communion with Him. We are all prone to be covetous, and it is a fearful sin. Covetousness is idolatry. It steals the heart from God, and sets it upon base and sordid things. It prevents our enjoying either temporal or spiritual blessings. A covetous man must be miserable, must be unholy, must be lost forever; well may our dear Lord say, "TAKE HEED, AND BEWARE OF COVETOUSNESS." It is sly and insinuating, it is deceitful and powerful; and if it once becomes rooted in the heart, nothing but omnipotent grace can root it out. Covet only the best gifts, spiritual blessings.

> Great things we are not here to crave;
> But if we food and raiment have,
>   Should learn to be therewith content:
> Into the world we nothing brought,
> Nor can we carry from it aught;
>   Then walk the way your Master went

Call upon me in the day of trouble. Psalm l. 15.

KEEP the straight path of duty, and if troubles come, or difficulties arise, thy God invites thee to call upon Him. He will come to thy help, and bring all His boundless resources with Him. He is always within call. His ear is never heavy, that it cannot hear; His arm is not shortened, that it cannot reach or save. He can make thy greatest troubles prove thy choicest blessings; He can give thee cause to bless Him through eternity, for thy sorest trials. Oh, trust Him, and fear not! Run not to creatures; but, "Arise and call upon thy God." Look not to others, until thou hast proved that He cannot, or will not help; and that will never be. His heart is too kind, His word is too faithful. Art thou in trouble this morning? If so, you have a SPECIAL invitation from thy God to pay Him a visit, and lay thy whole case before Him; expecting His sympathy, interference, and blessing; He says, "CALL UPON ME IN THE TIME OF TROUBLE. I WILL DELIVER THEE, AND THOU SHALT GLORIFY ME." He is faithful who hath promised. Oh, trust Him, for so you honor Him; expect from Him, and you cannot be disappointed. Wait for Him, and you shall not be ashamed.

Dear refuge of my weary soul,
 On Thee, when sorrows rise,
On Thee, when waves of trouble roll,
 My fainting hope relies.

NOVEMBER 1.

O Thou Preserver of men. Job vii 20.

WE have neither wisdom nor strength to pre‑
serve ourselves; we are daily liable to fall; and
unless God preserve us we certainly shall.
Our hearts are so deceitful, our corruptions are
so strong, and Satan is so vigilant, that we
need look to God as our PRESERVER every hour,
and call upon Him to uphold us every moment.
He can preserve, He doth preserve; but only in
the way of obedience. Except we are watchful,
prayerful, and walking humbly with Him, we
have no security; we may fall into the grossest
sins, and commit the greatest crimes. O be‑
liever, never think thyself safe, but as thou art
leaning on Jesus, calling upon thy heavenly
Father, and cultivating communion with the
Holy Ghost! Indeed thou art in danger;
Satan, the world, and thy corruptions are all
leagued against thee; nothing but omnipotent
grace can keep thee. Cease from man, trust
not thy own heart; but keep close to thy good
Shepherd. He is able to keep you from falling,
and to present you faultless before the presence
of His glory, with exceeding joy.

> Every foe must fly before Him,
> Earth and hell shall feel His power;
> Heaven and earth with joy adore Him.
> Hail the long expected hour:
> Hallelujah!
> Jesus has almighty power.

NOVEMBER 2.

They were tempted. Heb xi 37.

THAT is, they were tried; and the design of
their enemies by these trials was, to draw or
drive them from the Lord. Their trials were
of the most cruel kind, but they found that as
their day, so was their strength. Brethren, we
shall be tempted, Satan is not dead, no, nor
yet asleep; the world is not reconciled to godliness; nor are we free from indwelling sin. It
is not our sin to be tempted—this is our trial;
but it is our sin if we yield. God has promised
strength, wisdom, and grace; and we should
seek these, that we may be able to withstand,
and so overcome every trial. We may expect
to be tempted daily, for Satan goeth about;
and if at any moment we are off our guard, that
is the time he is most likely to beset us. Let
us keep close to Jesus the great Shepherd of
the sheep; let us keep our eye on our Father's
house, and let us aim in all things at God's
glory, and temptation shall not harm us.
" Blessed is the man that endureth temptation;
for when he is tried, he shall receive the crown
of life, which the Lord hath promised to them
that love Him." If the enemy come in like a
flood, we may still sing—

> His oath, His covenant, and blood,
> Support me in the sinking flood,
> When all around my soul gives way,
> Jesus is all my hope and stay.
> On Christ the solid Rock I stand,—
> All other ground is sinking sand.

NOVEMBER 3.

What would ye that I should do for you? Mark x 36.

So spake Jesus to the sons of Zebedee, and so He speaks to us. Beloved, have you your petition ready this morning? Jesus is at the pardon office; He is on His throne of grace; He is in a loving temper; He is ready to' bless. He says, "Ask, what shall I give thee?" O Jesus! give me sanctifying grace. Subdue my corruptions Purify my heart. Make me a vessel of honor, meet for Thy use Why should sin be allowed to work so powerfully? Why should Satan be permitted to have so much power over me? Why should the world attract and lead me astray? Lord, I would that thou shouldest make me holy, and make me useful; fill me with Thy Holy Spirit; write Thy word on my heart, and enable me to write out Thy precepts in my life. O Saviour! I would that thou shouldest make me like Thyself; as meek, as humble, as diligent, as disinterested, as useful to God and man. May I be holy, harmless, undefiled, and separate from sinners. Oh, make me shine, to the honor and glory of Thy free and sovereign grace.

Holy Ghost, no more delay;
Come, and in Thy temple stay;
Now Thine inward witness bear,
Strong, and permanent, and clear
Source of life, Thyself impart,
Rise eternal in my heart!

312

NOVEMBER 4.

They limited the Holy One of Israel. Ps lxxviii 41.

This was Israel's sin, and has it not often been ours? Our God is the Holy One, and will do what is most for His glory; He is the Holy One of Israel, and will therefore consult His people's welfare. We must not limit His wisdom, for it is infinite; we must not limit His power, for it is omnipotent; we must not limit His mercy, for it is as high as heaven and deep as hell; we must not limit Him to time, for He will display His sovereignty. He will not be tied to walk by our rules; or be bound to keep our time; but He will perform His word, honor our faith, and reward them that diligently seek Him. However tried, beware of limiting the Holy One of Israel; say not " It is too difficult, or it is too far gone;" this was the fault of Martha and Mary, but Jesus convinced them they were wrong. Rather say with Jonathan, " It may be that the Lord will work for us; for there is no restraint to the Lord to save by many or by few;" Jonathan honored the Lord by trusting Him, and the Lord honored Jonathan by giving him a victory over the enemies of Israel. Exercise unlimited confidence in God, for He will fulfil every promise He has made.

Wide as the world is His command,
Vast as eternity His love;
Firm as a rock His truth shall stand,
When rolling years shall cease to move.

NOVEMBER 5.

Be ye also enlarged. 2 Cor. vi. 13

CONTRACTION is a great evil, enlargement is **a** great blessing. We need to be enlarged in our knowledge—love—hope—liberality—faith—and every grace. Our God disapproves of contraction. The Apostles set a different example. Provision is made in the covenant to gratify enlarged desires. The promises warrant enlarged expectations. Jesus bids us ask largely. The gospel calls for enlargement in prayer—benevolence—pity—and compassion—and in our efforts for God's glory. Let us beware of narrow views or feelings, for the heart of God is large; the love of Christ is large; the provision of mercy is large; the gospel commission is large; and the mansions of glory are large. We are not straitened in God, nor in His gospel, but we are straitened in our own bowels. O Jesus, enlarge our narrow hearts; expand our contracted souls! Fill us with all joy and peace in believing, that we may abound in hope, by the power of the Holy Ghost. May we be full of goodness, able also to admonish one another. Oh, to be filled with the Holy Ghost and with power!

With holy fear, and reverent love,
  I long to lie beneath Thy throne
I long in Thee to live and move,
  And stay myself on Thee alone:
Teach me to lean upon Thy breast,
To find in Thee the promised rest.

Thou art no more a servant, but a son. GaL iv. 7.

It would have been a great mercy if God had made us His servants, after we had proved His enemies; but He has adopted us as His sons, and taken us to the bosom of His love. He is now our Father, and wishes us to call Him so; we are His children, and He wishes us to walk and act as such. We are not mere servants, therefore we should not be servile; we are sons, therefore we should love, obey, and delight in God as our Father. " Beloved, *now* are we the sons of God." We are delivered from bondage, introduced into favor, have the promise of eternal life, and should rejoice with joy unspeakable, and full of glory. It was free grace which adopted us; the Holy Spirit, by the word, begat us to a lively hope; and the gospel proclaims our privileges, and invites us to enjoy them. Let us to-day think, " I am a son of God My Father is holy, His children are holy, His word is holy, He loves holiness, and commands me to be holy; I will therefore lift up my heart to Him; seek grace from Hrn; and in all things aim to glorify Him."

> Pronounce me, gracious God ! Thy son,
>   Own me an heir divine :
> I'll pity princes on the throne,
>   When I can call Thee mine :
> Sceptres and crowns unenvied rise,
> And lose their lustre in mine eyes.

NOVEMBER 7.

Go forward. Exodus xiv 15.

BELOVED, there is no standing still in religion; we are either going forward or going back. 'Our Captain's command is, "GO FORWARD." This is our direction. Go forward in the Lord's way; in the Lord's work; to the Lord's kingdom. The command contains great encouragement. Go forward, remembering the Lord's wisdom; trusting in the Lord's power; and believing in the Lord's love Go forward in union with the Lord's people; with zeal for His glory; until summoned into your Master's presence. Go forward, notwithstanding difficulties, fears, and discouragements Go forward, because God has bidden you; He has promised to go with you; He will crown your journey's end. Let us imitate ardent and holy Paul, who said, "Not as though I had already attained, either were already perfect; but I follow after, if that I may apprehend that for which I am also apprehended of Christ Jesus." Let us look for, and hasten to the coming of the day of God. There is nothing behind us worth a thought, if compared with what is set before us by the gospel. .

Much in sorrow, oft in woe,
Onward, Christian, onward go ;
Shrink not, fear not, dare not yield,
Never quit the battle-field .
Forward press and win the prize,
Then to endless glory rise.

NOVEMBER 8.

As having nothing, and yet possessing all things
2 Cor. vi. 10.

THE Lord's family are generally poor ; men may look at them as having nothing valuable, important, or calculated to make them happy ; but in reality they possess all things, because God is theirs Our God has said, " I am their inheritance," and we say, " Thou art my portion, O Lord." His eternity is the date of our happiness—His unchangeableness, the rock of our rest—His omnipotence, our constant guard—His faithfulness, our daily security—His mercies, our overflowing store—His omniscience, our careful overseer—His wisdom, our judicious counsellor—His justice, our stern avenger—His omnipresence, our sweet company—His holiness, the fountain from which we receive sanctifying grace—His all-sufficiency, the lot of our inheritance—and His infinity, the extent of our glorious portion. This is the blessedness of the people of the Lord ; they have God for their Lord, and all His perfections engaged to make them blessed. O love the Lord ! Live upon the Lord ! Glorify God in the day of visitation ! Make Him your portion and everlasting all !

To us the privilege is given
To be the sons and heirs of heaven ;
Sons of the God who reigns on high,
And heirs of joys beyond the sky :
Oh, may our conduct ever prove
Our filial piety and love

NOVEMBER 9.

O God, Thou hast taught me from my youth
Psalm lxxi. 17.

THE Psalmist was called early, and he ascribes it to divine teaching. None but God can teach us experimentally; and the lessons He teaches are always useful and important He teaches all His scholars to know themselves—their depravity, poverty, and slavery. He teaches them His law—its purity, claims and penalty He teaches them His gospel—its fulness, freeness and suitability. He teaches them to know Himself: as a reconciled God, as their Father and faithful Friend His teaching is accompanied with power and authority. Are we taught of God? We may know divine teaching by its effects; it always produces humility, they sit at His feet; dependence upon Him; abhorrence of sin; love to God as a teacher; obedience to the lessons taught; thirst for further attainments; and brings us daily to Jesus Let us earnestly seek divine teaching; it preserves from dangers, sorrows, and snares; and if suitably improved, it brings great glory to God, and honor to the cause of religion. Our God says, "I WILL TEACH THEE." Lord, teach me, and make me entirely Thine!

Oh, let my heart be wholly Thine,
Thy property alone ;
No longer let me think it mine,
Or call myself my own.

NOVEMBER 10.

Behold the Lamb of God. John i 3C.

SIN requires a sacrifice, and the sacrifice must be in proportion to the offence, and the dignity of the offended; such a sacrifice could not be found, but God condescended to provide one, which was no less a person than His only-begotten Son. This Lamb was provided to expiate and remove sin; to honor the divine government, and reconcile us to God Let us daily direct our attention to the Lamb of God, who verily was fore-ordained before the foundation of the world, but was manifested in these last times for us. He is set forth to be a propitiation through faith in His blood, and to be the daily object of our faith, desire, and affection. Provided by God, He presented to God an infinite atonement; and we have redemption through His blood, even the forgiveness of our sins. The Lamb is to be presented daily to God by us, in our prayers and praises; and all our expectations are to be founded upon what He is, what He has done, and what He is doing now before the throne of God Take off your attention from all other subjects, and 'BEHOLD THE LAMB OF GOD."

Cast thy guilty soul on Him,
Find Him mighty to redeem,
At His feet thy burden lay,
Look thy doubts and fears away;
Now by faith the Son embrace,
Plead His promise, trust His grace.

319

NOVEMBER 11.

I say unto all, Watch. Mark xiii 37.

THE hour of death is uncertain, and the second coming of Jesus is equally so ; therefore we are commanded to be always ready, and to be on the WATCH. His coming is the grand object of our hope, and should be our daily desire and prayer. It will be awfully grand. We are deeply interested in it. It is certain, necessary, and will be sudden. We know not the day—month—or year. God has purposely concealed it, in wisdom, in mercy, and for our good. He commands us to AWAKE, and keep awake. To be at our post, and employed in our calling. In order to our watching we must be daily believing Jesus will come; thinking and praying to be found ready. We should watch the signs of the times; the workings of our own hearts; and over our daily conduct. We should walk as we wish death or Jesus to find us; and transact every business as though Jesus was at the door. Would you, beloved, wish to be found idle—contentious—at enmity—or murmuring—or indulging in any sin? If not, watch against these things; put off the old man, and put on the new.

Behold, the awful day comes on,
When Jesus on His righteous throne
  Shall in the clouds appear
With solemn pomp shall bow the sky,
And in the twinkling of an eye,
  Arraign us at His bar.

NOVEMBER 12.

The Lord is my helper   Heb xiii. 6.

THIS is a very encouraging view of the **Most High** God. He is the helper of His people, and therefore it is that they are more than conquerors Beloved, let us remember this, when called to perform self-denying duties, or to pass through great and sore troubles. We can do nothing right, apart from God ; but we can do all things through Christ who strengtheneth us. He will help us in every distress, bring us out of every trouble, lead us through the world with honor, and land us safe on the shores of the heavenly Canaan ; all this is promised to every one that trusts in Him, waits for Him, walks with Him, and aims habitually to glorify Him. What sweet encouragement is this ; we have an OM-NIPOTENT HELPER, God in the person of His Son is our DELIVERER : let us come up out of the wilderness leaning on our Beloved. Let us not grieve His love, or dishonor His grace. Let us keep a clear conscience, maintain a holy walk, exercise simple faith on our covenant God, and then we may boldly say, " THE LORD IS MY HELPER, I will not fear what man can do unto me."

To look to Jesus as He rose,
Confirms my faith, disarms my foes ;
Exalted on His glorious throne,
I see Him make my cause His own;
Then all my anxious cares subside,
For Jesus lives, and will provide

X

Speak evil of no man. Titus iii. 2.

SPEAK of no man from an unholy motive, or with a design to injure him : this is decidedly wrong. We are commanded by our beloved Saviour, to love our enemies ; to do good to them that hate us and despitefully use us ; to pray for them and seek their salvation. If we speak evil of them we dishonor God, bring guilt upon our consciences, grieve the Spirit, and spoil our peace of mind. If we can indulge in detraction without feeling guilty and distressed, our consciences must be blinded, and our hearts hardened through the deceitfulness of sin. Our tongues are not our own, they are bought with a price, and should be employed in the service of their proper owner. Never indulge yourselves in thinking evil of another, or in feelings of jealousy, envy, revenge, bitterness, anger, or malice ; for these are earthly, sensual, and devilish. How unlovely it is to hear one professor speaking evil of another ; the hearer speaketh evil of the minister ; the rich speaking contemptuously of the poor, the mistress of servants ; much more ministers of ministers Speak not evil one of another, brethren.

Whene'er the angry passions rise,
And tempt our thoughts and tongues to strife,
To Jesus let us turn our eyes,
   ht pattern of the Christian life !
   mild ! how ready to forgive !
   hese the rules by which we live !

NOVEMBER 14.

Consider how great things the Lord hath done for you.
1 Samuel xii. 24.

WE are very apt to dwell upon our miseries, and forget our mercies. If we are injured by man, how seldom we forget it; but if we are favored by God, how little attention we pay to it. Let us this morning consider how great things the Lord hath done for us. He gave His Son to be our ransom. He has given His Spirit to be our guide, and His word to be our directory. He called us by grace, when we were posting to perdition; wrought a change in our hearts, when we were enmity against Him; and pardoned our sins, when we expected to suffer His fiercest displeasure. He has given us faith to trust Him; promises to plead with Him; and proofs of His faithful regard, without number. He hath supplied us through all our journey, corrected our mistakes, conquered our foes, and no good thing hath He withheld from us. Let us consider these things, and praise Him for the past, and trust Him for the future. He that is our God, is the God of Salvation; He hath done great things for us, and He will do greater things, that we may glorify Him forever. My soul, consider thy obligations, and give glory to thy God.

Oh, may I ne'er forget
The mercy of my God;
Nor ever want a tongue to spread
His loudest praise abroad.

323

He will be very gracious. Isaiah xxx 19.

WE are often very miserable, always very un-worthy; but the Lord is very merciful, and He will be very gracious. He will glorify His grace before angels, men, and devils, in His exceeding kindness toward us; therefore if a sense of our deep depravity and entire unworthiness discourage us, let us appeal to the graciousness of our God, and rely on that. "He will be very gracious unto us at the voice of our cry; when He shall hear it, He will answer." He has said that when, forsaking our evil courses, we return unto Him, He will prove Himself gracious. "Then shalt thou call, and the Lord shall answer; thou shalt cry, and He shall say, Here I am." Yea, He will prove Himself very gracious, for He says, "Before they call I will answer; and while they are yet speaking I will hear." Oh, the infinite grace of a gracious God! Lord, keep it uppermost in our minds, and before our eyes continually; let it be our encouragement under all the discoveries of depravity we make, and our comfort under all the trials we endure. Let us endeavor to give our God credit for being "VERY GRACIOUS."

What from Christ my soul shall sever,
  Bound by everlasting bands?
Once in Him, in Him forever,
  Thus the word of promise stands:
    None shall pluck me
    From the strength of Israel's hands.

718

NOVEMBER 16.

Arise ye, and depart, for this is not your rest. Mich. ii. 10.

THERE is no permanent rest for the believer on earth; here briers and thorns will be with him; and a voice is daily sounding in his ears, "ARISE YE, AND DEPART." Here you are not to loll at ease, or to idle on your journey; here you are not to expect to find satisfaction, for it is an enemy's land, and you are only passing through it to your heavenly home. If your march is quick and your conduct scriptural, be not surprised if the dogs bark at you; they know you not, nor did they know your Master. He was pursued, annoyed, and at last put to death by them; and in agony of soul He cried out, "Dogs have compassed me; the assembly of the wicked have inclosed me; they have pierced my hands and my feet." Lay not up for yourselves treasures upon earth, where moth and rust doth corrupt, and where thieves break through and steal; but set your affections on things above, where Christ sitteth at the right hand of God. Use the world, but do not abuse it; pass through it, but never seek a home in it; remember it is peopled by the enemies of your God.

When snares and dangers line my way,
Jesus is all my strength and stay;
Cheerful I'll walk the desert through,
Nor fear what earth or hell can do:
Jesus will ease my troubled breast,
And shortly bring my soul to rest.

325

NOVEMBER 17.

Be ye reconciled to God. 2 Cor. v. 20

Is there anything but love between God and your souls? Theie ought not to be. God hates nothing but sin. He is offended with nothing but sin. This we profess to hate and forsake. We were once enemies, but Jesus died to reconcile us to God. We are now professedly friends, but do we act towards God, and speak of God, as though we were His friends? Are we offended at anything in God, or at anything done by God? Why should we be? His nature is love. His ways are all infinitely wise. His tender mercy is over all His works. He desires that we should be on the best terms with Him. How wonderful! He offers a pardon for all our sins, grace to sanctify our natures, and heaven to receive our souls! HE BESEECHES US TO BE RECONCILED. As though His tender love could not rest, as though He could not be happy, or content, unless we are friends with Him. Beloved, are you living or walking at a distance from God? Is there any shyness between God and your soul? God beseeches you by me, and I pray you in Christ's stead, " Be ye reconciled to God."

Sprinkled now with blood the throne,
Why beneath thy burdens groan?
See the curse on Jesus laid ;
Justice owns the ransom paid :
Bow the knee, and kiss the Son,
COME AND WELCOME, SINNER, COME!

NOVEMBER 18.

I will be as the dew unto Israel. Hos. xiv. 5.

OUR hearts by nature are like the dry, dead, and barren earth; there would be neither life, beauty, nor fruit, but for the grace of God. And even after regeneration, we are as much dependant upon God, as the earth in the east is dependant upon the dew. If there be no dew, there will be no fruit, and if there be no grace, there will be no real religion. But our God has said, "I WILL BE AS THE DEW UNTO ISRAEL." What the dew is to the earth, God will be unto His people. Does the dew cool and refresh the earth? So will the Lord cool and refresh our souls with the sense of His love and the tokens of His favor. Does the dew soften and break the clods of the valley? So will our God soften and dissolve our hard and impenitent hearts. Does the dew prepare the ground for the seed, and cause the same to vegetate and grow? So will our God prepare our hearts to receive the word, and cause it to grow and bring forth fruit. Does the dew fall insensibly, and in the evening, when most needed? So will our God come unto us, when we most need His quickening and fructifying operations.

Come, Holy Ghost, as heavenly dew,
　My parched soul revive;
The former mercies now renew,
　Quicken and bid me live·
Thy fertilizing power impart,
And sanctify my barren heart.

NOVEMBER 19.

It is good for us to be here.   Matt. xvii. 4.

So said Peter when on the mount with Jesus.
and so we have said when enjoying His presence
and His love. It is good to live and walk in
communion with God. It is good to be num
bered with God's people, and to occupy a place
in His church. It is good to be in the present
world, because we have an opportunity of bearing witness for Jesus, and against its course
we have talents to use, and opportunities for
usefulness, whereby we can glorify God. Is
Jesus honored by our patient suffering? Then
when on the bed of affliction, we should say
"Lord, it is good to be here." Is our God
glorified by our industry, forbearance, and tes
timony to the power and grace of Jesus? Then
when in our business, or in company with
those whom we are trying to benefit, we may
exclaim, "Lord, it is good to be here!" Yes
Christian, it is good to be anywhere, and any
thing, so that thy Jesus may be glorified, and
the end of thy creation, redemption, and sanc
tification, obtained. Oh, to aim always to hono
God, and then we may everywhere say, "Lord
IT IS GOOD TO BE HERE!"

> Great Comforter, descend
> In gentle breathings down;
> Preserve me to the end,
> That no man take my crown:
> My guardian still vouchsafe to be,
> Nor suffer me to go from Thee.

NOVEMBER 20.

Brethren, the time is short. 1 Cor. vii 29.

THEN our sufferings must be short, for they are bounded by time, and are confined to the present world. Consoling consideration this. Then our opportunities to glorify our God below, must be short; therefore we ought to seize them and improve them with all our might. Then the triumphing of the wicked is short, and the contradiction of sinners against us will soon be ended; let us therefore be patient, and prayerful, and diligent; for our redemption draweth nigh. The time is short; then we shall soon see our Jesus, enjoy the company of our sanctified brethren, and be forever with the Lord. The time is short, but eternity is long; let us therefore be laying up for ourselves treasures in heaven, where neither moth nor rust doth corrupt; and let us be daily preparing for our last remove. The time is short, it flies away, our dying day will soon be here; it remaineth therefore, that both they that have wives be as though they had none; and they that weep, as though they wept not; and they that rejoice, as though they rejoiced not; and they that buy, as though they possessed not.

Oh, may my soul maintain her ground,
From faith to faith go on!
At the last day in Christ be found,
And form the circles that surround
His everlasting throne.

NOVEMBER 21.

My peace I give unto you. John xiv. 27.

PEACE is an invaluable blessing, it is the gift of Jesus. None but believers know the sweetness of the peace He bestows. He made it by shedding His blood. He proclaims it in the everlasting gospel. He bestows it upon us when we believe, and it is enjoyed in the heart under the influence of the Holy Spirit. It is peace with God. A peaceful conscience. The beginning of heaven in the soul. He gives it often when in the midst of trouble; and it makes every burden light, every trouble less, and the sinner happy in every situation. O Jesus! give us thy peace this morning! Let it reign and rule in our hearts this day. Believer, look only to Jesus for peace, for "HE IS OUR PEACE." Believe His word, receive His atonement, trust in His perfect work, aim to show forth His praise, and peace which passeth all understanding shall fill your mind. Let it be your daily prayer, that you may enjoy this peace in death; for then you will die happy, honorably, and safely. Seek it as a gift of grace, and you shall enjoy it to the honor of God.

Close to my Saviour's bloody tree,
My soul untired shall ever cleave,
Both scourged and crucified for me,
With Christ resolved to die and live;
My prayer, my grand ambition this,
Living and dying to be His.

330

I will correct you in measure. Jer. xxx 11.

Sin procures correction, and love sends it. Every child is chastened, because every child sins. But though we are corrected for sin, yet not according to the desert of sin. Our Father chastens us in measure, not in wrath, but in love; not to destroy, but to save us. There is no wrath in His heart, for He has sworn that He will not be wroth with us; yet He will visit our sins with the rod, and our iniquities with stripes. He is reconciled to our persons, but not to our follies; therefore He says, " As many as I love, I rebuke and chasten; be zealous therefore and repent." Let us not despise His chastening, nor faint when we are rebuked of Him; for it is the common lot of all His children, and if it drives us to Him, and humbles us at His feet, it is evidently sent in love. It is a painful blessing; a mercy sent to purify and cleanse us. If we sin and are not chastened, our sonship is questionable; for what son is he whom his father chasteneth not? But if we are chastened, God dealeth with us as with sons; and our sufferings are the fulfilment of His promise.

> Though ten thousand ills beset thee,
> From without and from within,
> Jesus saith, He'll ne'er forget thee,
> But will save from hell and sin :
> He is faithful
> To perform His precious word.

NOVEMBER 23.

Open thy mouth wide, and I will fill it   Psalm lxxxi. 10 ✓

THE word of God affords all possible encouragement to earnest, fervent prayer; men ought
always to pray, and not to faint.   Believers should ask all they want of God as their
heavenly Father; they should ask of Him
because He has bidden them, and expect to
receive because He is faithful.   Are our wants
many this morning?   Our God bids us open
our mouths wide, and promises to fill them.
We should ask largely, for God considers Himself honored when we ask for much, and expect
much.   He rejoices over us to do us good.   He
looks upon us as His dear children, and pledges
Himself to give all that we want, or can use to
His glory.   Let us then ask for a supply of
every want; let us continue to plead His
largest promises; and let us continue to plead
in the name of Jesus until we receive.   Our
God heareth prayer: and if we, being evil,
know how to give good things unto our children, much more will our heavenly Father give
good things unto them that ask Him   Let us
therefore come boldly unto a throne of grace,
that we may obtain mercy and find grace

Thou art coming to a King,
Large petitions with thee bring ;
For His grace and power are such,
None can ever ask too much ·
He Himself has bid thee pray,
Therefore will not say thee nay.

7/12

NOVEMBER 24.

I will see you again   John xvi. 22.

THE presence of Jesus is the happiness of His people; when He is present manifesting His love, we are filled with joy and peace; but when He hides His face we are troubled. Nor is it any wonder, for then generally, Satan comes in with his temptations; our corruptions rise and trouble us; and for a time everything seems to be against us. But if Jesus hath once visited, He will come again; and He will manifest Himself unto us as He doth not unto the world. In every season of desertion and darkness, let us plead this precious promise given as by our adorable Lord; He sympathizes with us, and says, "Ye now therefore have sorrow; but I WILL SEE YOU AGAIN, and your heart shall rejoice, and your joy no man taketh from you." Precious Lord Jesus, let us this day enjoy Thy presence and Thy love; come and visit us, or rather, come and take up thy abode with us, to leave us no more forever. Our souls thirst for Thee; we long to enjoy Thy love, as we have done in days that are gone by. Oh, manifest Thyself unto us this day, and unite us closer than ever unto Thyself!

> Then let us sit beneath His cross,
>   And gladly catch the healing stream;
> All things for Him account but dross,
>   And give up all our hearts to Him;
> Of nothing think or speak beside;
> My Lord, my love, is crucified.

I trust in Thy word   Psalm cxix. 42.

I⟶ is unsafe and improper to trust our feelings or fancies; to listen to suggestions, or judge by appearances; the Christian's guide is God's word, and this should be the object of His trust. If we cannot take God's word and depend upon it, what can we trust? It is true; on all necessary points plain; it has been tried and always found faithful. We should believe it, rely on it, plead it, expect its fulfilment, and comfort ourselves with it; especially when surrounded with difficulties, when in darkness or filled with forebodings, because God delays and our prayers are not answered. Trusting in God's faithful word will bring peace to the mind, experience to the soul, and deliverance in every time of trouble: if we trust God's word we may be confident, for our supply is certain. Trusting a naked promise is difficult, but it is attainable, and truly desirable. The promise is God's bond, and is intended to set our minds at rest; if we trust it calmly and implicitly, we shall enjoy peace, quietness, and confidence. Trusting God's word, we need fear no foe, or dread any trouble; all is safe, and safe forever.

In Thee, O Lord, I put my trust;
Mighty, and merciful, and just,
  Thy faithful word I prove:
Thou canst, Thou wilt my helper be;
My confidence is all in Thee,
  The faithful God of love.

334

NOVEMBER 26.

An heir of God, through Christ. Gal iv 7.

By nature we are children of wrath; but union to Jesus exalts us to the highest pitch of honor and happiness. All our mercies flow through Jesus; we must ever look to Him as the medium of access to God, and of union with God. If we are one with Jesus, we are heirs of God; to us He has willed all the riches of grace, and all the riches of glory. The testament is made and sealed, and all is secured to us by the oath of God, and the blood of our dear Saviour. Oh, what an honor! To be the heirs of God! To possess and enjoy throughout eternity all that God can impart! Unutterable grace! We have enough secured to us while on earth; and we shall be put into full possession at the resurrection. Let us then ascertain beyond a doubt, that we are the sons of God; that we have received the spirit of adoption; that we are united to Jesus; and daily walk with God. Let us live expecting the day when we shall be put in possession, and preparing for that glorious event. Let us walk worthy of the vocation wherewith we are called, with all lowliness and meekness, watching unto prayer.

Let earth no more my heart divide
With Christ may I be crucified;
  To Thee with my whole soul aspire;
Dead to the world and all its toys,
To idle pomp, and fading joys,
  Be Thou alone my one desire!

I am the Good Shepherd   John x 11.

BELOVED, are you in the fold of Jesus? Are you numbered with His sheep? Are you feeding and resting among them? Jesus presents Himself to us this morning, in a very lovely character; He says, "I AM THE GOOD SHEPHERD." There is no other shepherd so good or so great as He. He has the tenderest affection for His flock. He affords them His powerful protection. He finds them plenty and suitable provision. He gave His life to redeem them. He sends His Spirit to sanctify them. He is preparing a place in heaven to receive them. He will eternally dwell among them and bless them. Oh, how great is his goodness! He is indeed abundant in goodness and truth. He says, "My sheep hear my voice, and I know them, and they follow me; and I give unto them eternal life; and they shall never perish, neither shall any pluck them out of my hand. My Father, which gave them me, is greater than all; and no one is able to pluck them out of my Father's hand. I and my Father are one." What glorious security! What honor is conferred on the flock of Jesus! GOOD SHEPHERD, keep us near Thyself. Never let us wander, no, not for a moment; but may we be always delighted with Thy love.

> The least, the feeblest of the sheep,
>   To Him the Father gave,
> Kind is His heart the charge to keep,
>   And strong His arm to save.

NOVEMBER 28.

The day shall declare it. 1 Cor. iii. 13.

THE day referred to is the day when the Lord Jesus shall be revealed from heaven in flaming fire, when the dead shall be raised, and the judgment commence. Oh, what a day will that be! Then every covering shall be removed, and every secret exposed. It will be a revealing day—a convincing day—a confirming day —a condemning day—a justifying day. Then our motives will all be discovered, and our intentions laid bare. Hypocrisy will be condemned, and deception punished. O beloved, let us live as having that day before us; let us act as though persuaded that then all will be discovered. Are we sincere?—the day will declare it. Are we aiming at God's glory, or self-exaltation?—the day will declare it. Are we conducting our business on Christian, or worldly principles?—the day will declare it. Are we honest and humble?—the day will declare it. Is our profession from principle, from faith in, and love to Jesus?—the day will declare it. Oh that that day may declare that we are humble, holy, watchful, diligent disciples of the Lord Jesus!

Before me place in dread array
The pomp of that tremendous day,
　When Thou with clouds shalt come
To judge the nations at Thy bar;
And tell me, Lord, shall I be there,
　To meet a joyful doom !

NOVEMBER 29.

I will mention the loving kindnesses of the Lord.
Isaiah lxiii 7

WHAT subject so suited as this to engage the thoughts, fill the memory, and flow from the lips of the Lord's people ? Let us mention the provision made for all His poor, for all their wants; the promises given to all His people, comprehending all their desires; the prayers answered in all times of trial, granting relief and defence Let us mention the loving-kindness of the Lord to those who are seeking Him, it will encourage them; to those who are complaining, it may silence them; to those who are tempted, it will support them; to those who have backslidden, it will convince, and perhaps restore them Let us speak of His kindness to ourselves, to check murmuring, produce gratitude, and raise hope Let us mention the loving-kindness of the Lord, at the Lord's throne, in pleading and intercession : in prayer and expostulation; in praise and thanksgiving. Let us often speak one to another, and let this be our daily subject, " THE LOVING-KINDNESSES OF THE LORD." This will comfort, strengthen, and sanctify our minds; it will bring us peace.

We'll speak of all He did, and said,
And suffer'd for us here below;
The path He mark'd for us to tread,
And what He's doing for us now;
Discarding every worldly theme,
Our conversation fill'd with Him.

7/15/24

NOVEMBER 30.

Return unto thy rest, O my soul. Ps. cxvi. 7.

THERE is no rest for the Christian but at the feet of Jesus; when we live near to Him, and exercise our faith upon Him, we are at rest. Conscience is silent, or commends us. The law has nothing to say against us. The world has but little influence over us. Satan is weak, and cannot overcome us. But if we wander we become weak, we lose our courage, and darkness, perplexity, and trouble, frequently fill our minds. But we MAY return, for Jesus is still inviting us; we MUST return, or we cannot enjoy peace; let us therefore return unto our rest this morning. O Jesus! we come to Thee! Receive Thy wandering sheep, restore unto us the joy of thy salvation, and let us find rest at Thy cross. Oh, to rest on Thy faithful word, with Thy faithful people. To rest from slavish fear, worldly care, and distressing anxiety; to rest in Thy boundless love, satisfied with the dispensations of Thy special providence. Return, return, my soul, from all thy wanderings, and find thy rest in Jesus; thy faithful Friend and Saviour. Sweet assurance, "He will receive us graciously."

Indulge me, Lord, in that repose,
Which only he who loves Thee knows:
Lodged in Thine arms I fear no more
The tempest's howl, the billow's roar:
Those storms must shake th' Almighty's seat,
Which violate the saints' retreat.

DECEMBER 1.

OUR God is the author of all good, the only object of religious worship and fear, the infinite, all-controlling Being. He can do all things, and do all things with ease—swiftness—certainty—and precision. He is on the throne,—His reign is merciful—just—glorious. He reigns universally over every empire—kingdom—state—parish—person—thing. Everything that takes place is either appointed or permitted by Him. Everything is overruled; for nothing escapes His notice—frustrates His purpose—or disorganizes His plan. All things are tributary, and bring honor to His name. Does the Lord God Omnipotent reign?—then let us fear to offend Him; aim to please Him well in all things; trust in and rely on Him; call upon and prove Him; live in the daily remembrance of His reign; this will conquer fear—prevent sins—strengthen faith—nourish all the graces of the Spirit—and inspirit us in our obedience. If the Lord God Omnipotent reigneth, be sure He will take care of His children. He will manage all their affairs. He will secure their best interests.

Behold the King of Zion rise
To endless glory in the skies!
Hail, Fount of blessings!—placed in Thee,
Our life, our strength, our all, we see.
While in thy God thy joys endure,
In Thee our blessings rest secure.

DECEMBER 2.

From this day will I bless you. Hag. ii. 19.

WHAT day? The day we begin to seek the Lord. The day we decide to be on the Lord's side. The day we publicly and honestly profess Him. The day we heartily engage in His work. The day we return from backsliding, and repent of our sin before Him. The day we identify ourselves with His people in heart and soul. What does the Lord promise? To bless us; He will bless our temporal mercies; He will bless our trials; He will bless our labors; He will bless our families; He will bless our souls; He will bless us with light—liberty—strength —peace—contentment—and success. Beloved, let us be decided for the Lord, and always walk in His ways. Expect His blessing, for He has given you His word, and confirmed it with a solemn oath. Be diligent in the use of all means. Constantly look to Jesus as the only medium through which all blessings flow. Plead this precious promise before thy God this morning, and many times to-day; yea, and every day; so shall thy peace be like a river, and thy righteousness as the waves of the sea. He will bless thee, and thou shalt be a blessing.

Then let no care perplex me now;
My only wish and care be Thou,
  Be Thou my sole delight,
Bid every sigh of rising thought,
And every pant of breath go out
  For Jesus day and night.

DECEMBER 3.

Believe the Lord your God 2 Chron xx 20

THE proper object of faith is God in Christ, not God as the God of nature. In Christ He is gracious unto us, ever with us ; ready to help us ; and takes pleasure in us He is our cove-nant God, all-sufficient, and ever propitious. We should believe in His word, which is true and faithful ; in His presence, for He will never turn away from us ; in His power, for nothing is too hard for Him ; in His character, which He will never allow to be dishonored ; and in His faithfulness, which is like the great mountains, and abideth forever. We should believe in God, though men rise up against us ; though Satan worry and distress us ; though doubts and fears arise within us. We should believe in God, for strength to perform duty ; deliverance out of every difficulty ; and for courage in every con-flict. Believing in God will produce content-ment, zeal, and humility. Let us have faith from God ; it is a gift which He is willing to bestow, and let us have faith in God, it is an exercise which He requires and approves. If the Son of man were to come would He find faith in our hearts ? O Saviour !— ·

Let us trust Thee evermore ,
Every moment on Thee call,
For new life, new will. new power ;
Let us trust Thee, Lord, for all !
May we nothing know beside
Jesus, and Him crucified !

342

DECEMBER 4.

I will go in the strength of the Lord God. Psalm lxxi. 16.

OUR own weakness would dismay us, but God's strength is offered to us; in His light we see, and in His strength we work We have duties to perform, difficulties to encounter, and foes to overcome ; let us therefore go in the strength of the Lord. It is promised to us and may be received by us; we must ask it of God, we must expect it in faith, and go forth believing that He is faithful who hath promised. Never let us attempt anything in our own strength ; if we do, we shall be sure to fail; let us first take up God's promise, rely on His veracity, and so go forth to duty, conflict, and danger. Then the battle is not ours, but the Lord's; then we are sure of success, succor, and victory. The Lord will then be our strength and song; our refuge and certain salvation. His strength is made perfect in weakness, and His grace is glorified in the unworthy. Let us not fear, let us not loiter, let us not despond, but let us go in the strength of the Lord, and we shall be more than conquerors. He giveth courage to the faint, and to those who have no might He increaseth strength.

I know the God in whom I trust,
 The arm on which I lean ;
He will my Saviour ever be,
 Who has my Saviour been :
Strong in His strength my foes I face,
 Assured of victory through His grace.

DECEMBER 5.

Create in me a clean heart, O God. Psalm ii 10.

SUCH a prayer implies a conviction of sin, a sense of pollution, a desire for holiness, a knowledge of weakness, grief for inconstancy, and the possession of true wisdom. It is the prayer of every Christian; let it be our prayer this day; let us lift up our hearts and voices to our God, and cry, "Remove guilt and pollution, produce purity and peace in our hearts. Cleanse us by Thy word, the blood of Jesus, and the influence of the Holy Spirit." Purity of heart can only be produced by God; it enters into the very essence of religion; we cannot be godly except we are holy. If we love sin, if we can indulge in sin, or if a sense of having sinned does not pain us, and cause us to adopt this prayer, our religion is spurious, we are destitute of the power of godliness. No real Christian can live in sin. He is called to holiness. He is the temple of the Holy Spirit. Holiness is his element and health. His God says, "Be holy, for I am holy:" and he cries, "Create in me a clean heart, O God." Let us be holy in all manner of conversation, looking for and hasting to the coming of Jesus.

Supreme High Priest, the pilgrim's light,
  My heart for Thee prepare,
Thine image stamp, and deeply write
  Thy superscription there.
Ah, let my forehead bear Thy seal,
My heart the inward witness feel.

DECEMBER 6.

And delivered just Lot 2 1 eter ii. 7.

Lot was a godly man, justified before God by faith, and justified before man by his good works. But he was a weak man. He chose to dwell in Sodom because it was a wealthy place; he aimed at a fortune, but he was vexed and grieved daily, by seeing and hearing of the unrighteous deeds of his neighbors. His children married into the world, and were ruined; and he himself, though delivered by a gracious and faithful God, suffered severely. His sons and their wives perished in Sodom; his own wife was made an example of on the plain; he was hurried away without a solitary servant, or any property of importance; and had to take up his dwelling in a cave. See the folly of being led by appearances; let not the heart follow the eye. See also the certainty of being chastened for sin —just Lot could not escape; the faithfulness of divine love towards its wayward children; and the importance of being distinct from the world. The Christian in the world is like Lot in Sodom, and if he choose his place from the same motives, the Lord may deal with him after the same rule.

Oh! to be brought to Jesus' feet,
  Though sorrows fix me there,
Is still a privilege, and sweet
  The energies of prayer,
Though sighs and tears its language be,
If Christ be nigh and smile on me.

DECEMBER 7.

Cast not away therefore your confidence.
Heb x. 35.

EVERY believer is confident that Jesus Christ is the Messiah, the sent of God; that He is the only Saviour, and the eternal God. He is confident that heaven is promised to all true believers, and is certain to all holy disciples. He gives credit to God's word, which reveals the same, is fully satisfied of its truth, and finds courage and boldness to profess the same. His confidence being produced by the Holy Spirit, and grounded on the divine word, will lead him to commit his all to the divine blessing; to surrender all to the divine will; to part with all in Christ's quarrel; and to rest on the word and veracity of the Lord Jesus. His confidence will often be assailed and sharply tried; but it must be maintained, for we are made partakers of Christ, if we hold fast the beginning of our confidence steadfast unto the end. It has great recompense of reward, in the present life a hundred-fold, for all it parts with for Christ; and in the world to come life everlasting. Beloved, let us hold fast our confidence and rejoicing of hope firm unto the end.

Protect me in the dangerous hour,
And from the wily tempter's power,
  Oh, set my spirit free!
And if temptation should assail,
May mighty grace o'er all prevail,
  And lead my heart to Thee.

346

DECEMBER 8.

I rejoice in Thy salvation. 1 Sam. ii. 1.

God's salvation is a deliverance from the worst of evils, of freest grace, for the best of purposes. He saves the poor and needy, the guilty and distressed, who call upon Him, and believe in Him. And we who have obtained mercy, should with Hannah rejoice in God's salvation, as those who have received an invaluable favor ; as those who are laid under, and are ready to acknowledge our infinite obligations. Salvation is the proper source of our joy and rejoicing; and while some rejoice in property, some in power, and some in earthly prospects, let us rejoice in the salvation of our God. It is a cause for rejoicing in sickness and health, in poverty and plenty, in life and in death. Although the fig-tree should not blossom, neither should fruit be in the vines; though the labor of the olive should fail, and the fields should yield no meat; though the flock should be cut off from the fold, and there be no herd in the stalls: yet we may rejoice in the Lord, and joy in the God of our salvation : for not one thing shall fail of all that He hath spoken. Delightful truth, " SALVATION IS OF THE LORD !"

Join, heaven and earth, to bless
The Lord our righteousness ;
In Him I will rejoice,
With cheerful heart and voice :
In Him complete I shine ·
His life and death are mine.

347

Walk in love. Eph. v 2

RELIGION is love; the love of God shed abroad in the heart, transforming our nature into love The blessing is bestowed to be exhibited; we are to let our light shine, and walk in love. Under the influence of love to God, for His mercy towards us; and love to man for God's sake. By the rule of love, doing unto others as we would they should do unto us. Seeking their spiritual and eternal welfare. Letting it be clearly seen, that we indulge no envy, jealousy, malice, or ill-will in our hearts against any; but that we wish them well, and desire to promote their best interests in any way we can. Love should run through the whole of our actions, and be the ruling motive in our souls. God acts towards us from love. The Holy Spirit is the Spirit of love; and love is the brightest and surest evidence of regeneration. Let us not be satisfied to feel that we love, but let us manifest it; let us "WALK IN LOVE;" this is the way to be happy, useful, and honorable. Bitterness, wrath, censoriousness, and selfishness, proves that we are under sin; but love is of God; and he that loveth is born of God, and knoweth God.

> May I from every act abstain,
> That hurts or gives my brother pain :
> Nay, every secret wish suppress,
> That would abridge his happiness ,
> And thus may I Thy follower prove,
> Great Prince of peace, great God of *love*

*Neither pray I for these alone · but for them also which shall·
believe on me.* John xvii 20.

BELOVED, when Jesus was praying for His disciples, He prayed for us; His prayer extended
to all who believe, however fearful, weak, and
timid He prayed that we may be one with
Himself; one with His church, as members of
the same body, children of the same family, heirs
of the same inheritance, and parts of the same
spiritual temple He prayed that we may be so
one as the Father is one with Him, and as He is
one with the Father; that we may have the,
same love influencing us; the same object always
in view; and may exhibit the same virtues.
What glorious privileges our Saviour here prays
that we may enjoy! What honors He seeks for
us! What unspeakable blessedness! Think of
being one with God; one with God as Jesus is;
one with the Father, Son, and Holy Spirit. To
be of one mind, one will, and, as it were, of one
soul. Gracious, gracious Lord, hasten on the
time when this all-comprehending prayer shall be
fully answered in our experience! Let us, beloved, daily pray for this blessing; nothing can
be greater, sweeter, or more important.

Thy revealing Spirit give,
Whom the world cannot receive:
Fill me with Thy Father's love;
Never from my soul remove;
Dwell in me, and I shall be
Thine through all eternity.

DECEMBER 11.

Why dost Thou strive against Him? Job **xxiii. 13**

A BELIEVER strive against his God! Yes, it is sometimes the case; he may strive against some of the doctrines of His word; or, against some of the dispensations of His providence; or against some of the commands He has issued But why dost thou strive against Him? His wisdom is infinite. His love is unchangeable His ways are all righteous. His methods may be mysterious, and His dispensations trying but His designs are all gracious and good. I is your duty to submit and be still. It is your privilege to believe and trust. It is rebellion and treason to strive against Him, for He giveth not account of any of His matters. It is the glory of God to conceal a thing. He is not accountable to any. He will not be questioned by the curious, or called to an account by the proud He demands our acquiescence on the ground of His perfections, promises, and word. He will make all clear and plain to us by-and-bye, and then we shall know as we are known, and be perfectly satisfied. He says, " Be still, and know that I am God" " Be silent, O all flesh, before the Lord."

Oh! let me live of Thee possess'd,
In weakness, weariness, and pain!
The anguish of my laboring breast,
The daily cross I still sustain,
For Him that languish'd on the tree,
But lived, before He died for me.

DECEMBER 12.

He is the Saviour of the body. Ephes. v. 23.

THE church is the body of Christ. Jesus and His people are one. They are His elect whom He hath chosen; His seed which He hath begotten; His portion which He hath received; His delight and glory, in which He constantly rejoices. He saves them by substitution; He took their place, their obligations, and their sins. He saves them by communication; giving them grace and His Holy Spirit, with every spiritual blessing. He saves them by instruction; for they are all taught of God. He saves them by separation, bringing them out of, and delivering them from this present evil world. He saves them by visitations; He grants them life and favor, and His visitations preserve their spirits. He saves them by translation; first out of the kingdom of Satan, into His kingdom of grace; and then out of the present world into His kingdom of glory. He saves them to display His perfections; confound His foes; exalt His name; satisfy His love, and from sympathy with them. All who are saved form part of His body. Salvation is entirely of God. What happiness to be saved thus!

Joyful truth, He bore transgression
In His body on the cross,
Through His blood there's full remission;
All for Him we count but loss·
Jesus for the sinner bleeds,
Nothing more the sinner needs.

351

DECEMBER 13.

Ask what I shall give thee. 1 Kings iii. 5.

WE are not straitened in our God; He has boundless resources, and is constantly calling upon us to ask and receive. What do we want this morning? Is it not more holiness? We want our understandings enlightened, our wills brought into perfect conformity to the will of God, and our affections fixed on holy and heavenly things. Let us agree to ask these things of our God. He will give freely, cheerfully, and plentifully. Let us ask as Solomon did, WISDOM; even that wisdom which cometh from above, which is pure, peaceable, easy to be entreated, full of mercy and good fruits. This wisdom will guide our hearts and direct our ways; it will lead us safely to a city of habitations; it will lead us to do God's will with pleasure, promptness, and delight. It will make us wise to escape from Satan's snares, to avoid temptation, and do good unto all men. How important is this wisdom! How necessary for us! Well, Jesus stands before us this morning, saying, "ASK WHAT I SHALL GIVE THEE:" in Him dwelleth all the treasures of wisdom and knowledge, and every one that asketh receiveth.

O sovereign Love, to Thee I cry;
Give me Thyself, or else I die;
Save me from death, from hell set free,—
Death, hell, are but the want of Thee·
My life, my crown, my heaven Thou art!
Oh, may I find Thee in my heart!

7/22

352

The author and finisher of our faith
Heb. xii 2.

ALL Christians have faith, but some of us have
but little faith. He who gave us what we have
can increase it, and He will if we apply to
Him, plead with Him, and wait upon Him.
We need more faith, to enable us to escape the
many dangers that are in our path; to do and
suffer the Lord's will with patience; to hold fast
the faithful word which we have been taught;
to grow in grace and holiness; to exercise
forgiving love towards those who have grieved,
offended, or injured us, and to honor God, by
believing His promise—trusting His providence
—expecting His interference—being active in
His service—and leaving our concerns in His
hands, to be arranged, directed, and brought
to pass. We are encouraged to pray for more
faith, by the nature of the request, and the design with which we ask it—by the promises
which God has given—by the precepts of His
holy gospel—by the examples of faith set before us in the word—by the well-known character of our God—and by the blessed results
which must follow from having such a prayer
answered.

Author of faith, I seek Thy face,
The work of faith in me fulfil,
Confirm and strengthen me in grace,
To do and suffer all Thy will:
From hell, the world, and sin secure,
And make me in my goings sure.

DECEMBER 15.

Make your calling and election sure. 2 Pet i 10.

Put your religion beyond a doubt: let there be no reason to question whether you are sincere or not. Calling separates us from sin, Satan, and the world; to holiness, Christ, and the church. Election is the root of calling; it is God's choice of us from others—in Christ—by grace—to holiness—for His glory. We know our election of God, by our being led to choose Christ, holiness, and heaven; to choose them, freely—heartily—and habitually. If we thus choose them, we shall use every means to obtain them. We know that we are called of God, by our calling upon God, secretly —heartily—constantly—for holiness—salvation —and fellowship with Himself. When we thus call on God we carefully avoid all evil, and follow after everything that is good. Let us give all diligence to know our election, for it is worth all the pains we can take, or the time we spend. Let us follow on to know the Lord—give up ourselves entirely to God—exercise ourselves unto godliness—seek the witness, earnest, and sealing of the Spirit, and cleave unto God with full purpose of heart.

Nothing is worth a thought beneath,
But how I may escape the death
  That never, never dies !
How make mine own election sure,
And, when I fail on earth, secure
  mansion in the skies !

DECEMBER 16.

The righteous shall hold on his way. Job xvii. 9.

THE way to the kingdom is rough and rugged, our strength is often small, and our fears are very many. But if we are justified by grace, sanctified by the Spirit of truth, and pursue a consistent course, there is no doubt of our safe arrival at our Father's house; for "the righteous shall hold on his way, and he that hath clean hands shall wax stronger and stronger." The true believer shall hold on, for the promise of God secures him; the fulness of Christ supplies him; the Spirit of grace influences him; the new nature urges him; occasional love-tokens encourage him; and attachment to the Lord and His people prevents him forsaking the right ways of the Most High. Beloved, let us be concerned to have a blameless conversation; let us live near to and walk with Jesus, then our graces will flourish; we shall become rooted in Christ; our daily conquests will give us courage; and our God will give as He hath promised, even grace and glory. It is not for us to be timid; it is not for the righteous to despond, FOR HE SHALL HOLD ON HIS WAY. "They go from strength to strength: every one of them in Zion appeareth before God." .

They may on the main of temptation be tost,
    Their troubles may swell like the sea;
But none of the ransom'd shall ever be lost
    The righteous shall hold on his way.

DECEMBER 17.

Let the word of Christ dwell in you richly.
Col iii 16

THE word which Jesus preached, or the word which His servants wrote, the whole word of God, is the word of Jesus. Believer, look at your Bible as containing the word of your best Friend—loving Saviour—and final Judge. Let it find a home in your memories—affections—and hearts. Let it keep house, ruling—feeding—and directing your souls. Let it dwell in you plentifully, and know how to apply the different portions to different persons, and different cases. Let it dwell in you richly. that you may have that to plead in prayer which God will notice—approve—and accept; to form—guide—and preserve your judgments; to curb—bound—and regulate your desires; to raise—confirm—and direct your expectations; to silence—enlighten—and purify conscience; to enable you to resist and overcome Satan; that you may be able to reprove sin, and speak a word in season to the weary. Let the word of Christ have the best room in your souls; let it be your daily meditation—food—and directory. "LET THE WORD OF CHRIST DWELL IN YOU RICHLY IN ALL WISDOM."

Still let Thy wisdom be my guide,
Nor take Thy light from me away;
Still with me let Thy grace abide,
That I from Thee may never stray:
Let Thy word richly in me dwell,
Inspiring me to do Thy will.

356

DECEMBER 18.

They are enemies of the cross of Christ.
Phil. iii. 18.

THE cross of Christ is the Christian's glory; and few things would give him more pain, than to be considered its enemy. It embraces the whole doctrine of salvation by grace; and is viewed by the Christian, as the foundation of his hope, and the object of his faith; as the end of the law, and the antidote of misery; as the centre of truth, and subject of the church's song; as mercy's sceptre, and the Saviour's throne; as the mirror, in which Jehovah displays all the perfections of His nature; and the key that opens the gates of the celestial paradise; as the glory of eternal wisdom, and the mystery of incarnate love; as the destruction of death, and the gate to everlasting life; as the object of the angels' wonder, and the cause of the devil's everlasting confusion. Beloved, let us fix our eyes and hearts upon this glorious, this surprising object; and never, never let us, by our conduct or conversation, bring a disgrace upon it; but let us endeavor to advance its triumphs, spread its glories, and bring sinners to admire, love, and trust in it. "God forbid that I should glory, save in the cross of my Lord Jesus Christ; by which the world is crucified unto me, and I unto the world."

Oh, may my single aim be now
To live on Him that died,
And naught on earth desire to know
But Jesus crucified.

357

DECEMBER 19.

If ye love Me, keep My commandments.
John xiv. 15.

HERE is the Christian's grand RULE of action, the commandments of his dear Saviour. Jesus commands us because He loves us; because He desires our present welfare; because He will prove the sincerity of our profession; and because He approves of the obedience of faith. He commands us to imitate Himself. He is our great pattern and example; and we should endeavor to imitate Him in His Spirit, and design, and actions. He commands us to believe Him, profess Him, obey Him, and continue in His love. Here we have the Christian's grand MOTIVE and spring of action—LOVE. Spiritual love is always loyal to the King of Zion; jealous for the glory of the Lord of Hosts; and determined in the cause of the Prince of peace. The obedience of love is easy—hearty—and thorough. Love is the strongest incentive to obedience; it conquers fear—furnishes with zeal—equips with courage—devises the means—surmounts difficulties—and triumphs over opposition. Let us inquire from what does our obedience spring? By what is it regulated? Is our motive and rule, holy love?

Love is the fountain whence
  All true obedience flows;
The Christian serves the God he loves,
  And loves the God he knows:
May love o'er every power preside,
And every thought and action guide.

358

DECEMBER 20.

I will give you the sure mercies of David.
Acts xiii. 34.

THE mercies of David are SUITED to a sinner's wants; they comprise all he needs for time, for body and soul; and all he will need through eternity. The mercies of David are COVENANT mercies; the Father has engaged to bestow them through the doing and dying of Jesus the Son has secured their bestowment by His vicarious sufferings and death; and the Holy Spirit will put the Lord's people in possession of them. They all flow from free grace, are revealed in the promises, and are stored up in the fulness of Christ. The mercies of David are SURE mercies; they are unconditionally promised to all comers; are received by simple faith; and are bestowed by Jesus as the appointed trustee and administrator of the covenant of grace. They are sure, for God has sworn, and will not change His mind, or remove His covenant of reconciliation. The mercies of David are GIVEN mercies; no desert is requisite to establish a claim; no hard conditions are laid down to entitle; no price is fixed, or money demanded; but it is, "COME AND RECEIVE FREELY."

Thy favors, Lord, surprise our souls;
  Wilt Thou indulge Thy creatures thus!
The stream of full salvation rolls.
  To strengthen, cheer, and comfort us;
How rich the grace! how kind the word!
All praise and glory to the Lord!

DECEMBER 21.

Oh, keep my soul, and deliver me   Ps. xxv. 20.

WHAT a mercy to have a God to go to, a throne
of grace set before us, and the precious name
of Jesus to plead. How encouraging the examples set before us in God's holy word. Let
us imitate them who spake as they were moved
by the Holy Ghost. We are going into the
world; the business of the day is before us; our
hearts are false and fickle; let our prayer be,
"OH, KEEP MY SOUL." Keep me from sin, let
me not indulge it in my heart, or commit it in
my life; keep me from Satan, suffer him not
to lead me astray from Thee; keep me from
men, let them not prevail against me. Keep me
in Thy way—in Thy truth—in Thy church.
Keep me by Thy word—Thy Spirit—Thy presence—or Thy rod. "DELIVER ME:" from guilt
and condemnation; from fear and shame. Keep
me at Thy footstool, and deliver me from my
own wandering heart. Let me be clothed in the
robe of righteousness—cleansed in the fountain
of my Saviour's blood—accepted in His glorious
person and perfect work—and be crowned with
loving-kindness and tender mercy. "Keep me
as the apple of the eye."

Ah, will not He who ransomed man,
  A Saviour's work fulfil?
Almighty is His power—He can·
  Boundless His love—He will.
Saviour Divine! deliver me,
Oh, keep my soul still near to Thee!

DECEMBER 22.

They shall not be ashamed that wait for Me
Isaiah xlix. 23.

WAITING for the Lord, supposes that we **want** Him to do something for us; bestow something on us; or fill some relation to us. It implies that we have sought Him, that He has promised, but that He delays to answer our request. It proves that no substitute can be found. This promise SUGGESTS that there may be fears, lest He should not come; lest after all we should be disappointed. This supposes, that there may be temptations to distrust the love, faithfulness, and goodness of God; to think they shall be ashamed of having sought, believed, or expected that the Lord would appear. But this precious promise SECURES the waiting soul from shame, disappointment, and confusion; it ASSURES us that the Lord will appear, answer, and bless in His own time, and in His own way. Are you tempted?—wait for the Lord. Are you afflicted?—wait upon God. Are you sorely tried?—wait patiently for the Lord; He will not suffer you to be ashamed. Abraham waited, and received the promise. Joseph waited, and was raised to honor. David waited, and had all his desire.

> Affliction is a stormy deep,
>   Where wave resounds to wave;
> Though o'er my head the billows roll,
>   I know the Lord can save:
> I'll wait, and bow beneath the rod;
> My hope, my confidence is God.

DECEMBER 23.

His soul shall dwell at ease. **Ps. xxv. 18.**

THE man that fears God must have faith in His word; love to His character; a desire to please Him in all things; a fear to offend Him in anything; a realization of His omniscience; and be looking forward to His appearing. Beloved, is this our character? It is said of such, "HIS SOUL SHALL DWELL AT EASE;" free from slavish fears—from soul-distressing cares and anxieties—in a state of contentment and solid peace. And well he may; for he has God for his portion—the eternal covenant as his stay—the precious promises as his security—the glorious atonement for his plea—a complete salvation for his shield—providence as his friend—Christ as his constant Advocate, Captain, and Man-of-war—daily fellowship with God as his relief—and heaven as his final home. His soul shall lodge, or dwell in goodness: so some read it. The goodness of God is the storehouse of every blessing, and will supply his every want—silence all his fears—contradict all his unbelieving doubts—and exalt him to peace and honor. Beloved, let us not be anxious about anything, but casting all our cares upon God, let us dwell at ease.

> Once the world was all my treasure;
>   Then the world my heart possess'd;
> Now I taste sublimer pleasure,
>   Since the Lord has made me blest;
>   I can witness,
>   Jesus gives His people rest.

DECEMBER 24

Whom resist, steadfast in the faith. 1 Pet **v. 9**

SATAN is the Christian's unwearied foe, he is
the enemy of all righteousness, and aims at our
destruction. He is especially the enemy of our
faith — comfort — prosperity — and usefulness
He is our enemy before God, and he gets access
to our hearts; he excites to sin, accuses of sin
and terrifies for sin. We are called upon to
resist him, steadfastly believing God's word—
faithfulness—and love. Steadfastly believing
what Christ is to us, as Satan's grand opponent
Is Satan a deadly serpent?—Jesus is the bra-
zen serpent which heals. Is Satan a roaring
lion?—Jesus is the lion of the tribe of Judah
who prevails. Is Satan a destroyer?—Jesus is
a Saviour. Is Satan an adversary?—Jesus is a
friend. Is Satan a wolf?—Jesus is the good
Shepherd. Is Satan a tempter?—Jesus is a De
liverer. Is Satan a deceiver and a liar?—Jesus
is the truth. Is Satan an accuser? Jesus is an
Advocate. Is Satan the prince of darkness?—
Jesus is the light of life. Is Satan a murderer
Jesus is the resurrection. Is Satan god of this
world?—Jesus is GOD OVER ALL. Resist the
devil in the faith of this. Jesus is all you need.

All power is to our Jesus given ;
  O'er earth's rebellious sons He reigns;
He mildly rules the hosts of heaven,
  And holds the powers of hell in chains.
Jesus, the woman's conquering seed,
Shall bruise for us the serpent's head.

DECEMBER 25.

I will be glorified. Lev. x. 3.

THIS is the great end Jehovah has in view in all He performs, and all He permits. He created and He preserves the world, that He might be glorified. He redeemed His people by the blood of His Son, and He will glorify His saints with Himself, to the same end. He will be glorified in His sovereignty, doing as He will—in His supremacy, commanding as He pleases—in His wisdom, disposing of His creatures to secure His design—in His grace, saving an innumerable company of the lost and wretched, to sound His praise forever—in His goodness, supplying the wants of all His creatures, though in rebellion against Him—in His justice, punishing the daring impenitent offender. Beloved, it is our duty to aim at the glory of our God in all things. Does Jehovah command?—then we should observe His commands and obey them. Does He graciously promise, and in wisdom and mercy provide?—then we should trust, rely, and depend on Him. Does He work in providence and grace?—then we should acknowledge His hand, submit to His wisdom, bow at His throne, fear to sin against Him, or grieve His love.

> Lord, turn the stream of nature's tide;
>   Let all our actions tend
> To Thee their Source; Thy love the guide
>   Thy glory be the end:
> In all we think, or say, or do,
> Thy glory may we still pursue.

364

This honor have all His saints. Ps cxlix. 9.

WHAT honor ? Of being redeemed by the blood of the Lamb, out of every nation, country, people, and tongue. Of being born again, not of corruptible seed, but of incorruptible; by the word of God which liveth and abideth forever. Of being acknowledged as the sons of God ; " Beloved, now are we the sons of God, and it doth not yet appear what we shall be ; but when He shall appear we shall be like Him, for we shall see Him as He is." Of being closely allied to Jesus ; He is not ashamed to call them brethren. Of being heirs of God ; " If children then HEIRS, heirs of God and joint-heirs with Jesus Christ." Of being delivered from slavery to serve God in liberty; " that being delivered out of the hands of our enemies we might serve Him without fear, in holiness and righteousness before Him all the days of our life." Of being appointed to sit in judgment with Christ; Know ye not that we shall judge angels ? " THIS HONOR HAVE ALL HIS SAINTS." Are we saints ? Do we walk as becometh saints ? Are we living under the influence of these great privileges ? Let us admire, adore, and obey.

> Pause, my soul, adore and wonder;
> Ask, " Oh, why such love to me ?
> Grace hath put me in the number
> Of the Saviour's family ;
> Hallelujah !
> Thanks, eternal thanks to Thee."

DECEMBER 27.

I would have you without carefulness.
1 Cor. vii 32

ANXIETY, or carefulness, is very injurious; it divides the heart, distracts the mind, chokes the word, leads to distrust, and destroys our peace. It is inconsistent with our profession; we have resigned all into the hands of the Lord, and should leave all to His blessing. We should do everything as for the Lord, and consider our families, our property, and our business, as the Lord's; so should we be holy and enjoy peace. Anxiety, or inordinate care, dishonors God; it reflects upon His sufficiency to supply all—upon His omniscience to discover all—upon His authority and ability to manage all—upon His mercy, bounty, and liberality, as if He would leave us to want—upon His veracity, fidelity, and immutability, as though His word may be forfeited or His promise broken. Carefulness injures our own souls—it is opposed to content-ment and resignation—it nourishes impatience and unbelief—it hinders our usefulness, and hardens our hearts—it cuts off supplies, and procures the rod and the frown. We should therefore aim to be without CAREFULNESS, for the Lord careth for us.

How sweet to have our portion there
Where sorrow never comes nor care,
    And nothing will remove !
We then may hear without a sigh,
The world's destruction to be nigh—
    Our treasure is above

DECEMBER 28.

Let us not be weary in well-doing. Gal. vi. 9.

It is not enough for us to be doing, we should be doing good. We are redeemed and new created for this very purpose. Let us ACT as before God, for the good of man; let us COM-MUNICATE advice, encouragement, or relief, in the fear of God, and for His glory. What is done well, is done in a good spirit, even the spirit of love—humility—and prayer; it is done from a good motive, even the love of Christ; is done by a good rule, the commandment of the ever-lasting God: is done to a good end, the glory of Him who hath called and commanded us. But we are prone to get weary of doing, especially if we are hasty—or meet with disappointments —or look at creatures—or consult our own ease But let us not lose heart in the work, neither let us give it over; for in due season we shal reap if we faint not. This is sowing time, bu reaping time will come; let us therefore go on ir divine strength—with holy fortitude—with fixed determination—and resigning ourselves daily to God. We shall reap in DUE SEASON if we fain not; for God is orderly—faithful—bounteous— gracious; He will not forget our work and labor of love; but will reward even a cup of cold water, given to a disciple in His name.

Put thou thy trust in God,
In duty's path go on;
Fix on His word thy steadfast eye,
So shall thy work be done.

367

DECEMBER 29.

All things work together for good. Rom. viii. 28.

ALL the Lord's people love God. They do not love Him as they desire, yet they cleave to Him and follow on to know Him. He is their God, and has called them according to His own purpose and grace, which was given them in Jesus Christ before the world began, and it becomes the Christian to view everything as having its place in God's economy; and its work to do in accomplishing God's purposes. Angels, men, and devils, but perform His pleasure. All things are connected by the infinite wisdom and good pleasure of the Most High. He superintends every movement of every one of His creatures; and directs them to answer His purpose and end. He overrules everything for our good; we never lose anything worth keeping by any of His dispensations. We may gain by all that occurs; we may gain wisdom—holiness—matter for prayer or praise—work for faith, patience, or hope. However, our best interests are secured; everything is working for the good of the church; and though it be a rough, it is a right way to our heavenly Father's house.

> All things on earth, and all in heaven,
> On God's eternal will depend;
> And all for greater good were given,
> And all shall in His glory end:
> This be my care! and this alone;
> Father, in me Thy will be done.

DECEMBER 30.

I will never leave thee, nor forsake thee.
Heb. xiii. 5.

IF the Lord is with us, all will be well; but He has promised to be with us always, even unto the end. Any one but our God would have left us long ago; but He is long-suffering, full of compassion, and of great mercy. He will be our God to all eternity, and will conduct us through life with safety. He will be with us in every trouble, to support us; in every trial, to comfort us; in every difficulty, to provide for us; in every danger, to deliver us; and under all circumstances, to bless us. He will be with us as our heavenly Father—as our firm and faithful Friend—as our God; and we shall be with Him by-and-bye, as His children, dependants, and jewels, to be glorified with Him forever. Beloved, let us rejoice in this, that God will never leave us; death may rob us, friends may leave us, troubles may come upon us; but our God will not forsake His people for His great name's sake, because it hath pleased the Lord to make them His people. Having loved His own, He will love them unto the end.

Since He has said, "I'll ne'er depart,"
I'll bind His promise to my heart,
    Rejoicing in His care;
This shall support while here I live,
And when in glory I arrive,
    I'll praise Him for it there.

A friend loveth at all times Prov. xvii. 17.

WHERE shall we find such a friend? He that redeems from slavery, and delivers from bondage, is such a friend—but Jesus does this. He that restores to the favor of the judge who condemned, or the Lord who delivered over to bondage, is such a friend—but Jesus does this. He that admits to intimacy with himself, out of pure love, notwithstanding disparity of condition, is such a friend—but Jesus does this. He who counsels in trouble, and gives the best advice in perplexity, is such a friend—but Jesus does this. He who rescues from foes and renders their attempts to injure us abortive, is such a friend—but Jesus does this. He who takes in the rejected and homeless, who clothes the naked and feeds the hungry, is such a friend—but Jesus does this. He who exposes Himself to pain, injury, insult, and death, to do us good, is such a friend—but Jesus has done this. He who expends all His property for our welfare, is such a friend—but Jesus did this. He who kindly reproves our faults in prosperity, and visits, comforts, and relieves in adversity, is such a friend—but Jesus does this. He who loves us through life, in death, and forever, is such a friend—but Jesus doth so. HE IS THE FRIEND WHO LOVETH AT ALL TIMES; changing scenes change not His affection. His friendship flows from purest love, and is founded in perfect knowledge of our persons—wants—

dispositions—and propensities ; His friendship is maintained by infinite patience—boundless pity—and the prospect of our being glorified with Him forever. He knows our frame consults our welfare, and is determined to do us good. He will not allow us to lose by any of His dispensations ; but will increase our spiritual wealth by all means. The friendship of Jesus secures all good, and prevents all evil; He will never fail us, nor forsake us. He commenced His friendship with a view to extend it through eternity ; and it is the same at the close of the year as it was in the beginning O Jesus ! let us love Thee with pure affection —walk with Thee in sweetest friendship—and prove ourselves Thy friends in every place Be Thou our Friend—Counsellor—Brother—Saviour—Lord—and God—in life, death, and forever. Amen.

One there is, above all others,
　Well deserves the name of Friend;
His is love beyond a brother's,
　Costly, free, and knows no end :
They who once His kindness prove,
Find it everlasting love!

Which, of all our friends, to save us,
　Could or would have shed his blood?
But our Jesus died to have us
　Reconciled in Him to God!
This was boundless love indeed—
Jesus is a friend in need.

IMPORTANT INQUIRIES.

Do you believe on the Son of God? Do you so believe on Him as to look to Him for salvation—trust in Him for life and peace—prefer Him to health, wealth, or pleasure?

Do you deny yourself, and aim to please God in all things—often asking yourself, Will this action, or this course, please God, and bring glory to His name?

Do you consider yourself a witness for God, being bound to witness against sin—and to the world, that the works of it are evil? Do you witness, by your daily walk and conversation? Do you always take God's side against sin and sinners—and plead with God for their salvation?

Do you live and act under the full persuasion that you must give an account of yourself to God? That your account may be demanded suddenly? That it may be called for to-day?

Are you walking close with God, relying only on the perfect work of Christ for justification and acceptance with God?

Are you living to self, or to God? Do you seek your own, or another's welfare? Do you distribute tracts, and speak a word for Jesus, whenever you have an opportunity?

Do you attend the means of grace on week-days? Are you justified in remaining at home when the Lord's people meet? Does not your conduct betray a lukewarm, indifferent state? God says, "Forsake not the assembling of yourselves together, as the manner of some is."

372

IMPORTANT INQUIRIES.

ARE you a decided Christian? Have you been born of the Spirit? Is there no doubt upon this point? Have you made your calling and election sure? You should do so.

Do you indulge in any known sin, or neglect any known duty? This is a dark sign, beware of it.

How do you feel towards perishing sinners? Can you see them perish without sympathy or concern? What are you doing to convince them of their danger and lead them to Jesus? What have you done for your relatives—your near neighbors? What have you done to-day? What are you going to do?

Are you praying for grace and gifts, with a view to do good? That you may watch for souls, and labor for God?

Were you ever the means of converting one soul to God? Did you ever pray that you might be? Do you use the means that are likely, under the blessing of God, to convert souls?

Which has most of your thoughts, affections, and money—worldly ornaments, or the conversion and salvation of sinners?

Do you know anything of travailing in birth for sinners until Christ be formed in them? Is it your heart's desire and prayer to God that they may be saved?

Are you willing to make sacrifices for Christ? Can you cheerfully give up your time, your money, your ease, and your many indulgences, for the good and salvation of souls?

IMPORTANT INQUIRIES.

ARE you reconciled to God? Can you approach Him as a Friend? Do you love Him as a Father? Do you obey Him as a Master? Do you love His word—His people—and His day? In vain do you profess to love Him, if you do nothing for Him.

Are you like Jesus, going about doing good? Do you visit the sick—pity the poor—and seek the salvation f all around you?

Do you consider your present life as an opportunity given you to serve and please God? Do you improve it as such? Jesus says, "Son, go work TO-DAY in my vineyard." Your work is day work, and should run through every day.

Do you daily live under the impression, "I AM RESPONSIBLE. I am responsible for my time—talents—and opportunities to do good?"

Are you growing in grace? Is the heart hard or soft? Is Christ precious? Are you willing to receive all He has, and to do all He bids? To make a complete Saviour of Him, imitating His example, as well as trusting in His blood?

Are you prepared for death? You will soon be summoned; how much better to be summoned from the field of labor than the bed of sloth! "Work while it is called TO-DAY, for the night cometh when no man can work."

Are you looking for the glorious appearing of the Lord Jesus, who will come to be glorified in His saints, and to REWARD every man ACCORDING TO HIS WORKS?

374

IMPORTANT INQUIRIES.

ARE you really a child of God? Have you really tl
Spirit of Christ? Do you live by faith on the Son ɩ
God?

Do you look to the Lord Jesus alone for life and sɩ
vation? Are you living upon Him as the bread of lɩ
—walking in Him as the way to the Father—and obe
ing Him as the Lord of all?

Are you regular in your attendance on the ordinanc
of the gospel? Or do you prefer ease, increasing wealt
or gratifying friends, to meeting with saints, obeyiɩ
Jesus, and seeking grace?

Do you confine your efforts and sympathies to a seɩ
or are you seeking the benefit of all?

Do you subscribe to the Missionary—Bible—aɩ
Tract Societies? Do you do so according to yo
ability?

Do you meet with the Church to pray, and unɩ
with the Church to work?—or are you only a cumbɩ
ground?

Do you ever ask, How will my present course appe
on a dying bed? or when I stand before the judgmeɩ
seat of Christ?

Are you keeping up that distinction between yoɩ
self and the world, which should always characteri
the Lord's people? "Have no fellowship with t
unfruitful·works of darkness, but rather reprove them."

Do you bear the image, delight in the law, and aɩ
always at the glory of Jesus?

375

TABLE OF TEXTS.

		Page			Page
Gen	xii. 2	281	Neh. iv. 14		233
	xv. 1	26	Job vii. 20		310
	xxii. 14	272		xvii. 9	355
	xxv. 22	106		xxxiii. 13	350
	xxx. 2	304		xxxiv. 32	125
	xxxii. 9	158	Psalm ix. 12		266
	xxxii. 12	117		ix. 18	232
	xxxii. 29	152		x. 14	287
	xxxiii. 10, 11	262		xi. 5	56
Exod. iii. 7		191		xxii. 6	14
	iii. 12	150		xxii. 11	74
	xiv. 15	316		xxiii. 1	96
	xxxii. 26	280		xxiii. 1	97
	xxxiii. 14	236		xxv. 13	362
Lev. x. 3		364		xxv. 20	360
Num. xi. 23		55		xxix. 11	197
	xxxii. 23	290		xxx. 5	83
Deut. iv. 31		187		xxxi. 15	42
	xxxiii. 3	94		xxxi. 23	257
	xxxiii. 3	175		xxxii. 8	30
	xxxiii. 25	170		xxxiv. 10	239
Jos. xvii. 14		138		xxxviii. 6	16
1 Sam. ii. 1		347		xl. 17	220
	xii. 24	323		xlii. 11	47
	xxix. 3	179		xlvi. 10	211
1 Kings iii. 5		351		l. 15	309
2 Kings iv. 23		144		li. 10	344
	iv. 26	20		lv. 22	271
1 Chr. xxix. 14		62		lvi. 3	201
2 Chr. xxx. 20		342		lvi. 9	45

		Page			Page
Ps.	lxvii. 6	240	Prov.	xx. 22	133
	lxxi. 16	343		xxiii. 26	185
	lxxi. 17	318		xxvii. 18	196
	lxxii. 17	230		xxviii 14	198
	lxxiii 24	209	Eccl.	vii. 14	231
	lxxviii. 41	313	Song	i. 4	286
	lxxxi. 10	332	Isaiah	i. 3	200
	lxxxiv. 11	168		ii. 22	93
	lxxxiv. 11	305		viii 10	192
	lxxxvi. 7	297		viii. 17	213
	lxxxvii. 7	155		xxvi. 4	277
	xci. 15	95		xxvii. 11	34
	cii. 27	19		xxx. 15	234
	ciii. 9	247		xxx. 19	324
	cxi. 5	222		xxxviii. 20	269
	cxvi. 4	227		xl. 8	256
	cxvi. 7	339		xl. 29	90
	cxix. 19	215		xli. 10	69
	cxix. 37	114		xli. 13	12
	cxix. 42	334		xliii. 12	163
	cxix. 94	186		xliii. 25	193
	cxix. 117	209		xliv. 5	92
	cxix. 106	268		xliv. 21	132
	cxxx. 7	165		xlv. 21	208
	cxxxix. 23	48		xlv. 22	5
	cxliii. 9	98		xlvi. 4	264
	cxliv. 3	78		xlvi. 10	195
	cxlv. 18	235		xlviii. 16	223
	cxlv. 20	237		xlix. 23	361
	cxlix. 9	365		li. 12	122
Prov.	iii. 6	153		lii. 7	80
	iii. 26	294		liv. 5	65
	xii. 13	156		liv. 17	137
	xvii. 17	370		lv. 4	199

			Page
Isaiah	lxi.	2	258
	lxii.	4	49
	lxii.	11	298
	lxiii	7	338
Jer.	iii.	13	283
	iii.	22	129
	iii.	22	291
	xxiii.	6	157
	xxv.	6	282
	xxx.	11	331
	xxx.	17	292
	xxxi.	20	71
Lam.	iii.	24	167
	iii	25	248
	iii.	33	135
Hosea	x.	2	189
	xiv.	4	254
	xiv.	5	327
Joel	iii.	16	184
Jonah	ii.	9	173
Micah	ii.	7	275
	ii.	10	325
	iv.	9	128
	vi.	8	116
	vii.	7	296
	vii.	18	57
	vii.	19	111
Zeph.	iii.	17	103
	iii	17	142
Hag.	ii.	19	341
Zec.	ii.	8	188
	iii.	5	169
	xiii.	10	37
Mal.	ii.	15	146

			Page
Mal.	iii.	17	46
	iii.	17	139
Matt.	i.	23	36
	v.	8	204
	vi.	24	25
	vi.	32	279
	xi.	28	15
	xi.	28	85
	xii.	50	23
	xiv.	16	72
	xiv.	18	89
	xiv.	22	143
	xv.	23	82
	xvi.	24	11
	xvii.	4	328
	xvii.	5	73
	xxi.	28	306
	xxii.	42	273
	xxv.	5	246
	xxvi	36	13
Mark	iv	40	27
	v.	40	177
	v.	36	68
	vi.	6	293
	vii.	27	162
	x.	36	312
	xi	22	118
	xiii.	37	320
Luke	i.	17	24
	vi.	20	8
	vi.	21	141
	vii.	48	88
	viii.	25	87
	x.	19	149

378

		Page				Page
Luke	x. 42	102	John	xvi. 22	333
	xii. 15	308		xvi. 24	91
	xvii. 5	104		xvii. 20	349
	xvii. 32	183		xix. 5	121
	xviii. 7	238	Acts	ix. 5	302
	xxii. 35	31		ix. 6	161
	xxii. 40	206		xi. 23	38
	xxii. 44	130		xiii. 34	359
	xxiv. 34	84	Rom.	iii. 17	210
	xxiv. 38	108		iii. 24	245
	xxxii. 40	206		v. 11	35
John	i. 36	319		vi. 4	301
	i. 50	229		vi. 14	267
	v. 6	259		vi. 14	278
	v. 39	33		vii. 4	244
	vi. 20	99		vii. 21	21
	vi. 35	119		vii. 21	22
	vi. 37	253		viii. 26	242
	viii. 49	61		viii. 28	368
	x. 11	336		viii. 31	164
	x. 15	260		viii. 33	176
	xiii. 7	221		viii. 33	288
	xiv. 1	171		xi. 20	250
	xiv. 2	172		xi. 26	249
	xiv. 14	147		xii. 1	241
	xiv. 15	358		xii. 12	255
	xiv. 18	174		xiii. 8	225
	xiv. 21	285	1 Cor.	i. 31	216
	xiv. 27	330		iii. 13	337
	xv. 4	207		iv. 7	120
	xv. 5	100		vi. 19	28
	xv. 14	29		vii. 29	329
	xv. 26	190		vii. 32	366
	xvi. 14	105		x. 13	178

			Page
1 Cor.	xi.	28	151
	xiv.	1	194
2 Cor.	i.	10	214
	iii.	5	113
	v.	7	140
	v.	20	326
	vi.	1	212
	vi.	2	52
	vi.	10	317
	vi.	13	314
	vi.	18	126
	xii.	9	182
	xii.	9	295
	xii.	11	123
Gal.	i.	4	226
	ii.	20	58
	ii.	20	59
	iii.	20	7
	iv.	7	315
	iv.	7	335
	v.	1	115
	vi.	9	367
Eph.	i.	6	134
	i.	13	252
	ii.	7	159
	ii.	7	160
	iii.	8	243
	iv.	30	50
	v.	1	270
	v.	2	348
	v.	15	18
	v.	23	351
Phil.	iii.	8	43
	iii.	9	154

			Page
Phil.	iii.	9	284
	iii.	18	357
	iii.	20	148
	iv.	4	136
	iv.	6	10
	iv.	19	251
Col.	ii.	10	109
	iii.	1	77
	iii.	2	110
	iii.	11	60
	iii.	15	6
	iii.	16	356
1 Thess.	ii.	12	70
	v.	17	131
	v.	18	303
1 Tim.	iii.	16	81
	iv.	10	218
	vi.	12	265
2 Tim.	ii.	13	107
Tit.	iii.	2	322
Heb.	ii.	15	9
	iii.	1	274
	vi.	9	217
	vi.	15	300
	vi.	20	112
	viii.	10	51
	x.	35	346
	xi.	37	311
	xii.	2	353
	xii.	5	219
	xii.	28	67
	xiii.	5	276
	xiii.	5	369
	xiii.	6	321

TABLE OF TEXTS.

		Page			Page
James	i. 4	261	2 Pet.	ii. 7	345
	i. 6	17		iii. 11	181
	ii. 5	228		iii. 18	127
	iv. 6	145	1 John	ii. 1	32
	iv. 7	66		ii. 15	64
	v. 8	53		iii. 2	75
1 Pet.	i. 8	205		iii. 2	76
	i. 19	40		iv. 16	307
	ii. 7	41	Jude	21	289
	ii. 9	180	Rev.	i. 5	203
	iv. 7	263		i. 18	63
	iv. 16	79		ii. 9	124
	v. 5	202		iii. 2	44
	v. 7	54		v. 12	1C1
	v. 9	363		xix. 6	340
2 Pet.	i. 1	39		xxii. 13	166
	i. 4	86		xxii. 20	224
	i. 10	354			

CPSIA information can be obtained
at www.ICGtesting.com
Printed in the USA
LVHW082020160422
716403LV00026B/269

9 780530 199924